The Tree Key

PUBLISHER'S NOTE

This compact field reference book, devised and written by a distinguished authority, presents all the important features of the trees *commonly* found throughout Western Europe and the temperate-climate regions of North America. The careful balance between text and illustration makes it a book of particular practical usefulness to those who care for trees and wish to know more about them.

It is a particular sadness that Herbert Edlin did not live to see the publication of his work and the fulfilment of all the painstaking care he took in its compilation.

The major contribution of artist Ian Garrard will at once be apparent and was especially valued by the author.

HERBERT LEESON EDLIN

Herbert Edlin's death at Christmas 1976 will be sadly felt not only by his relations, friends and colleagues, but also by a great many people who received both pleasure and interest from his very popular illustrated lectures, and by the even greater number who read and enjoyed his many books on forestry, woodland life and country crafts.

After training at Manchester, Edinburgh and Oxford, Herbert Edlin's career as a professional Forest Officer covered an unusually broad spectrum of activities including rubber planting in Malaya, work in the New Forest, Chairman of the South Eastern Division of the Royal Forestry Society, Business Editor of *Forestry* and over thirty years as Publications Officer with the Forestry Commission. This wide range of experience gave him a wealth of woodland knowledge and a breadth of view seldom equalled, so that his many writings were not only full of interest but also faithfully reflected much of his own excellent character—his enthusiasm for all the wonders of trees, plants and the countryside, his care and respect for country people and their crafts and his unfailing kindness and good humour so helpful to many.

As an author Mr. Edlin had a long association with Frederick Warne and Company resulting in the publication of *The Observer's Book of Trees* and *Wayside and Woodland Trees*; the spontaneous style of his writing, which makes his books so interesting and so readable, undoubtedly resulted from meticulous care and concentrated effort on the part of the author. Although, unhappily, he did not see the completion of this book, we hope not only that its published form will be as he envisaged, but also that it will prove to be a fitting tribute to his memory.

THE TREE KEY

A guide to identification in garden, field and forest

77 Genera including 235 species compiled and described by
Herbert Edlin

Illustrated by
Ian Garrard

CHARLES SCRIBNER'S SONS
New York

To
MARGARET

1 3 5 7 9 11 13 15 17 19 I/P 20 18 16 14 12 10 8 6 4 2

Printed in Holland

Library of Congress Catalog Card Number 78-54995
ISBN 0-684-15890-6

Contents

Acknowledgements

The first requirement for any tree book is an exhaustive supply of living material for direct study. I have been fortunate here in having available the resources of the Forestry Commission of Great Britain, the Royal Botanic Gardens at Kew near London, the Royal Horticultural Society Gardens at Wisley and numerous forests and arboreta in France, Switzerland and North America.

Observations require exacting checks against those of other scientists, and my search has ranged from the precise botanical Latin texts of Linnaeus, circa 1733, to the racy descriptions of Alan Mitchell, published as recently as 1974. Leading French, German, American and Canadian textbooks have all been consulted, and I am indebted to the librarians of the Forestry Commission and the Commonwealth Forestry Institute at Oxford for their ready help. Over sixty tree books have been needed for confirmation of details, some obscure, some so obvious that few writers have troubled to set them down!

The illustrator has done a fine job of work in the limited space available for each subject. I am particularly grateful to Maurice Nimmo, who provided most of the bole-and-bark photos from a collection he has amassed during fifty years of travel to forests, gardens and botanical collections.

This book owes much to the long-standing encouragement of my sister, Ada McKeehan, of Brewster, Massachusetts, and also to the enthusiasm of her grandson, David Wilson, who introduced me both to the Arnold Arboretum at Boston and his own fascinating woodlot in the mountains of Maine.

Lena Birchall has coped admirably with the typing of an intricate manuscript and Clare Gaskin, my niece, has given imaginative secretarial help. My wife, Margaret, has proved an excellent tree-finder, and has shown exceptional patience whilst yet another specimen was recorded, photographed or sketched.

1976   *Herbert Leeson Edlin*

Foreword

This book is the outcome of a long search for a way of presenting, by text and pictures, all the important features of common trees to observant enquirers. Fortunately the method devised has fitted the publishers' plans for their 'Key' series.

Trees are large subjects, often known from afar by their form or branch pattern. They also hold much fine detail, in shoot, bud, leaf, flower or fruit, which can be even more critical for identification. Their character and colour vary with the time of year, and while trunk, branch, and bark are always present, the leaves of many kinds are seasonal. Flowers and fruit are unknown on young trees, short-lived on older ones. As individuals, trees grow remarkably in size, yet even the tallest oak or redwood began life as a small seed and seedling, which the expert forester must be able to identify, even in its youngest stages.

There are literally thousands of kinds of trees, broken down by botanists into families, genera, species and varieties. The effective unit of study is the *genus* and a consistent pattern of about ten features is presented, in text and pictures, for seventy-seven genera, embracing two-hundred and forty-seven species or major varieties. Once you can tell each genus with certainty, usually by some unique combination of only two or three features, you can progress to the further details that distinguish its component species and varieties.

For each typical genus, a common representative kind, a *species*, is taken, and its characters are presented—on the illustration pages—in a simple and logical way. Across the top of the page you will find the full view of the whole tree, usually in three differing phases, the bare branches of winter, the green leafy crown of summer, and the rich brown or orange colours of autumn. Different individual trees are usually featured here. This, rather than the same specimen over again, helps bring out the tree's range of form.

Across the centre of the page comes a similar seasonal succession of close-up detail. Flowers, which usually open in spring, often ahead of the leaves, will be found on the left. A summer leaf, or a group of smaller leaves, appears in the centre. Autumn fruits, often revealing ripe seeds, are shown on the right.

The bottom third of each page holds specialized drawings that show finer detail more precisely than colour pictures could do, on this scale. The winter state is represented again on the left by leafless twigs and buds, which give surprisingly accurate clues to tree identity, once the code is known. In the centre, a seedling tree is shown at the end of its first summer's growth, before any seed-leaves, helpful for identification, have fallen away. Usually a single seed is illustrated too, as a further guide.

This general pattern is varied, for example, in the case of evergreen trees, which do not display bare branches or autumn colour.

Usually only one species represents its genus, but several large

7

genera, with many varying species, have been given the fuller treatment they deserve. The distinguishing features *of various allied kinds* are shown in the spaces that follow those that give full treatment to the leading species.

Everywhere the stress is on what the naked eye sees, but may not note without expert guidance. Features that can only be appreciated by lens or microscope study are omitted for in practice they are rarely used or needed.

The text sequence breaks, deliberately, the conventions of standard textbooks, though those are apt and proper for their particular purposes. In a standard account you must read all about a holly tree's bark and shoots before you discover that it has prickly dark green leaves. Then you must go through its flower pattern before you find that it has red berries. Here, in the spirit of a simple key, you are told at once that if a tree has evergreen, prickly leaves and red berries it is probably holly—check the rest later! You work, like a practical forester or nurseryman, by *headmark characters*.

The positioning of text opposite pictures makes this approach sensible and practical, and it has also simplified descriptions of illustrations. There is little need for cross-references to distant pages where the same account must inevitably be repeated. Further features of certain kinds, squeezed out of the main illustrated section, will be found on the opening text pages.

The choice of trees for inclusion has been made on an international basis, to cover western Europe and the temperate-climate regions of North America. The two continents share a common heritage of native trees, often differing only slightly in characters. For nearly five hundred years trees have been ferried, as seeds, plants, or cuttings, across the seas. Every tree found on each side of the Atlantic is nowadays cultivated on the other, sometimes only in botanical gardens, but often in vast orchards or commercial timber plantations. American arboriculturalists naturally wish to know how the introduced trees they tend grow wild in Europe; many indeed have run wild in North America. Equally, a European forester cannot appreciate the requirements of an American or Canadian tree unless he has studied its growth pattern in, let us say, its Rocky Mountain homeland.

Fortunately, the Latin scientific names are standard for both regions. Differences in popular names are surprisingly few, and are noted wherever they occur. Home-made American names often fit the trees better than their older English counterparts. *Basswood* aptly describes the bast-rich bark of limes, *cottonwood* the downy seeds of poplars, *buttonwood* the fruits of plane trees, *redwood* the rich-red, very thick bark of sequoias, and *buckeye* the seed of the common horse chestnut.

Inevitably, many fascinating trees, on the fringe of those described, have had to be omitted. For if these were brought in, *yet more* on the outer fringes would clamour, mutely, for admission, extending this pocket book to the size and price of a five-volume treatise. I have thought it better to give a full picture-show and text for a limited number of commonly-encountered trees, rather than adopt the compromise solution often adopted elsewhere. That method displays a flower of one kind here, a fruit of another elsewhere, and adds a brief mention of a third sort which merely whets the appetite for something more factual.

For the record, out of seventy-seven genera featured here, thirty-eight, or close on half, have native species in both Europe and North America. Nineteen were originally found only in North America and ten only in Europe. The balance consists of six from Asia, two from South America, and one each from Australia and New Zealand. There is even one African species, the Atlas cedar from Morocco.

Frequency of encounter has been a guiding principle of choice, rather than rarity. I trust that this book will serve as a really practical guide for all who seek trees in forests, parks or gardens, on mountains or along highwaysides, on either side of the Atlantic.

Herbert Leeson Edlin

NOTE BY MRS. EDLIN

It is fortunate that this book was well under way before my husband's death and I hope that the decision made and the work done to bring the book to publication are as he would have wished. He had always felt that there was a great need for a book on tree identification which would in particular be of use to the layman and be easy to use. He had high hopes for this book which I feel he prepared with even more meticulous care and hours of work than perhaps any of his previous books.

I would like to thank Frederick Warne (Publishers) Ltd. for their help in the extra work this has entailed; Ian Garrard who has carried out the art work with such care from the plans prepared by my husband; and particularly I would like to record my thanks to our very old friend, Maurice Nimmo, for all the time and help he has given in checking the art work and choosing the bole photographs so that the book could finally appear.

Margaret Edlin
July 1977

Classified Index

FAMILIES, GENERA AND SPECIES DESCRIBED

Text and pictures are arranged in ninety-four openings, each of two facing pages, in a sequence of botanical families and genera. Each specific name is usually followed by an "authority" for it, usually abbreviated. "L" stands for Linnaeus, leading Swedish botanist. The sign × before a name indicates a hybrid between two species.

Genus	Title, Species Described	Page
	FAMILY: ROSACEAE	
Crataegus	HAWTHORNS *C. laevigata* DC., *monogyna* Jacq., *crus-galli* L.	132
Sorbus	MOUNTAIN ASH TREES *S. aucuparia* L., *americana* Marsh	134
Sorbus	WHITEBEAMS, WILD SERVICE TREE *S. aria* Crantz., *intermedia* Pers., *torminalis* Crantz.	136
Malus	APPLE *M. sylvestris* Mill.	138
Pyrus, Cydonia, Mespilus	PEAR, QUINCE AND MEDLAR *Pyrus communis* L., *Cydonia oblonga* Mill., *Mespilus germanica* L.	140
Prunus	PLUMS *P. domestica* L., *cerasifera* Ehrh., *spinosa* L., *americana* Marsh	142
Prunus	PEACH AND ALMOND *P. persica* Batsch., *amygdalus* Batsch.	144
Prunus	CHERRIES *P. avium* L., *padus* L., *serrulata* Lindl., *serotina* Ehrh., *virginiana* L.	146
Prunus	CHERRY LAURELS *P. laurocerasus* L., *lusitanica* L.	148
	FAMILY: LEGUMINOSAE	
Cercis	JUDAS TREE, REDBUD *C. siliquastrum* L., *occidentalis* Torr., *canadensis* L.	150
Gleditsia	HONEY LOCUST *G. triacanthos* L.	152
Laburnum	LABURNUM *L. anagyroides* Med., *alpinum* Bercht. et Presl., × *vossii* Hort.	154
Robinia	ROBINIA, BLACK LOCUST *R. pseudoacacia* L.	156
	FAMILY: SIMARUBACEAE	
Ailanthus	TREE OF HEAVEN *A. altissima* Swingle	158
	FAMILY: BUXACEAE	
Buxus	BOX *B. sempervirens* L.	160
	FAMILY: ANACARDIACEAE	
Rhus	STAGHORN SUMAC *R. typhina* Torner	162
	FAMILY: AQUIFOLIACEAE	
Ilex	HOLLIES *I. aquifolium* L., *opaca* Ait.	164
	FAMILY: CELASTRACEAE	
Euonymus	SPINDLE TREE, WAHOO *E. europaeus* L., *atropurpureus* Jacq.	166

CHAPTER ONE

How Trees are Known and Named

Since speech first began among our remote, forest-dwelling ancestors, men have put names to trees. Such names are found, and used with greater or lesser precision, in every language of the world. The reasons for this are simple. As a food-gatherer man had to convey to his fellows the concept of a fruit-bearing tree like apple or a nut-bearer like hazel. As a user of tools and weapons he had to distinguish between a tough yet smooth timber, such as ash and a hard but brittle one such as beech. Among the conifers, all with similar needle-shaped leaves, he got to know that resinous pine made good fire brands, and supple yew the best bows for firing arrows; he could not substitute one for the other.

Knowledge of trees had survival value. In Europe those people who recognized sweet chestnut trees as a source of winter food had an advantage over any who did not. South American Indians discovered that monkey puzzle trees shed nutritious seeds, a staple, easily stored foodstuff. Tribes who made their bows from yew wood shot their arrows farther, killed more game, and won more battles than those who used other timbers.

Because he moved among these trees the whole year round, early man understood the seasonal patterns of their existence. In winter he would pick out various trees by differences in bark—smooth and metallic grey on beech, furrowed on ash, flaky and pink-tinged on Scots pine. In summer, leaf shapes revealed differences of kind at once—the hazel bore broad simple leaves, the ash larger compound ones, made up of many leaflets, and the pine and yew narrow needles that persisted through winter. Flowers, fruits and seeds were even more revealing. Apples bore gay petals followed by soft round edible fruits holding pips, hazel and beech had cat-kins and nuts of contrasting shapes, ash bore winged seeds in bunches, pine produced smaller winged seeds hidden within cones, yew had bright red berries.

Such easily observed and remembered features are the basis for this book, but as science developed a more formal approach was required. Trees attracted the attention of scholars, the first academic botanists, who, usually being countrymen and often landowners as well, knew their material at first hand.

Genus

Their first task was to agree on names that would be common currency in all countries, for every language group had developed different names for the same tree. Oak, for example, was *Eiche* in German, *chêne* in French, *ek* in Swedish and *derw* in Welsh. Because all learned people of this age, the sixteenth to eighteenth centuries, knew Latin, they decided to standardize on the word that the ancient Romans used, which was *quercus*. This was later formalized into the 'scientific' name of a genus or group of allied trees, and distinguished with a capital initial letter, so: *Quercus*.

Species

There are many kinds of oaks in different countries, so a second word was needed to distinguish between them. This again has a Latin form, and is called the **specific** name. It always follows the main **generic** name and nowadays always starts with a small letter. As examples, *Quercus robur*, the 'timber oak' which loses its leaves in winter, is the main European kind. An evergreen species that grows further south is called *Quercus ilex*, the 'holly oak'. Early settlers in North America found a leaf-shedding species with distinctly red foliage; when specimens were sent to Europe botanists naturally named it *Quercus rubra*, the 'red oak'. The convention when printing these generic and specific names is to set them *in italics*.

Authority

In order to define a species, a full description of it is needed. This too was, and still is, written in Latin. Because more than one botanist might describe the same tree believing he was the first to deal with it, each 'authority' appended his own name to the species and this is printed in roman type. Most of the pioneer work was done by the great Swedish naturalist Carl von Linné, who wrote his own name in Latin form as Linnaeus. His fellow botanists paid him the compliment of citing his 'authority' by the single initial letter 'L'. For convenience, all authority names in this book are confined to the Classified Index on pages 10–15.

Variety, Cultivar and Hybrid

Species of trees produce varieties quite naturally and these are identified by a third Latin word preceded by the abbreviation 'var.', thus, *Pinus nigra* var. *maritima*, the Corsican pine, a variety of the Black pine, *Pinus nigra*. Variants occurring in cultivation are now called cultivars and are indicated by the new name in Roman letters enclosed in single quotes, thus: *Fagus sylvatica* 'Pendula', a cultivar of Common beech, *Fagus sylvatica*. A hybrid arising from the crossing of two species is shown by placing a capital ' × ' in front of the new name as in *Larix* × *eurolepsis*, the Hybrid larch.

Family

Further studies showed that trees belonging to different genera could be conveniently grouped in 'families' that showed a general resemblance and had clearly shared some common ancestor. Some of these families consisted only of trees and shrubs, others included smaller non-woody plants. For example, the large rose family, or Rosaceae, includes cherry trees, rose bushes, and strawberries, but the birch family, Betulaceae, holds only trees like birch, alder and hornbeam, which have similar catkins. This classification is a great help to everyone, because related trees can now be grouped together. A family sequence is followed through this book.

But all these family groupings depend on the structure of flowers, and even so are highly technical. Trees bear flowers for only a fraction of the year, and a still smaller fraction of their lifetime.

Little is gained by a study of the floral features that **distinguish tree families**, except by a professional systematic botanist, armed with his microscope and text books. This aspect of tree identification is, therefore, not discussed in any depth in this simple *Key*.

Natural Order

Families, in their turn, fall into a few much larger natural orders, which have major distinguishing features fairly easy to see. Two large and four smaller orders embrace all trees that grow in temperate climates. As always, there are exceptions to any broad description, but the following pattern fits those included here.

Broadleaved Trees

These are also called **Hardwoods** and **Angiosperms** (meaning 'hidden seeded'). They have **broad-bladed leaves** (exception: tamarisk with narrow ones). They develop their seeds from ovules that, at first, lie enclosed within a seed-box called an **ovary**. Most are **deciduous** and shed their leaves each autumn, but some are evergreen. Typically, their timber is hard but exceptionally, as in willows, it is **soft**. Seedlings always have two seed-leaves, giving rise to yet another name: **Dicotyledons**.

Coniferous Trees

These are also called **Softwoods** and **Gymnosperms** (meaning 'naked-seeded'). All have narrow needle-shaped leaves. They develop their seeds lying exposed on the scales of their woody cones, which, however, conceal them until they become ripe. Most **conifers** (an alternative name) are evergreen (exceptions: larch, swamp cypress, dawn redwood). Typically, their timber is **soft**; exceptionally as in pitch pines, it is **hard**. Seedlings may have two, three, or many seed-leaves, up to twenty or so, depending on their genus. Conifers are usually **resinous** in some or all of their structure—needles, cones, bark timber, or seed.

Monocotyledonous Trees

Here these comprise only palms and cabbage-trees, which have slender leaves with a simple unbranched vein system; their stems likewise seldom branch. Seedlings have only one seed-leaf, hence the name **Monocotyledon**. Seeds develop within an enclosed ovary so they rank as **Angiosperms**, as do the Broadleaved Trees.

Wood, composed of bundles of fibres, with no annual rings, is soft.

Taxads
Yews, genus *Taxus*, are the only common examples. They resemble conifers in their narrow leaves, but bear berries, not cones.

Ginkgoales
These are represented only by the maidenhair tree or *Ginkgo*, described in full later.

Tree Ferns
Ferns with fronds at the top of a woody stem, not considered further here.

OUTLINE OF TREE CLASSIFICATION

1	**Order**	Broadleaved Trees (Hardwoods, Angiosperms, Dicotyledons)	(Five other orders)
2	**Family**	Beech family Fagaceae	(Many other families)
3	**Genus**	Beech, *Fagus*	(Many other genera)
4	**Species**	Common European beech, *Fagus sylvatica* L.	(Many other species, eg American beech, *Fagus grandifolia* Ehrhart.)
5	**Variety**	Fern-leaved beech, *Fagus sylvatica* variety *laciniata*	(Other varieties)
6	**Cultivar**	Purple beech, *Fagus sylvatica* 'Rivers Purple'	(Other cultivars)

Fig. 1 *An outline of tree classification showing, within the 'box', the genus and species which are the main units described throughout this book.*

The 'box' of this diagram encloses the units described and illustrated in full on the descriptive pages. The **genus**, here numbered '3', is the key unit for recognition. Once you know its characters, you can say whether or not a particular tree, or in many instances just a part of a tree, 'fits'.

For point '4', the **species**, a common representative kind is described and shown in full, so that a firm determination can be made. Wherever possible, other important species are covered in less detail.

With this information, you can extend your search towards a wider knowledge of units outside the 'box', looking sideways at other related genera and species, downwards towards varieties and cultivars, or upwards to the tree's position in its family and natural order. The genus remains the starting point of your identification study, on which any wider knowledge must be built.

Confusion of Names

A great advantage of Latin scientific names is that they are linked to precise descriptions and can only be applied to closely related trees. Common names have no such close links, and the same word is often used to cover trees that are *not* nearly related, but have only one or two features in common.

Cedar and *cypress* cause most problems. When the first settlers found new trees in North America they had only one English word to describe several new evergreen conifers bearing fragrant foliage. So they gave this name, 'cedar', to trees that the botanists place in three separate genera, namely *Chamaecyparis, Thuja* and *Calocedrus*. All three are distinct from the true or Lebanon cedars, *Cedrus*, of the Old World.

The name 'cypress', which originated with the Italian cypress, *Cupressus*, was given to other unfamiliar conifers, including Florida's swamp cypress, *Taxodium*, and California's Lawson cypress, a western *Chamaecyparis* species, as well as to America's own *Cupressus* trees.

All this is clarified in the appropriate descriptions. Names of timbers are not so simple. American timber merchants often sell Douglas fir, *Pseudotsuga*, as 'Oregon pine' because its timber looks like that of pine, *Pinus*, and behaves like pine, which is all the customer wants. In Europe the timbers of spruce, *Picea*, and silver fir, *Abies*, are marketed together as 'whitewood', because both have similar properties and uses. Trade names for timber trees must, therefore, be handled with caution.

Fortunately, most trees of any one genus carry the same English name in Britain and America. An exception arises with the name 'sycamore', which is applied to a maple, sycamore maple or *Acer pseudoplatanus* in Britain, and to plane trees, of the genus *Platanus*, in America. All such exceptions are explained in the relevant texts; if doubts arise the Index will help resolve them.

CHAPTER TWO

Tree Structure and Life History

Every part of a tree contributes to the life of the individual or else to the reproduction of its kind. There are no spare parts! Identification becomes easier when you know, for example, why leaves are sometimes green, sometimes brown, and sometimes not there at all. The keyword here is **function**. Following chapters will outline the character and purpose of each element—leaves, wood, bark and so on. Let us look first at the tree as a whole, with all these elements living together in mutual support and balance. *See* Fig. 2.

A tree is a large land plant that lives for many years and forms, or tries to form, a single firm central woody stem. This simple definition isolates trees from all non-woody plants, from woody shrubs with much-divided branch systems, and from woody climbers whose wandering stems lack rigidity.

Trees start life as seedlings, and in their first year each has only a slender, weak, non-woody stem, like that of any common plant. But wood formation begins early, at or before the start of the second year of life for every shoot. Buds that form at shoot tips in autumn break next spring and extend the main upright shoot or **leader**, or else diverge to form side branches, so building up, eventually, the tree's **crown**. All these woody stems form both physical links and lines of transport between the tree's essential organs of nutrition, leaves and roots.

Roots at Work

Large tree seeds hold only enough nourishment to support a seedling for a few weeks, while very small seeds can only sustain seedling growth for a matter of days. Growth begins with the intake of water through the seed coat. As the next step towards independence from its founding seed, the seedling puts down a root that fixes it in position and draws in, through fine root-hairs, the larger water supply essential for life and growth. With this water come minute quantities of dissolved mineral salts, particularly those of the elements nitrogen, phosphorus and potassium, all essential for life and growth. As the tree gets larger, the first small root divides, becomes woody, and develops into a root system that will extend for a distance around the tree roughly equal to the tree's height. Large woody main roots, which live for many years, bear innumerable but individually short-lived **root-hairs** that actually tap the soil. The system as a whole remains remarkably shallow. A tree 50 m (150 ft) tall may have roots that descend no more than 2 m (6 ft) below ground level. **Tap roots**, striking deeper, are much more common in textbooks than they are in forests!

Because roots are for the most part hidden below ground, they play next to no part in practical tree identification, even though the wood of each kind is recognizably distinct under the microscope. With rare exceptions, such as the swamp cypress, roots can only live in soil that contains air. Like all other parts of the tree, they must breathe in oxygen, which is not available to them from waterlogged soil.

In order to extend, roots need nourishment from the leaves. This gives rise to the two-way traffic found in all woody stems, with root sap rising through inner layers of **wood** and the sugar-sap descending through the thin outer layer, just beneath the bark, called **bast**.

Leaves in Action

Every living green leaf is a marvellous chemical workshop that uses the energy of sunshine to **fix**, that is render into solid form, the carbon element that is always present in the atmosphere around us. Because light is needed, the process is called **photosynthesis**, meaning 'building up through light'. The carbon is found in the shape of carbon dioxide gas, CO_2, which makes up only 0·03 per cent of an average sample of air. Large volumes of air must therefore pass through leaf-blades, before any worthwhile quantity of 'fixed' carbon can be obtained. Because the process only works in the presence of water, correspondingly large quantities of root-sap must be sent up by the roots. Most of this is evaporated, or **transpired**, to the atmosphere. Only a small fraction is returned to the roots in the downward stream of sugar-sap that runs through the bast.

Why do the leaves of most broadleaved trees, the **deciduous** or 'leaf-shedding' ones, fall in autumn? Simply because they could not get enough water from very cold or frozen soil to maintain transpiration. In tropical countries with hot, dry seasons leaves fall off then for a similar reason. In both circumstances the leaves are sacrificed after the nutrients they hold have been absorbed into the tree's stems. A fresh set of leaves must be produced each year. **Evergreen broadleaved trees** have specially constructed, thick, leathery leaves with waxy surfaces that resist water loss. Coniferous trees, mostly evergreen, have narrow, thick-skinned leaves called **needles**, which also resist such losses and transpire the least possible amount of water. The leaves of evergreens persist for several years, but eventually fade and fall.

The process of photosynthesis is best explained by the accompanying diagram. In simple terms, as air flows through the leaves, a natural chemical catalyst called **chlorophyll** comes into play, provided daylight is present to provide energy. The word 'chlorophyll' is simply Greek for 'green of the leaf'. All green leaves hold it in active form, though it is sometimes obscured by other colourings, as in copper beech. Chlorophyll causes the carbon dioxide gas to interact with water, in appropriate proportions, to form glucose sugar, a soluble carbon compound that can flow to any part of the tree where it is required.

The chemical formula for this process, on which all life on earth depends, is:

$$6CO_2 + 12H_2O + \text{light} \quad = \quad C_6H_{12}O_6 + 6O_2 + 6H_2O$$
(carbon dioxide) (water)   (glucose sugar) (oxygen) (water)

The oxygen is lost to the air. The sugar, dissolved in water, flows to every part of the tree. It is the source of all the varied carbon compounds that make up the tree's tissues, from wood to flowers and seeds.

Breathing

The energy that the tree needs for life and growth is obtained by **breathing**, which involves the oxidation of carbon compounds. The simplest formula is:

$$C \quad + \quad O_2 \quad = \quad CO_2 + \text{energy}$$
(carbon)   (oxygen)   (carbon dioxide)

Obviously growth is only possible if the amount of carbon obtained by photosynthesis exceeds that lost through breathing. Every part of the tree breathes, and must therefore have access to the air that provides it with oxygen, as well as to sugar-sap.

Some of the energy obtained by breathing is used to drive root-sap up from the roots to the crown of the tree. This sap is impelled from one wood cell to another, higher one, through microscopic pits in cell walls. Only living stems can raise sap; physical forces need the aid of breathing cells.

Veins and Woody Stems

Within the leaves, young stems and other soft green parts of a tree the transport of sap takes place through **veins**, which are structures designed for two-way transport. Each vein holds **xylem** cells which carry root-sap out towards the leaves and shoots, and also **phloem** cells that carry sugar-sap in from the leaves to other parts of the tree, including the roots. The two tissues lie side by side in a **vascular bundle**. *See* Fig. 3A.

In the woody parts of the tree the arrangement is quite different, as Figs. 3–6 show. The xylem tissues are concentrated in the inner zone, where they form a solid cylinder of **wood**. The phloem tissues lie outside, just under the bark where they form a hollow cylinder of **bast**. The term 'cylinder' is used here for simplicity; actually the structures taper towards the top of the stem. Between the two cylinders lies a very narrow hollow cylinder of rapidly dividing cells called the **cambium**. During the active growing season this cambium 'splits' off more **bast cells** on its **outer surface**, so that the bast layer becomes larger, in proportion to the increasing size of the tree. On its **inner surface** the cambium splits off more **wood cells**, so that the central core of wood grows steadily stouter. *See* Fig. 4.

If a woody stem is cut across a little of its marvellously intricate structure is revealed. Alternate bands of light and dark tissues are visible. Each pair of light and dark bands make up an **annual growth ring**. In spring, when much root-sap is needed by expanding shoots and leaves, the cambium forms a pale layer of

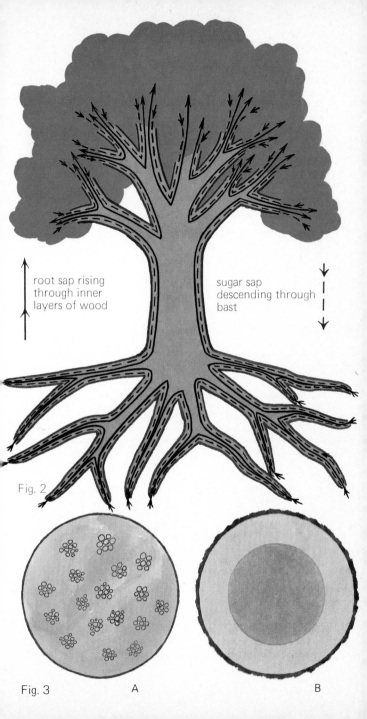

root sap rising
through inner
layers of wood

sugar sap
descending through
bast

Fig. 2

Fig. 3   A   B

springwood; the cells of this have thin walls and broad conductive channels. In summer, when less sap is needed, but more support is required, the cambium produces a harder, darker band called **summer wood**; the cells of this have thicker walls and narrow conductive channels. *See* Fig. 5.

As the years go by, the inner portion of the stem is gradually closed off from active sap movement. It ceases to become **sapwood** and is transformed into **heartwood**. Chemical changes take place which in some trees, though not in all, render it more durable. Its only function thereafter is to help support the tree's crown. In many trees the heartwood is distinctly **darker** than the sapwood, though logs left lying in the woods sometimes give the opposite impression, because fungi invade the sapwood and stain it dark grey. Fig. 6 shows heartwood formation.

Living sapwood is a storage tissue, as well as a supporting and transporting one. When leaves fall from broadleaved trees in autumn their woody trunks hold the food reserves that enable them to recommence growth next spring.

Surrounding both wood and bast lies the outer **bark**, a protective tissue. It holds moisture within the stem, and resists injury by insects, larger animals, chance blows, and the extremes of heat or cold. It also checks the entry of harmful fungi which are spread by airborne spores. As the woody stem gets stouter, its bark becomes thicker and often more rugged: this growth is effected by a special layer called the **cork cambium** that lies outside the bast. On its outer surface, bark bears breathing pores, called **lenticels**, that enable the trunk to breathe. These are hard to see on many trees but on others they help, like the bark itself, in identification.

Buds—the Growth Points

Tree growth in temperate climates is seasonal. During the summer each tree stores up food reserves for growth in the spring of the following year. At the same time **winter resting buds** are formed at the tips of most shoots. Within any bud you can find, in autumn, the structures that will expand suddenly in six months time. Future shoots, leaves, and possibly flowers are all in being, packed into a tiny space. They are protected from adverse weather and enemies, such as fungi or insects, by bud scales, which fall away when the buds open. Buds, though small, vary markedly in detail and provide valued clues to identification.

The shoots that spring from buds are, in their first months of life, soft and non-woody. Their veins, which contain both xylem and phloem elements, form a ring of vascular bundles, as shown in Fig. 3, at A. But after a few months of growth, these bundles are linked up by a wood cambium layer, also shown in Fig. 3, at B.

Limits of Size and Age

Once growth begins, with the sprouting of the seed, a tree can increase its size indefinitely. Spreading roots obtain more water and mineral salts from the soil to match the growing demands of

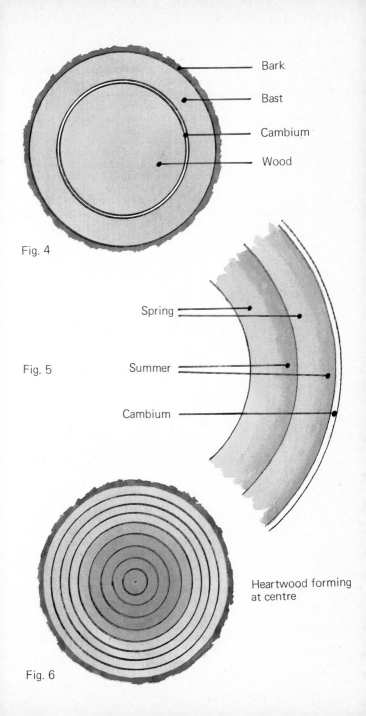

Bark
Bast
Cambium
Wood

Fig. 4

Spring

Fig. 5

Summer

Cambium

Heartwood forming
at centre

Fig. 6

the developing crown of foliage. This in return sends ever-increasing supplies of sugar sap down to nourish the roots. Buds, formed afresh each year, make possible the continued expansion of the crown. The two cambiums, for wood and bark respectively, that run through the outer layers of all the woody stems, increase the extent of wood, bast, and bark every year. The cambiums themselves grow larger to match, increasing in diameter just as the stem does.

Exceptional sizes and life-spans can result. Size records are held by the Californian sequoias, which exceed 120 m (394 ft) in height and 24·3 m (80 ft) in girth, at ages of about 3,000 years! Bristle-cone pines approach 5,000 years in age. But most trees have far shorter lives, a few hundred years at best. Few exceed 50 m (150 ft) in height or 10 m (30 ft) in girth. Usual causes of death are windblow and invasion by fungal diseases, which weaken the stem internally until it finally collapses under its own weight—aided perhaps by a gale; or it may be felled by a forester, keen to harvest its timber. Trees perpetuate their kind usually by seeds, sometimes by offshoots, which enable the whole life cycle to be repeated indefinitely.

Reproduction

Trees rarely flower until they are well-established. Typical ages for first flowering are fifteen years for larches, thirty for beech. Some kinds, such as maples, give regular annual seed crops. Others yield bumper crops followed by years of scarcity, or no seed at all; oaks and apples behave in this way.

Some trees bear showy flowers that attract pollinating insects; cherry and tulip trees are good examples. Such flowers have green outer *sepals* that protect the inner elements in the bud, and gaily coloured **petals** to attract the insects. These may also be lured by scents and are always rewarded with nectar. But many trees rely on wind for pollination. Their flowers in consequence lack attractive features and consist only of sexual organs surrounded by green **bracts**. Usually they arise in **catkins**, with male blossoms in one cluster, females in another. Indeed some varieties have distinct male and female trees—the willow is one of these.

The resulting seed is, in good seed years, produced in lavish abundance. Every year, for perhaps one hundred years, a vigorous birch may shed enough seed to multiply itself ten thousand times! Out of a million seeds produced in that time, only one need grow successfully to replace its parent, and in the wildwoods this is enough. Under cultivation diligent foresters and nurserymen tend both seed and seedlings to ensure a more profitable rate of success. Even so, four or five seeds must be sown to obtain one tree worth planting out in forest or garden.

All normal trees bear seed, but some, such as most elms and plums, are able to reproduce by root **sprouts** or **sucker shoots** that spring up from their underground roots and continue to live after the parent dies. Nurserymen naturally make use of this easy way of increasing stocks.

Other trees will strike root readily as **cuttings**, severed from parent branches and planted in moist soils. Alternatively, live shoots of desirable varieties, called **scions**, can be **grafted** on to the living stems of less valuable kinds, called **stocks**. Increase by suckers, cuttings, and grafts is called **vegetative reproduction** and every tree that results from this method is exactly like its parent. This makes possible the identical repetition of exceptional ornamental strains, such as the weeping ash.

The other main form of reproduction involves a **sexual** process, normally with two parent trees. The resulting offspring show both the resemblances and the variability that one associates with a human family. The male element of each flower, the **stamen** with its **anthers**, provides the pollen that is carried, by the wind or by an insect, to the female element of another flower, usually on another tree. This female element, called the **pistil**, has three parts. At its tip comes the **stigma**, which transmits the pollen through a stalk called the **style**, to the **ovary** at its base. Here, within or upon the ovary, lie the **ovules**, or seed elements, which develop, after fertilization, into seeds. This may take only a few weeks, a few months, or even two years.

As the seeds ripen, the flower that bears them changes into a **fruit**, which may hold one or many separate seeds. Most or all of the flower parts, having served their purpose, now fall away. Even the ovary may disappear, leaving fruits that consist of one or two seeds and nothing more. As a rule, however, the fruit is a well-developed, recognizable structure, like a juicy pear holding many seeds, or a dry pod, as in laburnum.

Pods split and scatter their seeds. Juicy fruits are attacked by birds that distribute the seeds they find within, either casually or by swallowing them, and then voiding them later. Large seeds like acorns roll away or are carried by nut-eaters such as woodpeckers or squirrels. Winged seeds, which have either tufts of hairs or membranous wings, are wafted away by the winds.

Once the seeds alight on moist ground they are ready, given the warmth of spring, to draw in water, put down roots, send up shoots and expand the leaves that take nourishment from the surrounding air. The whole life cycle now begins again, for a new generation of tall trees.

CHAPTER THREE

Identification by Leaves

This chapter and the two that follow it show you how to set about naming any unknown tree by the features that are illustrated in the general descriptions of individual genera, which make up the main body of this book. The approaches set out here cut across conventional text-book keys and definitions based on academic botany. They take you straight to easily observed features.

Many component parts of trees are produced so plentifully that you can gather them without endangering your subject. Leaves, twigs, flowers, fruits and seeds can usually be picked in the small quantities needed for study. There are of course botanical gardens and similar places where no collection is permitted—here a camera, or better still a sketch-book, will be useful for making a working record. In order to sketch you must note structure, which is invaluable for all identification work.

Most soft tree parts are easily preserved, if required, by pressing them between sheets of newspaper placed under the moderate weight of a large book. Polythene bags keep specimens fresh until you get them home.

Always be wary of linking fallen tree parts, particularly leaves, with the nearest tree. One leaf, however faded, that remains still firmly attached to its twig, is better evidence than a hundred fallen ones, which may have drifted in with the wind from another tree elsewhere.

Leaves

Where choice allows, select a leafy twig from an average branch, avoiding both the outer twigs and ageing material near the tree's trunk. Note carefully the **placement** of leaves on the twig. Trees with **opposite paired leaves and twigs** form a small distinctive group.

Remove a single leaf from the twig and check that it **really is a single leaf.** Compound leaves, such as those of the ash (page 194), can be mistaken for leafy shoots, because their separate leaflets look very like whole leaves themselves. The test is that **a leaf never ends in a bud**; a shoot always ends in a bud, flower or fruit.

Next, note whether the leaf has a long stalk, a short stalk, or none at all. Each point is usually distinctive.

In the following paragraphs, leaves are grouped in eighteen separate slots, a handy form linking them with their representative illustrations in Figs. 7 and 8.

If your leaf has a **broad blade** you are probably dealing with the **broadleaved trees** described in the first group of main text descriptions, pages 88–205. As exceptions to this, you may encounter a maidenhair tree, *Ginkgo biloba* (page 260); a palm (page

204); or even a cabbage tree (page 204), all of these have **parallel veins** which are not found on truly broadleaved trees (see **Slot 1**).

The alternative type is the narrow **needle-shaped leaf** or **needle**, found on the conifers described on pages 206–262 of the main text, and which are dealt with later. The only common 'broadleaved' trees with such needles are the tamarisks, described on page 182.

EVERGREEN BROADLEAVED TREES (SLOT 2)

These are easily known because their leaves look like the 'durable goods' they truly are. Tough, hard, thick and leathery, they have glossy surfaces and remain the same the whole year round. Only a few genera bear leaves like these. Check with evergreen oaks (page 112), magnolia (page 122), true laurel (page 126), cherry laurel (page 126), box (page 160), holly (page 164), strawberry tree or madrone (page 190), and olive (page 196). All these evergreen broadleaves are **simple** in character; they have oval blades without lobes or smaller leaflets. **Spiny leaves** distinguish hollies (*Ilex*, p. 164). Under cultivation certain evergreens, especially hollies, exist as variegated varieties or cultivars. They have yellow, white or pink foliage but always belong to some common species that normally bears green leaves.

DECIDUOUS BROADLEAVED TREES: MAIN LEAF SHAPE CLASSES (SLOTS 3–7)

The leaves of deciduous broadleaved trees, which fall in autumn, have relatively thin, delicate blades. Leaf shapes fall into five clear types. *See* Figs. 7 and 8. These are:

(Slot 3): Simple, undivided leaves which are usually oval in outline, but may be oblong, round, diamond-shaped or triangular. Veins may spread out from the base, or branch off at intervals from a central main vein or midrib, as in beech (*Fagus*, p. 102 and southern beech, Nothofagus, p. 102).

(Slot 4): Palmately-lobed leaves, as in those of the maple (*Acer* p. 170), have their leaf blade extended into three, five or seven projections or lobes. Their main veins run out at angles from the end of the leaf stalk, on to each lobe.

(Slot 5): Pinnately-lobed leaves, as in the deciduous oak (*Quercus*, pp. 106–11), have several lobes projecting from either side. Each lobe has a vein running towards it from the central midrib.

(Slot 6): Palmately compound leaves are divided into separate leaflets that radiate from the main stalk. The only common examples are horse chestnut or buckeye (*Aesculus*, p. 176), and laburnum (*Laburnum*), p. 154.

31

(Slot 7): **Pinnately compound leaves** bear from five to twenty-one leaflets, that spring from a long central stalk. Walnut, (*Juglans*, p. 88) is a good example.

As always with handy rules there are a few exceptions. Leaves of certain poplars (*Populus*, p. 80), elms (*Ulmus*, p. 114), fig (*Ficus*, p. 120) and sassafras (*Sassafras*, p. 126), which are normally simple, may occasionally be lobed, especially on vigorous shoots. The early or juvenile leaves of most trees that bear lobed or compound leaves later, are **simple**, but this feature is confined to **seedlings**, described further on page 61, and shown later for each kind.

Nearly all broad-bladed leaves can be assigned to one or another of the seven slots, 1–7 described above. Do this before you go any further. Next check whether the leaf's placement is isolated, paired, or possibly **clustered**, as in oaks (*Quercus*, pp. 108–111). This will enable you to place your leaf in a further sub-division of its main slot. Next, look at the stalk, to narrow the range of possibilities still further.

Minor Leaf Shape Details

Within the main shape classes, minor shape features are specified by classic textbooks with an exactitude rarely matched by the actual living tree. Rather perversely, the leaf may vary in actual outlines even on the same branch, and certainly will from one branch to another. Here we must rely on illustrations of typical leaves to give the general picture.

Practical points to note are the character of the **leaf top**, which may be sharply-pointed, bluntly-pointed, round or even cut-off, as in the tulip tree (*Liriodendron*, p. 124). The **leaf-base** may be tapered, rounded, squared-off, or hollowed out. These features are fairly constant for each species, but not invariable.

Many leaves have **toothed edges**; some have doubly-toothed ones. This **serration** is a handy guide too, though its degree is too variable for precise description.

Leaf Size

Representative sizes for leaves are only given here where they are exceptionally large or small, and therefore a real aid towards identification. Most simple leaves average 5–15 cm (2–6 in.) in length and breadth, with wide variation on the same tree at the same time. Small seedlings and the twigs of under-nourished trees naturally bear small leaves. Vigorous shoots bear much larger ones. Compound leaves, which really behave like side shoots, may become enormous, up to 60 cm (24 in.) in length. Shape is always more significant than size.

Hairiness

Most leaves bear small hairs on their under surfaces, especially within the angles of their veins. Despite careful descriptions published by diligent botanists, this feature rarely helps people to distinguish trees; the hairs often disappear as the leaves age. A few trees, however, such as evergreen oaks (*Quercus*, p. 108) and medlar (*Mespilus*, p. 140) have exceptionally hairy surfaces that are a valuable diagnostic feature.

Fragrance

A few broad leaves proclaim the identity of their parent trees by the fragrance of essential oils held in special cells. Crush them and you will know their names at once. Examples are walnut (*Juglans*, p. 88), true laurel (*Laurus*, p. 126) and eucalyptus trees, (*Eucalyptus*, p. 186).

Leaf Colour

This is inconstant and must be interpreted according to the season of the year. Even the dark green leaves of evergreens like cherry laurel (*Prunus laurocerasus*, p. 148) begin with brighter, paler shades. The general march of colour for deciduous leaves is from bright, pale, emerald shades in spring to rich true or deep green around midsummer. Variegation, in the form of yellow or white patches, occurs on some deciduous broad leaves: this indicates a freak variety, never a genus or species.

In autumn, when the leaves fade, their green chlorophyll breaks down and bright pigments called *carotenes* become obvious as yellow, orange or scarlet shades. More rarely, another pigment group called *anthocyanins* colour the leaves purple or crimson, as in liquidambar or sweet gum (*Liquidambar*, p. 128). Though this colour display varies from one autumn to another, it is a handy guide to many trees at that time of year. At the least it eliminates those few, like alders (*Alnus*, p. 96) which simply turn dull brown or black. Colour clues are therefore given in the text for all appropriate species.

NEEDLES ON CONIFERS (SLOTS 8–18)

These, though at first sight much alike, fall on closer inspection into a few clear-cut groups. *See* Figs. 7 and 8.

It is important to ignore shoot tips, which often have foliage patterns that are unlike each tree's characteristic type.

(Slot 8): Fern-like foliage in which all the needles clasp the twigs, hide them completely and also hide the buds, is found in incense cedars, red cedars and white cedars, cypresses, and certain junipers. These belong to the genera *Calocedrus*, *Chamaecyparis*, *Cupressus* and *Juniperus*, described respectively on p. 246, p. 250, p. 254 and pp. 246–256.

(Slot 9): Sharp, stiff, stalkless, pointed, scale-like needles radiating in spiral fashion all round twigs, which they conceal, indicate monkey puzzle (*Araucaria*, p. 208); giant sequoia (*Sequoiadendron*, p. 236), *Japanese cedar (Cryptomeria*, p. 240), and many junipers (*Juniperus*, pp. 256–259).

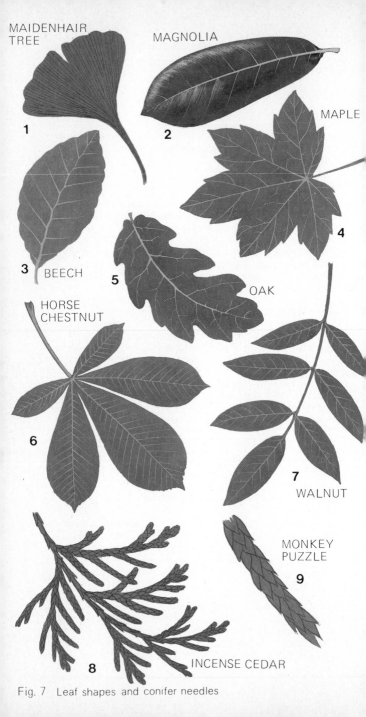

MAIDENHAIR TREE **1**

MAGNOLIA **2**

MAPLE **4**

BEECH **3**

OAK **5**

HORSE CHESTNUT **6**

WALNUT **7**

INCENSE CEDAR **8**

MONKEY PUZZLE **9**

Fig. 7 Leaf shapes and conifer needles

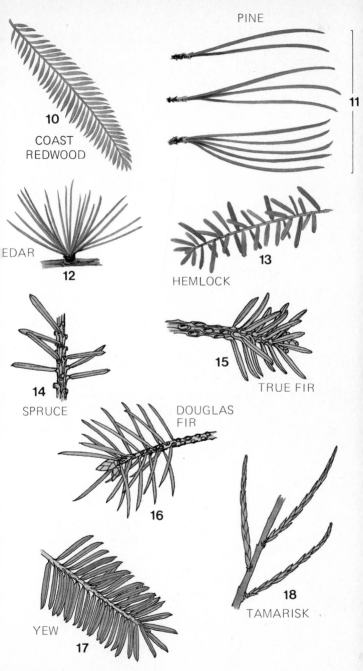

PINE

10
COAST
REDWOOD

11

EDAR

12

13

HEMLOCK

14

SPRUCE

15

TRUE FIR

16

DOUGLAS
FIR

17

YEW

18

TAMARISK

Fig. 8   Conifer needles

(Slot 10): Short, boat-shaped sprays of foliage, with needles varying in length in orderly progression—short at each end, longer at centre, indicate evergreen coast redwood (*Sequoia*, p. 236), deciduous swamp cypress (*Taxodium*, p. 242) or dawn redwood (*Metasequoia*, p. 244), also deciduous.

(Slot 11): Grouping of needles in twos, threes or fives marks out the huge genus of pines (*Pinus*, pp. 210–219).

(Slot 12): Grouping of many needles together, radiating from **short shoots**, indicates the evergreen true cedars (*Cedrus*, p. 220), and the much commoner deciduous larches (*Larix*, p. 222).

(Slot 13): Needles of irregular lengths, all jumbled together, point to hemlocks (*Tsuga*, p. 228).

(Slot 14): Needles with regular lengths, grouped in fairly flat planes extending on either side of the twig, with **every needle mounted on a tiny woody peg**, identify the very common spruces (*Picea*, pp. 224–227).

(Slot 15): Needles in very flat ranks, affixed to the twig by **stalkless leaf bases** that leave a **round scar** when detached, show a conifer to be a true fir (*Abies*, pp. 232–235). True firs have short blunt buds, often resinous.

(Slot 16): Needles as above, but with a **short narrow stalk** at their base, identify Douglas firs (*Pseudotsuga*, p. 230). Douglas firs have long pointed buds that lack resin.

(Slot 17): Green twigs bearing non-resinous needles of even lengths with pale green undersides, in two ranks making a flat plane mark out yews (*Taxus*, p. 206).

(Slot 18): The needle-leaved tamarisk (*Tamarisk*, p. 182), technically a broadleaved tree, stands out from the true conifers by its non-resinous leaves, set spirally along wiry, red-brown twigs.

Fragrance in Conifer Needles

Many conifers have leaves with distinctly fragrant leaves but in fact the absence of odour, as in yew, is often more helpful towards recognition than its presence. Typical 'nose pointers' are those of western red cedar (*Thuja*), smelling of pineapple; junipers (*Juniperus*) smelling of gin; and white spruce (*Picea glauca*) scented like blackcurrant jam. Crush a few needles to test for scent. Once smelt, they are never forgotten!

Sizes of Conifer Needles

Size is rarely diagnostic. Most needles are very small, only 1 or 2 cm (say 0·5–1 in.) long, by about 2·5 mm (say 0·1 in.) broad. Exceptions do occur with certain pines (*Pinus*; p. 210) which bear needles, still very narrow, up to 50 cm (20 in.) long.

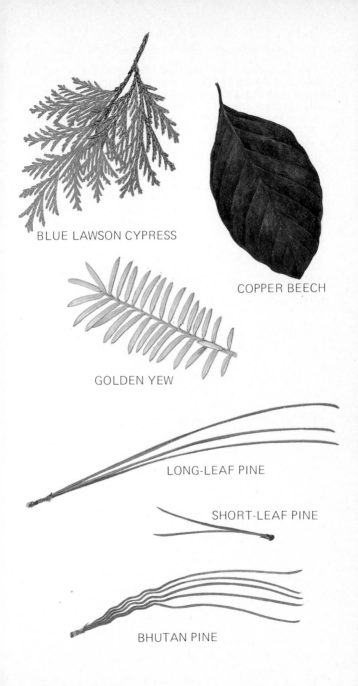

BLUE LAWSON CYPRESS

COPPER BEECH

GOLDEN YEW

LONG-LEAF PINE

SHORT-LEAF PINE

BHUTAN PINE

Fig. 9   Unusual foliage features

DECIDUOUS NEEDLE-LEAVED TREES

Most conifers are evergreen, and bear stiff, thick, waxy-surfaced needles. A few stand out because they are deciduous, and bear thin-textured needles with a seasonal march of colour—bright green, then mid-green, finally yellow, orange or rust-red. These are the larches, swamp cypress, dawn redwood, and also certain tamarisks (*Larix*, p. 222; *Taxodium*, p. 242; *Metasequoia*, p. 244 and *Tamarix*, p. 182).

Conifer Needle Colour

Exceptional colour varieties exist in many species of evergreen conifers. Commonest are those usually termed *glauca*, with blue foliage, and *aurea* with yellow foliage. This rarely helps identification of species or genus. In fact it usually confuses the issue, making the trees harder, rather than easier, to name.

Unusual Foliage Features

Figure 9 illustrates colour variations, foliage patterns found in hedgerows, and easily recognized differences among the three-needled pines (Slot 11).

CHAPTER FOUR

Identification by Twigs, Bark and Timber

The features described in this chapter are particularly useful for practical identification because you can find them, usually within reach, low down, and **all the year round**.

Twigs

Attention is concentrated here on the twigs of **deciduous trees**, because they are the best clue to the identity of trees when they stand leafless in winter. Bare twigs are extensively illustrated in the descriptive texts for the separate genera, which appear later.

The twigs of **evergreen trees** are seldom used for identification, because their leaves, which naturally have more scope for variation, are available all year round.

Twigs spring from buds as soft green shoots, but this phase is rarely used for sorting out the various kinds of trees. It is easier to work with harder **woody twigs**, and with buds in their winter resting stage. All our illustrations show twigs in this winter state.

During the short spring season of active growth, when buds are bursting and shoots elongating, twig-and-bud identification is, frankly, difficult. At this time of year it should be supported by the evidence of other features, such as bark, leaf, and possibly flower.

Twigs harden into their woody state by midsummer and the buds for next year's growth are formed remarkably early. From June onwards it is usually possible to name a genus from its 'winter twig' features.

The **terminal** bud on every **tree** twig is **always solitary**. Shrubs differ in this—lilac, *Syringa*, has paired terminal buds. Check to see if the **side** buds stand in opposite pairs along the twigs. If so, the leaves and branches will also be paired. Only a handful of genera have such paired characters—look up: maples, *Acer*; ash trees, *Fraxinus*; spindle trees, *Euonymus*; dogwoods, *Cornus*; elders, *Sambucus*; and blackthorns, *Rhamnus* and *Frangula*.

Buds and leaves in threes point clearly to catalpa trees, *Catalpa*. **Buds clustered at shoot tips** indicate oaks, *Quercus*.

Placement of buds as **solitary** structures along the twigs is the rule for a large number of genera. These trees are best sorted out by other features, such as leaves, bark, flowers or fruit; but the twig pictures will help.

Exceptionally fine twigs are found on birch, *Betula*. Remarkably **stout ones** grow on staghorn sumac, *Rhus typhina*, fig, *Ficus*, walnut, *Juglans*, and hickory, *Carya*.

Hairy twigs occur on staghorn sumac, *Rhus typhina*, and on medlar, *Mespilus*. The sumac is easily known by its reddish hue.

Twig colour is sometimes an aid to identification. It often varies from one side of the same twig to another. Sunlit sides tend to be coloured red or purple, while shaded sides remain green. Lime, *Tilia*, hawthorn, *Crataegus*, and plum, *Prunus domestica*, have **crimson twigs**, or at least crimson sunlit surfaces. The lime has two-scaled buds (see below, under Buds), the hawthorn has spines, while the plum lacks both those features.

Pith Distinctions. A cut across a stout twig, best made on the slant, may reveal distinctive pith features. Elder, *Sambucus*, has exceptionally thick, light, white pith. Walnuts, *Juglans*, and hickories, *Carya*, have pith divided into chambers, by cross walls which look like a little ladder when exposed. Tree of heaven, *Ailanthus*, has orange pith.

Square twigs are found on spindle tree, *Euonymus*. **Corky twigs** distinguish field maple, *Acer campestre*, and certain elms, *Ulmus*.

Buds

The buds themselves often supply clues to identity (Fig. 10). They are therefore illustrated in detail on the winter twig pictures in the main text describing genera.

Examine a bud carefully to see if it is enclosed by only one or two outer scales, or by many. A **single oval outer scale** indicates willow, *Salix*. A **single conical outer scale** points to a plane tree or American sycamore, *Platanus*. Two scales, one larger than the other, are characteristic of the limes, lindens or basswoods, *Tilia*.

Stalked buds, which actually have narrow bases, not true stalks, are found in alders, *Alnus* (purple buds) and tulip tree, *Liriodendron* (green buds).

Long, tapered, brown, pointed buds are found on beech, *Fagus*.

The buds of evergreen conifers have helpful peculiarities too. All true pines, genus *Pinus*, have **large buds**, in which are packed the multitude of needle groups—twos, threes or fives, that will burst forth the following year. Such buds are big enough to show features that point to a particular species of group of species. For example, maritime pine, *P. pinaster* bears bud-scales with **reversed tips**, Scots pine, *P. sylvestris*, has **blunt buds**, and Corsican pine, *P. nigra* variety *maritima*, has broad buds that taper suddenly to a **sharp point**. Pines and certain other conifers have **resinous** buds; but in some other conifers the buds lack resin.

Spines

Very few trees bear spines (Fig. 10, foot); these are usually placed close beside buds. Paired spines identify the locust tree or false acacia, *Robinia*. **Spines in threes** are a peculiarity of honey locust, *Gleditsia*. **Single spines associated with paired buds** mark out buckthorn, *Rhamnus*. **Single spines near solitary buds** indicate blackthorn, *Prunus spinosa*; hawthorn, *Crataegus*; wild pear, *Pyrus*; or crab apple, *Malus*.

A simple colour key helps to separate out the four last-named genera:

Black twigs—blackthorn, *Prunus spinosa*; Crimson twigs—

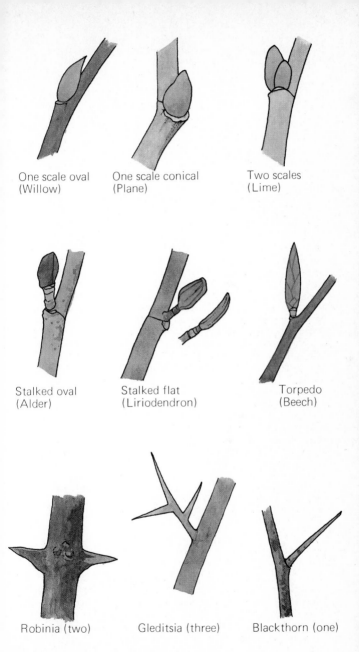

One scale oval (Willow)

One scale conical (Plane)

Two scales (Lime)

Stalked oval (Alder)

Stalked flat (Liriodendron)

Torpedo (Beech)

Robinia (two)

Gleditsia (three)

Blackthorn (one)

Fig. 10 Buds and spines

hawthorn, *Crataegus*; Brown twigs—wild pear, *Pyrus*; Purplish-grey twigs—crab apple, *Malus*.

Bark

Bark provides a fascinating, instant means of naming certain trees (Fig. 11), though bark patterns are shared by several sorts of trees. Its textures are hard to describe in words, so an array of photos has been assembled here to display them. Bark sometimes helps to distinguish a genus, but at other times it separates species **within** the same genus.

To see why bark is so useful, yet why it must be looked at with so much care, we must consider its purpose, and how it develops. Bark is a waterproof layer made of cork, that surrounds woody stems to maintain their water content and shield their delicate outer layers from casual damage, sudden changes of temperature, insect attacks and fungal diseases. It is nearly air-proof, and therefore has breathing pores, either obvious or concealed, to allow the air that the stem needs to pass through it. Bark is formed, and constantly extended and renewed, by a thin layer of cells called the bark cambium. *See* Fig. 4.

As the woody stem grows stouter the bark cambium expands also. The outer layers of the bark, formed earlier, are split into various patterns by the overall expansion of the woody stem. Because the waterproof envelope must never be broken, the cambium produces new layers of cork cells beneath the outer ones. This process gives bark its depth and characteristic patterns, because the splitting **takes different trends on different kinds of trees**.

All young twigs bear smooth bark, because there has been no cause, as yet, for their outer layers to break up. As each twig grows older, cracks and splits appear, and on many trees these develop into fissures, separated by ribs. When examining bark, it is best to observe this gradual development. The most distinctive patterns are found in the **adolescent bark** of developing branches and tree trunks. This is the intermediate stage between the **juvenile bark** of twigs and slender young branches, and the **senescent bark** of very old trunks. The last-named is often exceptionally thick and rugged but can lack diagnostic features.

TYPICAL BARK GROUPS

Smooth bark, retained to a great age and size, is found on relatively few trees, notably beech, *Fagus*, and southern beech, *Nothofagus*.

Flaking bark, in which patches break away as they age, occurs on plane or American sycamore, *Platanus*; sycamore maple, *Acer pseudoplatanus*; horse chestnut, *Aesculus*, and several other trees.

Peeling bark, in which strips break away horizontally as they grow older, is characteristic of birch, *Betula*.

Smooth: beech, *Fagus sylvatica*

Flaking: European sycamore, *Acer pseudoplatanus*

Peeling: paper birch, *Betula papyrifera*

Smooth, with prominent breathing pores: cherry, *Prunus avium*

Network of fissures and ribs: hybrid poplar, *Populus* 'Eugenei'

Broken ribs and fissures: pedunculate oak, *Quercus robur*

Thick, fibrous: Monterey pine, *Pinus radiata*

Tight, stringy: Japanese cedar, *Cryptomeria japonica*

Resin blisters on grand fir, *Abies grandis*

Fig. 11 *Bark characters*

Smooth bark with prominent breathing pores, also called **lenticels**, occurs on wild cherry, *Prunus avium*, and certain garden cherries.

Networks of fissures and ribs, which criss-cross at sharp angles like expanded metal, are characteristic of willows, *Salix*, and certain poplars, *Populus*.

Broken ribs, cut off by horizontal gaps, are usual on most oaks, *Quercus*, and give them their famed rugged appearance.

Thick, fibrous, ribbed-and-furrowed bark develops on many common conifers, notably pines, *Pinus*, and larches, *Larix*. It becomes exceptionally thick and soft in the coast redwood, *Sequoia* and the giant sequoia, *Sequoiadendron*.

Tight, stringy bark occurs on certain conifers, notably Japanese cedar, *Cryptomeria*.

Resin blisters are characteristic of the smooth juvenile bark on young stems of silver fir, *Abies*, and Douglas fir, *Pseudotsuga*. Prick these oval swellings, and clear white resin, with its highly distinctive scent, will ooze out. As the bark ages, these blisters disappear, leaving no trace on older stems.

Bark colour is distinctive in a few instances. Most birches, *Betula*, have peeling **white** bark, approached only by the greenish-white, non-peeling bark of white poplar, *Populus alba*. Olive-green bark marks out laburnum, *Laburnum* genus. Pinkish orange hues, in its adolescent stages, distinguish the bark of Scots pine, *Pinus sylvestris*, from that of nearly all other pine trees. Many cherries, *Prunus avium* and allies, and mountain ash, *Sorbus aucuparia*, bear purplish-grey bark.

In general the bark of most trees has prevailing shades of brown or grey. These are hard to define in words and are not constant, even for the same tree. Sometimes a regular progression of colour occurs. Silver birch, *Betula pendula*, has purplish-brown, smooth, juvenile bark, then white peeling adolescent bark, and finally black, ribbed-and-fissured senescent bark.

Bole

The bole or tree trunk (Fig. 12) that bears the bark may manifest peculiar features too. The bole photos on pages 264–71 always show the base of the tree, to bring these out and to provide a common standard for comparison.

Buttresses

These are **projections at the base of the tree trunk** that serve to give it support, like the buttresses of some great cathedral. Never found on young trees, they may develop markedly with age. Though useless, therefore, for naming a sapling, they are often a quick clue to the identity of a veteran. Common trees that frequently develop buttresses are beech, *Fagus*, and spruce, *Picea*.

Very broad ones grow at the base of the swamp cypress *Taxodium*, to help support it on marshy soil.

Flutes

These are projections that **run up the trunk**, and give it an irregular outline. Hornbeam, *Carpinus*, provides the commonest and most conspicuous example. Flutes are also common on hawthorn, *Crataegus*, and yew, *Taxus*.

Timber

Though every trunk and branch of a tree consists of timber, being hidden by bark it is only rarely visible to the observer. Exposures of the wood below, useful for identification, are however, reasonably frequent in woodlands. Logs felled for sale, the stumps that are left, and chance breakages caused by wind or by one tree falling across another, reveal surfaces that tell, by their colour or texture, a great deal. Fresh exposures are naturally best. As time goes by colours are faded, textures become weathered, and fungi may change the original contrasts. Heartwood, normally darker than sapwood, may appear **lighter** if certain fungi stain the sapwood around it. But other fungi stain only the inner heart of the tree.

The first point to look for is the colour contrast, if any, between inner heartwood and outer sapwood. *See* Fig. 6. Some trees, such as beech, *Fagus*, and spruce, *Picea*, show no distinction, being as a rule a uniform pale brown throughout. In others, it is marked. Yew, *Taxus*, has a thin white sapwood zone that changes abruptly into a bright rust-red to purplish-red heartwood—quite unmistakeable.

Next, sapwood colours are rarely distinctive, but **heartwood colours** can be so. Larch, *Larix*, has terra-cotta or red-brown heartwood. Apple, *Malus*, is dark purplish-brown. Pear, *Pyrus*, is warm dark pinkish-brown, and cherry, *Prunus avium*, greenish golden-brown.

Annual rings (Figs. 5 & 6) are very prominent in certain timbers, such as Douglas fir, *Pseudotsuga*, and certain pines, *Pinus*, which always develop distinct dark summerwood zones. The width of the rings, however, has no diagnostic value at all; it depends on the rate of growth, not on the kind of tree.

Some timbers have pores, large enough to be visible to the naked eye, disposed in a circular fashion along the course of the rings. Examples are ash, *Fraxinus*, walnut, *Juglans*, and hickory, *Carya*. *See* Fig. 13 left.

A few trees, including oaks, *Quercus*, have easily-seen *rays*, which show up on cross sections as **bright, very narrow bands radiating from the heart** of the tree. *See* Fig. 13.

Resin, oozing from pores in the wood, is a sure sign of a coniferous timber, or softwood, but it is not evident in **every** conifer. Where present, it is a clear, transparent, sticky fluid when it first emerges, but it soon hardens and turns black. If you touch

Flutes and buttresses: western red cedar, *Thuja plicata*

Flutes and buttresses: hornbeam, *Carpinus betulus*

Fig. 12 *Bole characters*

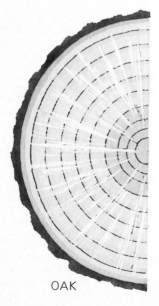

OAK

ASH

Fig. 13 Timber

fresh resin with your fingers they will turn black too! The **turpentine odour** of resin, due to its actual turpentine content, is unmistakeable, but if it has dried you may have to break its surface to freshen the smell.

Occasionally the **hardness** of a timber provides a clue to its name. Test this by trying to indent it with a fingernail. Most **hardwoods**, the timbers of broadleaved trees, resist this, but a few, notably poplars, *Populus*, and willows, *Salix*, are very soft. Most **softwoods**, the timbers of coniferous trees, can be indented by finger-nail pressure. The summerwood zones of a few conifers, particularly Douglas fir, *Pseudotsuga* and certain pines, *Pinus*, resist it.

CHAPTER FIVE

Identification by Flowers

Flower structure is the basis of all plant classification. In theory, therefore, it should be easy to identify any tree by examining its flowers. This is broadly true, but of limited practical help, because flowers are only available for short periods of the year, and for only a fraction of a tree's life-time. During their seedling, sapling and young adult stages, most trees bear no flowers at all, yet the nurseryman, forester and field botanist must be able to name them. Once flowering begins, blossoms are only available, on average, for one month out of twelve, against the need to identify trees all the year round.

A further complication is that in certain genera, notably poplars, *Populus*, and willows, *Salix*, each tree bears only male, or only female, flowers. You need, therefore, to know the characters of both sexes before you can put a name to them. In other genera, such as maples, *Acer*, and ash trees, *Fraxinus*, you may find on the same tree or even in the same flower-cluster, individual flowers that are male, female or hermaphrodite, holding fertile organs of both sexes. Individual trees may only bear male flowers one year, but only female flowers the next. Flowers of one sex may open ahead of those of the other, though an overlapping period is essential to ensure pollination of the females by the males. Do not, therefore, expect to find on living trees the regularity of 'ideal' flowers, which tend to be more frequent in the textbooks than the forest.

Season of Flowering

Season of flowering is another clue that you should handle with caution. In the descriptions that follow, this is stated in general terms, because exact statements of months seldom fit observed facts. Obviously, trees tend to flower later the farther north you go, throughout the northern hemisphere. They also flower later, even in the same place, during a 'late' spring, when weather remains wintry far into March or even April.

There is a general relationship between the time of flowering and the time of leaf opening, but it is not constant for all trees in all years. Cherries and plums, members of the large *Prunus* genus, open their snowy white blossoms ahead of their leaves during late, cold springs. But in an early warm spring their leaves expand at the same time as the flowers, or even ahead of them. Flowering here is linked to day-length which increases constantly every spring. But leafing-out depends on temperatures, which vary from one year to another.

It is useful to recognize a group of trees that always open flowers well ahead of their leaves, on bare branches. All have catkins or catkin-like flowers, usually all-male or all-female, and are wind-pollinated. Pollination by wind is more efficient early in the year, because there are then no leaves to check the drift of pollen from male to female flowers.

Trees That Always Flower Early, Well Ahead of Leaf Opening

Willows—with a few exceptions, *Salix* genus; poplars—all, *Populus*; alders—all, *Alnus*, hazels—all, *Corylus*; elms—all, *Ulmus*; maples—a few species, *Acer*; yews (evergreen), *Taxus*.

If, therefore, you find a tree displaying flowers or catkins on leafless branches between January and the end of March, you can safely concentrate your search for its name within this small group of genera.

Two exceptional trees flower **in autumn**. One is the *Cedrus* genus, comprising the true cedars. You will find their yellow male flower-clusters, which look surprisingly like little cones, from September onwards, and search may reveal bud-like female flowers. The other is the strawberry tree *Arbutus*.

All other trees open their flowers between the time they leaf-out, normally April, and midsummer. The four months April, May, June and July see the whole panorama of blossoms unfolding. Descriptions of the separate genera say whether they bloom early or late, **with** the leaves or **after** them, but cannot be more precise. Species, varieties or cultivars, and even individual trees, show differences both in time of flowering and the length of their display.

Types of Tree Flowers

Having found your flower, at any season of the year, it is helpful to assign it to one of three broad groups. These take no particular heed of academic botanical classifications.

1 Perfect Flowers, Bearing Petals: These resemble the familiar flowers of smaller plants, with green sepals, white or brightly-coloured petals, male stamens and a female pistil. Exceptionally, the male or female organs may be lacking.

2 Broadleaved Tree Catkins, Without Petals: In this group there are no easily-known petals to guide you. All the flowers, with rare exceptions, are entirely male or entirely female. (Sweet chestnut, *Castanea*, has male and female flowers on one catkin.)

3 Conifer Flowers: This catkin-like group are always male or female throughout each cluster. It is handy to distinguish them from the Broadleaved Tree group above, because you will usually find them associated with needle-shaped, evergreen leaves. (Exceptionally, in larches, *Larix*, swamp cypress, *Taxodium*, and dawn redwood, *Metasequoia*, they may open just ahead of deciduous needles.)

Group 1—Easy Keys to Flowers with Petals

Characters of the component parts of a perfect, petal-bearing flower often give 'short-cut' clues to the name of the tree that bears it. The green sepals seldom help here, and the central pistil needs a lens for the determination of critical points. Petals and stamens tell us most.

Colour of Flower Petals

A large proportion of petal-bearing trees have **white** flowers, or else white-flowered varieties have been developed in cultivation. Whiteness is therefore of little use as a clue, but any variation from it can prove diagnostic.

Clear-yellow petals indicate laburnum, *Laburnum*, Cornelian cherry, *Cornus mas*, or certain American buckeyes, *Aesculus*.

Greenish-yellow petals are typical of maples and European sycamore, *Acer*, tulip tree, *Liriodendron*, and spindle trees, *Euonymus*.

Purple petals are found on Judas trees and redbuds, *Cercis*.

Green petals occur on tree of heaven, *Ailanthus*, and buckthorns, *Rhamnus* and *Frangula*.

Red petals, and **petals flushed with pink** are characteristic of trees in the rose-tribe, or Rosaceae, particularly: hawthorns, *Crataegus*; apples, *Malus*; quinces, *Cydonia*; medlar, *Mespilus*; plums, cherries, peaches and almonds, *Prunus*. They also occur on some horse chestnuts or buckeyes, *Aesculus*.

Number of Petals

A large proportion of petal-bearing trees bear **five** petals in each flower. Double varieties grown in parks and gardens may have many more.

Trees whose flowers **only have four petals** are holly, *Ilex*; box, *Buxus*; spindle, *Euonymus*: buckthorns, *Rhamnus* and *Frangula*, dogwoods, *Cornus*.

Trees whose flowers have **six petals** are tulip trees, *Liriodendron*, magnolia, *Magnolia*, and cabbage tree, *Cordyline*.

Symmetry

As a rule, petals are arranged in perfect symmetry, all of one shape, around the heart of the flower. Asymmetrical flowers, with petals of different shapes and sizes, giving a lop-sided flower, therefore stand out.

Asymmetrical flowers occur on: Judas trees and redbuds, *Cercis*; honey locust, *Gleditsia*; laburnum, *Laburnum*; robinia or black locust, *Robinia*; horse chestnuts or buckeyes, *Aesculus*, catalpas, *Catalpa*. In all these, the asymmetrical shape of the petals is followed by the stamens and the central pistil.

Stamen Number

Stamens may be recognized by their position in the flower, just within the ring of petals, and by their shape, typically a pair of oval anthers, yellow with pollen, on a long white stalk. Their numbers are highly diagnostic. *See* Fig. 14.

PEAR (Numerous)

LAUREL (12)

ROBINIA (10)

HORSE CHESTNUT (6)

MAPLE (8)

CATALPA (5)

ASH (2)

DOGWOOD (4)

Fig. 14 Stamens

Numerous stamens, difficult to count, are found in all the genera of the rose tribe or Rosaceae, namely: hawthorns, *Crataegus*; mountain ashes and whitebeams, *Sorbus*; apples, *Malus*; pears, *Pyrus*; quinces, *Cydonia*; medlars, *Mespilus*; plums, cherries, peaches, almonds and cherry laurels, *Prunus*. They also occur in tulip tree, *Liriodendron*; magnolia, *Magnolia*; limes or basswoods, *Tilia*; and eucalyptus trees, *Eucalyptus*.

Twelve stamens: true laurel, *Laurus*.

Ten stamens: Judas tree and redbud, *Cercis*; honey locust, *Gleditsia*; laburnum, *Laburnum*; robinia or black locust, *Robinia*; strawberry tree and madrone, *Arbutus*.

Eight stamens: maples and European sycamore, *Acer*.

Six stamens: sassafras, *Sassafras*; horse chestnuts and buckeyes, *Aesculus*; cabbage tree, *Cordyline*; true palms, including *Trachycarpus* and *Chamaerops*.

Five stamens: sumac, *Rhus*; tamarisks, *Tamarix*; elder, *Sambucus*; catalpa, *Catalpa*.

Four stamens: box, *Buxus*; hollies, *Ilex*; spindle tree, *Euonymus*; persimmon, *Diospyros*; buckthorns, *Rhamnus* and *Frangula*; dogwoods, *Cornus*.

Two stamens: ash, *Fraxinus*; olive, *Olea*.

Group 2—Catkins of Broadleaved Trees

Catkins and catkin-like flowers must first be classed as **male** or **female**. Male catkins consist of numerous bracts, with stamens that shed yellow pollen from anthers that are easily seen. Females, usually much smaller and bud-shaped, are difficult to find and identify.

Shapes of Male Catkins (*See* Fig. 15)

Long, drooping, 'lamb's tail' male catkins, bearing clusters of bracts and flowers along a central stalk, indicate:
poplars, *Populus*; hickories, *Carya*; alders, *Alnus*; hazel, *Corylus*; walnuts, *Juglans*; birches, *Betula*; hornbeam, *Carpinus*; sweet chestnut, *Castanea*.

Short, oval, woolly male catkins, with anthers emerging through a coating of 'fur', point to willows, alias 'pussy willows', of the genus *Salix*.

Tassel-shaped catkins, with groups of male flowers, set at intervals along their stalks, or springing from a twig, indicate:
beech, *Fagus*; elms, *Ulmus*; oaks, *Quercus*; ash, *Fraxinus*.

(Elm has both male and female elements; ash may have both.)

Round catkins on long stalks belong to one of these genera: mulberries, *Morus*; sweet gum, *Liquidambar*; planes and American sycamore, *Platanus*.

Shapes of Female Catkins (*See* Fig. 16)

Some trees have female catkins that mimic those of males, so: **long, drooping, 'lamb's tails'**, with many flowers projecting from a central stalk: poplars, *Populus*.

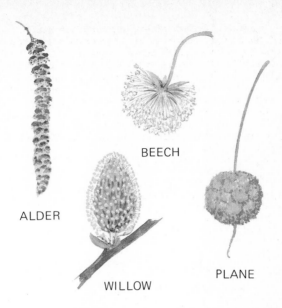

Fig. 15 Male catkin shapes

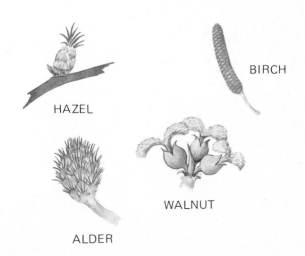

Fig. 16 Female catkin shapes

Long, tight cylindrical catkins: birches, *Betula*.

Short, oval, woolly catkins, with 'pussy' fur: willows, *Salix* (like the males, but show no yellow pollen).

Tassel-shaped female catkins: elm, *Ulmus*; ash, *Fraxinus*. (Elm has both male and female elements; ash may have both.)

Round female catkins on long stalks: mulberries, *Morus*; sweet gum, *Liquidambar*; planes and American sycamore, *Platanus*.

Bud-shaped female catkins: hazels, *Corylus*; oaks, *Quercus*.

Club-shaped female catkins: alders, *Alnus*.

Groups of three flask-shaped female flowers: walnuts, *Juglans*; hickories, *Carya*.

Group 3—Conifer Flowers

Male flowers of conifers give few formal clues for telling one genus from another. They grow in catkins, set a little way back from the shoot tips. Each flower consists of bracts and anthers, and when they open they all become yellow with pollen. Monkey puzzle, *Araucaria*, has long, cylindrical, catkin-like, yellow male flowers. Size varies, but there are rarely any marked structural differences between the male flowers of one conifer genus and those of another.

Differences of general appearance can prove helpful, and typical flowers for each genus are therefore illustrated in all the main-text conifer descriptions. Note that all these pictures show the flowers at the critical stage of pollen dispersal. Pictures of partially opened male flowers are frequent in textbooks, but are misleading, as they confound comparisons between one genus and another.

Female conifer flowers give better clues to identification. Most, but not all, foreshadow the variable shapes of ripe cones, into which they will develop. The main-text pictures of female flowers and cones clarify this. Female conifer flowers always open at or near twig-tips.

All female conifer flowers are illustrated here at the stage of pollen reception. The pictures differ, in consequence, from those in many standard textbooks which really show developing, previously fertilized cones.

Pines, *Pinus*, bear odd female flowers, **unlike** their cones. They open **at the very tips of newly-expanded shoots**, ahead of the still-opening needles. Each is a bright red globe, smaller than a pea. They take two years to mature fully. After one year each cone has become a round, hard, pea-sized, brown structure, now **at the base** of an extended annual shoot. During the following season it enlarges rapidly, and passes through a soft green stage to become a hard, brown woody cone, of the shape peculiar to its species.

Silver firs, *Abies* genus, and Douglas firs, *Pseudotsuga*, have curious female flowers, unlike their cones. A mass of green bracts, one, long or short, per cone-scale, makes many of them look like round tufted brushes, or fox's tails.

CHAPTER SIX

Identification by Fruits, Seeds and Seedlings

Most trees ripen their fruits and seeds in autumn, and fruiting material is usually available to aid identification until midwinter. A few exceptional trees, notably: poplars, *Populus*, most willows, *Salix*, elms, *Ulmus*, and certain kinds of cherries, *Prunus*, ripen fruits early in summer; these naturally disappear sooner. Seedlings of these early-fruiting trees commonly sprout in the summer of ripening. The great majority of seedlings of late-fruiting trees, do not sprout until the following spring. Seeds of some kinds of trees lie dormant in the soil for eighteen months after ripening.

Fruits and seeds are highly distinctive for each kind of tree. Unfortunately, like flowers, they are only available for a limited season of the year, and only over a fraction of the life-time of each individual tree. Trees too young to bear flowers cannot develop fruits or seeds. Certain trees, particularly large-seeded ones like oaks, *Quercus*, and beeches, *Fagus*, have irregular **seedless years**, long after they have reached an age of size suitable for regular seeding.

FRUITS, SEEDS AND SEED NUMBERS

Useful technical definitions distinguish **fruits** from **seeds**. **A fruit is the product of a single flower**. If the flower was one of a bunch, the fruits will be bunched also: solitary flowers likewise develop into solitary fruits. Each individual fruit may hold one seed or several seeds.

A seed may be a solitary element in a fruit, one of a small group, or one of a multitude. **The seed is the vital element from which a new tree can develop**.

Single-seeded fruits are comparatively rare, and therefore help one to identify the genus of tree concerned. Fruits with two, three or four seeds also distinguish certain genera, but one must be careful here, because some members of each group may fail to develop. A 'three-seeded' fruit, for example, may appear to be one-seeded. The following brief lists may help:

Fruits Clearly One-seeded

Hard Fruits (when ripe)
Walnut, *Juglans*; hickory, *Carya*; hazel, *Corylus*; beech, *Fagus* and *Nothofagus*; sweet chestnut, *Castanea* (on occasion).

Oaks, *Quercus*; horse chestnut, *Aesculus*; lime, *Tilia*; elm, *Ulmus*; ash, *Fraxinus*.

Soft Fruits (*when ripe*)
Some hawthorns, *Crataegus*; plums, cherry laurels and cherries, *Prunus*; palm, *Trachycarpus*; yew, *Taxus*; maidenhair tree, *Ginkgo*.

Fruits Clearly Few-Seeded

More than one seed, less than five
Beech, *Fagus* and *Nothofagus*; sweet chestnut, *Castanea* (when all seeds develop).
Maples, *Acer* genus; two seeds arise as a pair from each flower.
True laurels, *Laurus*; sassafras, *Sassafras*.
Some hawthorns, *Crataegus*.
Holly, *Ilex*; spindle tree, *Euonymus*.
Buckthorns, *Rhamnus* and *Frangula*; dogwoods, *Cornus*.
Cabbage tree, *Cordyline*.

Fruits, or Fruiting Bodies, with Many Seeds

Five or more in each conventional fruit, catkin, or cone
Willows, *Salix*; poplars, *Populus*; birches, *Betula*; alders, *Alnus*; elms, *Ulmus*.
Mulberries, *Morus*; figs, *Ficus*; magnolias, *Magnolia*; tulip tree, *Liriodendron*.
True laurels, *Laurus*; sassafras, *Sassafras*; sweet gum, *Liquidambar*; plane or American sycamore, *Platanus*.
Mountain ash and whitebeam, *Sorbus*; apple, *Malus*; pear, *Pyrus*.
Judas tree or redbud, *Cercis*; honey locust, *Gleditsia*; laburnum, *Laburnum*; robinia, *Robinia*.
Tree of heaven, *Ailanthus*; box, *Buxus*; sumac, *Rhus*; tamarisk, *Tamarix*; tupelo, *Nyssa*; eucalyptus, *Eucalyptus*.
Strawberry tree, *Arbutus*.

Cones of conifers always hold many seeds.

Fruit Characters: Soft or Hard?

Certain trees develop soft, succulent pulp around their seed or seeds. This attracts birds and beasts who eat it and in so doing accidentally spread the active seeds. The presence, colour and character of soft pulp is a handy means for identifying the genera listed below. All other tree fruits are hard.

TREES WITH SOFT FRUITS SORTED OUT BY COLOUR

The colour of the pulp or skin of a succulent fruit is often diagnostic, but some trees have cultivated varieties with odd-coloured fruits. In the following broad assortment these multi-coloured genera are mentioned twice or even three times: only the fully-ripened colour is quoted.

Green: fig, *Ficus*; olive, *Olea*; almond, *Prunus amygdalina*; plum, *Prunus domestica*.

Yellow: pear, *Pyrus*; apple, *Malus*; quince, *Cydonia*; medlar, *Mespilus*; peach, *Prunus persica*, persimmon; *Diospyros*; maidenhair tree, *Ginkgo*; fig, *Ficus*.

Orange: mountain ashes and whitebeams, *Sorbus*.

Pink: spindle tree, *Euonymus*.

Crimson; hawthorns, *Crataegus*; some plums, *Prunus domestica*.

Clear red: apple, *Malus*; some cherries, *Prunus avium* and cultivars; holly, *Ilex*; strawberry tree and madrone, *Arbutus*; elder, *Sambacus racemosa*; yew, *Taxus*; mulberry, *Morus*.

Blue or Purple: sassafras, *Sassafras*; some plums, *Prunus domestica*; fig, *Ficus*; tupelo, *Nyssa*; elder, *Sambucus* species; palm, *Trachycarpus* (blue-black); juniper, *Juniperus*.

Black: true laurel, *Laurus*; mulberry, *Morus nigra*; cherries, *Prunus avium*, *P. padus*; buckthorns, *Rhamnus* and *Frangula*; dogwood, *Cornus*; olive, *Olea*.

White: cabbage tree, *Cordyline* (bluish-white).

GUIDE TO CONIFER CONES

The genus to which a coniferous tree belongs is often shown by the character of its cones.

A   Cones with Overlapping Scales (*See* **Fig. 17**):

Pines, *Pinus*, have a **marked swelling on every cone-scale**, often carrying a prickle. **Asymmetric** or lop-sided cones are frequent in pines, rare in other genera. Many pine cones are nearly **conical**, rather than cylindrical.

Silver firs, *Abies*, bear **cylindrical upright cones** that **fall to pieces** when they ripen in autumn, leaving an upright central stalk.

Douglas fir cones, *Pseudotsuga*, are egg-shaped, droop downwards, do not shatter, and bear a **three-pointed bract** behind every scale.

Spruce cones, *Picea*, droop downwards, and have no apparent bracts; they are **cylindrical**—both long and short cylinders occur in different species.

Larches, *Larix*, bear **barrel-shaped cones**, with hollow tips.

Cedars, *Cedrus*, also have barrel-shaped cones, larger than larch cones, with **very shallow visible scale surfaces**.

Hemlocks, *Tsuga*, open short, oval, drooping cones, with scales that soon spread outwards.

The rarely seen cone of the monkey puzzle, *Araucaria*, is known at once by its **large size, pineapple shape, bristle-tipped oval scales** and **big-seeds**.

Slender scales that **diverge from the cone-base**, are found on cones of the western red cedar, *Thuja*, and the incense cedar, *Calocedrus*. *Thuja* has wings on both sides of its seed; *Calocedrus* has a single wing on one side only.

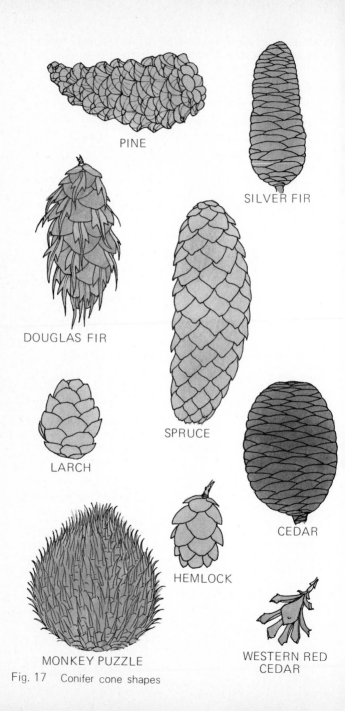

PINE

SILVER FIR

DOUGLAS FIR

SPRUCE

LARCH

CEDAR

MONKEY PUZZLE

HEMLOCK

WESTERN RED
CEDAR

Fig. 17   Conifer cone shapes

B   Round or Oval Cones, with Scales that radiate from a central stalk without overlapping (*See* Fig. 18):

Cypresses, of the genera *Cupressus, Chamaecyparis* and *Cupresso-cyparis*, are the commonest bearers of round knobbly cones; each scale has a stalk below its centre. If detached it resembles a small umbrella.

Coast redwood, *Sequoia*, and giant sequoia, *Sequoiadendron*, bear oval cones with **crumpled scale-faces**, depressed at the centre.

Japanese cedar, *Cryptomeria* is easily known by its **frilly cones**; each scale bears little points and is fixed to a bract that has a reversed tip.

Swamp cypresses, *Taxodium*, bears **truly round cones** with **diamond-shaped (rhombic) scales**, that meet at their edges. Dawn redwood, *Metasequoia*, bears similar but less regular cones; their scales have grooved, swollen ends.

SEED CHARACTERS, WINGED OR WINGLESS

A large proportion of tree seeds bear wings or hairs, to help their spread by wind. It is easy to assign these wings to one of three types, so: A **tufts of hairs**; B membranous or papery **wings attached to one end of the seed only**, and C membranous or papery **wings affixed to both sides of the seed grain** or else **all round it**. *See* Fig. 19.

Hairy-tufted Seeds

Poplars, *Populus* (from pods); willows, *Salix* (from pods), planes and American sycamore, *Platanus* (from a 'ball'); tamarisk, *Tamarix* (from pods).

Seeds with Membranous, Papery Wings Affixed at One End only

Tulip tree, *Liriodendron*; hornbeam, *Carpinus*; maples, *Acer*; ash trees, *Fraxinus*.

Many conifers, including: monkey puzzle, *Araucaria* (wing is rudimentary); pines, *Pinus*; true cedars, *Cedrus*; larches, *Larix*; spruces, *Picea*; hemlock, *Tsuga*; Douglas fir, *Pseudotsuga*; silver firs, *Abies*; incense cedar, *Calocedrus*.

In pines, the seed is **lightly attached** to the wing, which grips it by **two narrow prong-like processes**. In spruces, the seed is again lightly attached, but lies in a **spoon-shaped hollow**. The other genera named have seeds firmly attached to their wings.

Seeds with Membranous, Papery Wings Affixed to Both Sides of Seed or All Round it

Alder, *Alnus* (small); birches, *Betula* (tiny); elms, *Ulmus* (broad); tree of heaven, *Ailanthus* (long, free); catalpa, *Catalpa* (hairy wings, from pods).

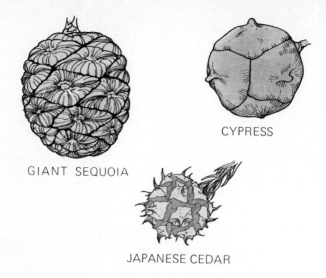

GIANT SEQUOIA

CYPRESS

JAPANESE CEDAR

Fig. 18   Conifer cone shapes

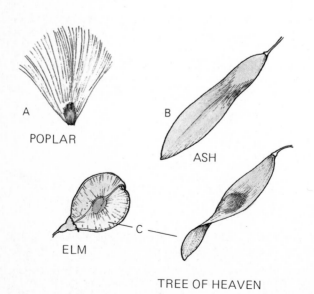

A

POPLAR

B

ASH

C

ELM

TREE OF HEAVEN

Fig. 19   Types of winged seed

Certain conifers notably: giant sequoia, *Sequoiadendron*; coast redwood, *Sequoia*; Japanese cedar, *Cryptomeria*; swamp cypress, *Taxodium*; dawn redwood, *Metasequoia*; fern-frond cypresses, *Chamaecyparis*; true cypresses, *Cupressus*; western red cedar, *Thuja*.

Hard Seeds Enclosed in Pods

A few trees ripen small, numerous hard seeds, wholly enclosed within slender, long, leathery pods, which eventually open to release them. Common pod-bearing genera, with wingless seeds, are:
Judas tree, rebud, *Cercis* (long pod); honey locust, *Gleditsia* (long pod); laburnum, *Laburnum* (long pod); robinia or black locust, *Robinia* (long pod); box, *Buxus* (round, papery pod); eucalyptus, *Eucalyptus* (hemispherical capsule).

Hard Nuts Grouped in Husks that Split

In this very distinctive fruit group, one seed or a group of two, three or four seeds, ripens within a thick, tough, and often spiny husk, which splits to release them. Found in:
beech, *Fagus*; southern beech, *Nothofagus*; sweet chestnuts, *Castanea*; horse chestnuts, *Aesculus*.

Solitary Nuts

Nuts are the seed-grains of one-seeded fruits, which lack all the peculiarities described above. They have no wings and no distinctive spines or husks, and they lack soft juicy flesh. Typical genera are:
walnuts, *Juglans*; hickories, *Carya*; hazel, *Corylus*; beech, *Fagus* (may have 1 or 2 seeds); likewise southern beech *Nothofagus*; sweet chestnut, *Castanea* (1, 2 or 3 seeds); sumac, *Rhus* (hairy); limes, *Tilia* (grouped on **short stalks** arising from long stalks).

Spiky Nuts Grouped on Hard Balls

Sweet gum, *Liquidambar*.

SEEDLING CHARACTERS

Tree seedlings are small, yet each kind develops in a way that reveals its identity. Classic textbooks ignore this, but its value is well stated in the following passage by E. J. H. Corner, in his: *The Natural History of Palms* (Weidenfeld, London, 1966):

"No land plant can be fully appreciated until the developmental sequence of its leaves is known. As the eye is accustomed to the juvenile stages, the main characteristics then appear. Seedling identification has to be learnt by the ecologist, and foresters have made of it a practical art."

As a practising forester and field ecologist I endorse Corner's

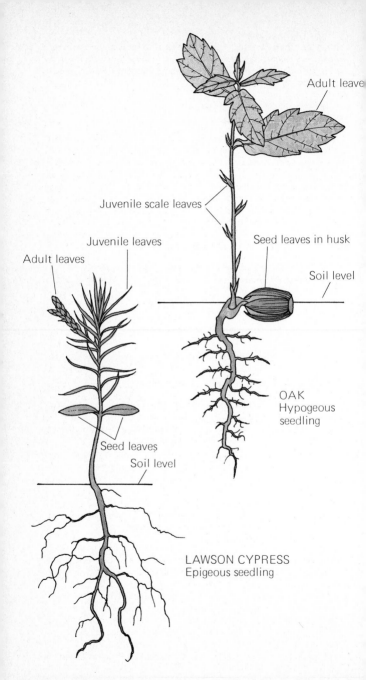

Adult leave

Juvenile scale leaves

Seed leaves in husk

Soil level

OAK
Hypogeous
seedling

Adult leaves

Juvenile leaves

Seed leaves

Soil level

LAWSON CYPRESS
Epigeous seedling

Fig. 20   Seedling characters

view wholeheartedly. Here I have aimed to show what seedlings actually look like. All are sketched at the end of their first season of active growth, and show the three typical elements *a*, *b* and *c* usually present. *See* Fig. 20.

a   Seed-leaves or Cotyledons

These were originally present within the seed when it ripened. In a few trees they do not emerge from the husk, but serve only as food reserves, which nourish the emerging seedling when it sprouts. Such germination is called **hypogeous**, meaning 'below ground'. Examples are: walnut, *Juglans*; sweet chestnut, *Castanea*; oaks, *Quercus*, and among conifers: monkey puzzle, *Araucaria*.

The majority of trees show **epigeous** or 'above-ground' germination, in which the seed-leaves are raised into the air by the stalk that bears them and carry the seed-husk with them. They then expand and split the husk, which falls away. The seed-leaves, now exposed to light, next turn green and start to nourish the tree through photosynthesis.

In broadleaved trees, which are botanically classed as **dicotyledons**, there are **always two seed-leaves**. Our few **monocotyledon** trees, palms and cabbage-palms, have **only one seed-leaf**.

Conifers may have **two, three, four or many seed-leaves** according to their genus. Large numbers are much commoner than small ones.

b   Juvenile Leaves of Seedlings

These peculiar structures, widely ignored in conventional textbooks, are of great value to foresters and ecologists who must name seedlings in the woods. They can prove misleading because they differ from the typical adult leaves of the same tree and may resemble those of some unrelated kind.

Either their shape or their arrangement, or both, may be exceptional. Thus young maples, *Acer*, have **triangular or oval leaves**, not lobed ones, while young pines bear their **needles singly**, not in the twos, threes or fives of the adult state.

Juvenile leaves usually mimic the leaves of the tree's remote ancestors. Palms, for example, bear juvenile leaves like broad blades of grass. Some trees however bear **no** juvenile leaves. They proceed instead directly from the seed-leaf to the adult leaf pattern.

c   Adult Leaves of Seedlings

These follow the characteristic pattern of the tree concerned, but are naturally smaller in size on the seedling than on the full-grown tree.

CHAPTER SEVEN

The Tree in its Surroundings

Many trees can be identified, even at a distance, by their general form and situation, but it is difficult to express the distinguishing features in words. This book therefore includes pictures of representative trees in full leaf and, where appropriate, in their leafless winter condition. All these illustrations are based on actual photos of identified specimen trees.

NATURAL FORMS OF OPEN-GROWN TREES

A tree can only develop its representative form or individuality, if it is allowed to grow in the open, without artificial pruning or any competition from neighbouring trees: in natural forests this rarely happens, because trees spring up closely together, and their side branches die off early through overshading by their neighbours. Only the more successful trees, in the struggle for existence, eventually get their heads free above their competitors. At that point, but not before, they start to develop their characteristic form free from restraints.

The same thing happens in a man-made plantation. The forester spaces his trees with parade-ground regularity, and, though he thins them out as they grow larger, he only allows their crowns to develop, free from competition, during the later stages of the plantation's life. All the same a plantation of any one kind of tree develops a 'personality' different to that of another. Experienced foresters can distinguish a stand of spruce, seen on the skyline, from one of pine, though both are evergreen conifers; but the way they do this cannot easily be put into words or even into illustrations.

The finest examples of open-grown trees usually occur in both private and public parks. Here specimen trees have been planted with full clearance all round, protected from animals, and tended by a succession of zealous gardeners or foresters. As there are no cows or deer to bite their side branches back, these branches grow out naturally right down to ground level. Such trees are said to be 'fully furnished'—they are rare in the wilds.

The shape of a naturally-grown tree's crown is, and can only be, an expression of the bud pattern on its twigs. If the buds are set in pairs and point away from the twig at acute angles, then the resulting crown will develop as a series of paired branches, inclined away from their neighbours in a sharply angular arrangement. Ash trees, *Fraxinus*, and maples, *Acer*, both develop in this way. *See* Fig. 21.

If the buds are set singly, and follow closely the trend of the twig, they result in a closely-ranked crown, with many fine

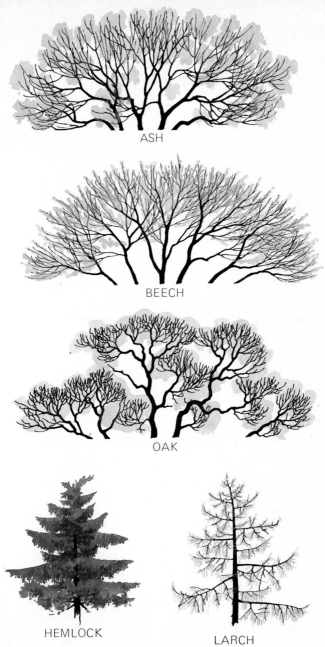

ASH

BEECH

OAK

HEMLOCK

LARCH

Fig. 21 Crowns of open grown trees

branches forming a feathery fringe at its outer surfaces; this is well shown by beech, *Fagus*.

If the buds are clustered at the twig tips, as in oak, *Quercus* or arranged in some random way as in black locust, *Robinia*, then an irregular pattern of branching must result; the tree's crown will have a remarkably intricate outline, with twigs criss-crossing each other in all directions.

All these arrangements are naturally much more easily observed in the winter, where the branches are leafless, than in the summer, when the twigs are clad in leaves.

Certain trees, called 'shade-bearers', have leaves that show a much greater tolerance of shade than do others. Their twigs are therefore much more closely ranked, which results in a solid, dense crown. Examples, drawn from conifers, are yew, *Taxus*, and hemlock, *Tsuga*. Conversely, some sorts of leaves cannot thrive in the shade of others growing nearby. Larches, *Larix*,' are strong 'light-demanders'. Hence the crowns of larch trees are always light and open. *See* Fig. 21.

These differences become apparent in quite distant sightings, once you known what to look for. They may reinforce the differences due to bud patterns. In the examples given above, the 'stand-apart' frameworks of branches in ash, maple, and larch are related to both angular, widely-spaced bud-groupings and intolerance of shade. The 'close-together' look of beech and hemlock is linked to close bud spacings, with one bud at each branching-out point, and shade-tolerant foliage.

ARTIFICIALLY IMPOSED TREE FORMS
(*See* Fig. 22)

Trees are often forced to grow in unnatural ways by artificial lopping and pruning, or occasionally by grafting. The commonest cause of strange growth patterns is called **coppicing**, which means cutting a tree branch back to its stump. Side buds around the rim of this stump then grow out into separate stems, which take the place of the original single one. Few conifers will coppice, but most broadleaved trees can do so. Coppice form is, in consequence, of limited value for the identification of trees. A few trees, especially hazel, *Corylus*, do however grow as a group of sprouts, or small limbs, rather than as a single-boled sturdy tree. Sweet chestnut, *Castanea sativa*, is often grown as a coppice crop, in Britain and Europe, because its durable small poles are highly valued for fencing and hop supports; chestnut is then seen as a regular stand of bunches of thin stems, springing from large cut-over stumps.

Pollarding, the next most important cause of artificially-shaped trees, consists in lopping them at a convenient height, commonly 2 m (6 ft) above ground level. The word comes from Norman French *pol*, meaning 'head', and the tree, now called a **pollard**, responds by sending out a head or bunch of stems at that point. The

SWEET CHESTNUT — COPPICE

OAK — POLLARD

ASH — WEEPING

PRUNUS — FASTIGIATE

Stock grows faster than scion

Scion grows faster than stock

Fig. 22 Imposed tree forms

practical advantage is that this regrowth is out of reach of browsing cattle. Hence cows, sheep, and horses can be allowed to graze below pollarded trees, whereas they would stop the regrowth of coppice unless fenced out.

Pollarding is rarely practised today but pollards are 're-juvenated' trees. Cutting back, followed by sprouting, restores their lost youth, and many live for centuries and achieve bizarre forms, often with hollow trunks. The genera that were most often pollarded, to create such 'golliwog' trees, are oak, *Quercus*, beech, *Fagus*, hornbeam, *Carpinus*, and willow, *Salix*. Other broadleaved trees can be, but rarely are, pollarded successfully. Yew can be pollarded but few true conifers respond to this drastic treatment.

Close clipping and training as hedges will completely destroy the natural form of any tree and as like as not stop it flowering and fruiting. You are then driven back on twig and leaf characters to effect an identification. The extreme case of branch and form suppression is reached when trees are subjected to **topiary**, which involves their being shaped in decorative forms such as pillars or peacocks! Yew and box are the main species concerned.

Changes in form due to grafting very often affect either **weeping** or upright, that is **fastigiate**, varieties of trees. Most trees with branches that 'weep' or droop downwards are exceptional cultivars. Weeping willow, however, droops naturally. The others are usually grafted on an upright **stock** of some related tree that has grown in the normal fashion. This gives them a start in life some 2 m (6 ft) above ground level. The existence of a graft is **always** revealed by a disparity between the bark of the stock at the base and that of the scion that was grafted on to it. Even if the two kinds of bark, above and below the graft, are similar, a broken line, running all round the trunk, will show up. Often there is a difference in diameter on either side of this grafting point; either the scion or the stock may grow faster than the other partner. Weeping varieties that need grafting exist in many kinds of trees; they are common in ash, *Fraxinus*, elms, *Ulmus*, and hemlock, *Tsuga*.

Upright varieties, with multitudes of twigs following the trend of the main stem or leader, require grafting except for Lombardy poplar, which is increased by cuttings. Here the grafts are naturally made low down just above ground level. The commonest trees of this kind are the Dawyck beech, *Fagus*, the Irish yew, *Taxus*, and the Japanese cherry cultivar called *Prunus* 'Amanogawa', meaning 'the milky way'.

Besides these changes in form imposed with the idea of **helping** the tree to grow, though possibly in some strange shape, there are others designed simply to control it, or even suppress it. Trees that have been crudely lopped when they grew too big for their situations are only too frequently seen in gardens and along highways. As sprouts appear around the edges of each cut, each tree behaves as though it had been repeatedly pollarded at several points.

Many broadleaved trees growing in old, neglected woodlands often prove to have arisen from stumps, and have multiple stems just like coppiced trees.

SEASONAL CHANGES

The annual march of the seasons creates many changes among the appearance of trees, and such changes are often diagnostic. The difference between the summer and winter states of deciduous or 'summer-green' trees, and their contrast with the more constant aspect of the evergreens, is obvious to all. Lesser changes call for comment.

Some deciduous trees reveal their identity in spring by opening leaves very early. Weeping willows, *Salix babylonica* and others, are conspicuous examples—these willows also hold their leaves late into the fall of the year. Hawthorns, *Crataegus*, expand leaves early and so do larches, *Larix*, the only common deciduous conifers.

Conversely, certain trees regularly open their leaves **very late** in the year, remaining leafless with bare branches far into late spring, or even early summer. Conspicuous late-leafers are: ash, *Fraxinus*; walnut, *Juglans*; black locust, *Robinia*, and catalpa, *Catalpa*.

A number of trees reveal their identities very clearly at certain seasons of the year, by features that stand out from all other kinds. Examples follow.

Midwinter: January–February

Conspicuous lambs' tail catkins open on hazel, *Corylus*, still leafless.

A 'haze' of purple blossom is seen on bare branches of elms, *Ulmus*.

Early Spring: March–April

Bright acid-green flowers open on bare branches of certain maples, such as Norway maple, *Acer platanoides*, and sugar maple, *Acer saccharum*.

Leafless branches of certain willows, *Salix*, carry golden male, and greyish-white female, furry or 'pussy' catkins.

Lawson cypress, *Chamaecyparis lawsoniana*, opens crimson-and-brown male flowers, in crowded bunches, alongside tiny blue female ones.

Late Spring: May–June

Whitebeam, *Sorbus aria*, displays white undersides on opening leaves.

Pines, *Pinus* species, expand long shoots carrying young needles, pale green at their opening stages, and male and female flowers.

Midsummer: July–August

The high season of late flowering trees, such as catalpa, *Catalpa*.
Poplars, *Populus*, which have flowered early, now shed clouds of tiny seeds tufted with white hairs; so do willows, *Salix*.

Early Autumn: September–October

Autumn leaf-colour begins with horse chestnut, *Aesculus hippocastanum*, whose dark green leaves turn to rust-red.

Cones ripen on many conifers, particularly larches, *Larix*.

Most broadleaved trees ripen fruits or nuts.

Late Autumn: November–December

Late leaves fall from deciduous trees. Among the last to go are those of alders, *Alnus*, which turn from dull green to black before dropping; ripening cones are then visible on alders' bare branches.

A few evergreens, such as strawberry tree, *Arbutus*, continue flowering during mild spells all winter through.

Instances of conspicuous features that should be looked for at particular seasons are frequently quoted in the main text that follows. Always ask yourself: 'If this tree is what I think it is, what should it be showing at this season of the year?' Positive evidence, in the form of remarkable catkins, flowers, leaf colour and so on, is of course more valuable than the **absence** of any particular feature.

NATURAL SURROUNDINGS

The kind of ground on which a tree is growing in a wild state can give useful, though not decisive, clues to its identity. Willows, *Salix*, and alders, *Alnus*, are typically trees of watersides. This is not an accident. Their tiny seeds can start life readily on the damp mud of banks that are occasionally flooded, but elsewhere they fail to compete with lush weeds.

Pines and birches are at home on dry heaths, again because their seedlings readily strike root in bare places where poverty of soil prevents herbs, grasses, and heaths from growing vigorously and choking them out.

A small, but distinctive, group of trees are only common on chalk or limestone soils, which have a strongly alkaline reaction. These include box, *Buxus sempervirens*, purging buckthorn, *Rhamnus cathartica*, and whitebeam, *Sorbus aria*.

On a broader geographic scale, certain trees have limited spreads due either to their **need for high temperatures**, or **intolerance of them**. Olives, *Olea*, for example, do not occur naturally north of the Mediterranean zone of France. Jack pine, *Pinus banksiana*, the commonest kind across northern Canada, is rarely found as a wild tree south of the St Lawrence River.

Exposure to sea winds restricts the variety of trees that grow naturally near coastlines. Maritime pines, *Pinus pinaster*, Sitka spruce, *Picea sitchensis*, evergreen oak, *Quercus ilex*, elms, *Ulmus* species, and white poplar, *Populus alba*, are examples of salt-tolerant trees.

Low rainfalls limit the spread of certain trees, particularly deciduous broadleaves like limes and beeches, which cannot prosper under the summer droughts of southern Europe or California.

All this means that there are 'likely' and 'unlikely' places to find any tree growing wild. If you come across one in an unlikely area, or on a type of ground unsuited to its known needs, you should make doubly sure of its identity, as expressed by standard features of leaf and bark, flower and seed.

Conventional maps of natural distribution, which figure largely in some textbooks, especially in America, should be treated as a guide, but nothing more. Many such 'distributions' have been plotted far more accurately in the drawing office, than they were ever surveyed in the field. Furthermore, trees are very often planted, or become naturalized, far outside these original limits.

USUAL PLANTING SITUATIONS

The distribution of **planted** trees follows a mixture of needs and fashions. It has been fashionable to plant yews, *Taxus*, in churchyards for several hundred years, though nobody can say they are necessary. If you see a dark evergreen bearing berries in a graveyard it is unlikely to be anything else than a yew.

Another vogue concerns the planting of lime trees, *Tilia*, in long straight avenues leading towards mansion houses. Poplars, *Populus*, are planted on odd patches of wet ground, because they make effective use of otherwise valueless land, by providing a quick timber yield. You will also find them on camping sites because of their welcome summer shade.

Shelterbelts, in any particular region, are naturally planted with trees that have been found, by experience, to grow under severe exposure to the elements. Austrian pine, *Pinus nigra* variety *nigra*, is often intermixed with beech, *Fagus sylvatica*, to make reliable upland shelterbelts in Britain. It is rarely planted elsewhere, having few merits either for timber or decoration.

The typical city-square tree, both in Europe and America, is the London plane, *Platanus* × *hispanica*, a vigorous hybrid between American sycamore, *P. occidentalis,* and oriental plane, *P. orientalis*. It is chosen for tolerance of town smoke and hard pavements, and no tree with dappled bark in urban surroundings is likely to be anything else.

The planters of roadside trees often show strong preferences for cherries, whitebeams and mountain ashes, all members of two large genera *Sorbus* and *Prunus*, because they rarely grow too large for their station, and need little pruning. An attractive range of leaf colour, flowers, and fruits increases their desirability. So if you have to name a roadside tree, it is a good idea to consider these genera first.

Timber growers naturally have sound economic reasons for planting selected kinds of trees on particular kinds of ground in various districts—though they do not always follow them! In the colder, wetter, more northerly regions of Europe and North America, spruces, *Picea*, are planted on a vast scale as the most reliable quick producers of large volumes of wood for sawmills and paper mills. Further south, where it is hotter and drier, pines, *Pinus*, take the lead.

Larches, *Larix* are often preferred locally on hillsides, where they are known to grow well. Typical broadleaved timber trees— oak, ash, maple, beech, and elm—are cultivated on richer soils. Beech is often the leading tree on chalk or limestone hills.

Prudent foresters, whether they are planning vast national forests or the smaller-scale woodlands of private estates, usually avoid committing the whole area to one kind of tree. So you should expect occasional changes of species, even in man-made forests aimed at production for the needs of the market.

All this adds up to a challenging range of trees for you to find, under the attractive surroundings of wood, park, or wayside. Study them closely until you can, with assurance, give each its name.

Descriptions of Trees

WILLOWS I: WHITE WILLOW

SALIX ALBA   SALICACEAE

Most willows bear **long narrow leaves** but some have broader ones. One constant feature distinguishes all members of the large willow genus, *Salix*. Buds, which **hug the twigs**, are covered with **only one exterior scale** which completely envelopes them. Easily seen, easily checked by peeling it off. Only two exceptions: the very different conical bud of the plane tree, or American sycamore, genus *Platanus*, which **never** hugs the twig, and the **projecting** bud of the *Magnolia* genus, which is **pinched in** at its base.

White willow, *Salix alba*, is a typical representative of this large group. Native across northern Europe, it was an early introduction to North America. Now naturalized in New England, frequently planted elsewhere. Long, slender, symmetrical leaves about six times as long as broad, averaging $7 \cdot 5 \times 1 \cdot 25$ cm ($3 \times \frac{1}{2}$ in.) each with short stalk, toothed edges, prominent mid-rib, fine point at drawn-out tip. Pale bluish-green with scattered white hairs, **white with silvery hairs beneath**, set at any angle to twig. Buds very small, pointed, on long **slender** olive-brown twigs.

White willow usually grows along riversides where its shapeless crowns spread widely, and its foliage reflects sunlight when stirred by wind. Thick grey-brown bark develops characteristic **network of criss-crossing ribs and fissures**. Timber with white sapwood, pinkish white heartwood, is exceptionally light, but has profitable commercial uses. Cricket-bat willow, cultivar 'Coerulea', distinguished by **bluish-grey-green** leaves on **purple shoots**, and **conical crown**, is grown at high speed on fertile riverside land to yield exceptionally tough timber, the only kind accepted for cricket bats; also used, because of strength with light weight, in artificial limbs.

Nearly all willows bear male and female catkins on separate trees; growers propagate them by cuttings to ensure true strains and same sex. Catkins, in most kinds, open before leaves, and bear nectar; pollination by wind, helped by bees. White willows bear long, slender catkins, without the 'pussy' down found on some other willows. Yellow males consist of numerous, crowded simple flowers, each a bract bearing two golden stamens, on a long central stalk. Green females hold numerous, less close-packed, separate flowers, each a bract with a flask-shaped pistil. Fertilized females ripen before midsummer into green seed-pods, which burst and release masses of **white cottony seeds**. Every seed is a tiny black grain tufted with white hairs. Seed only survives if it falls on damp earth within weeks of ripening. Seedling has short, spreading, hair-like roots; a squat stalk bears two oval seed-leaves; short true leaves follow, then normal slender ones.

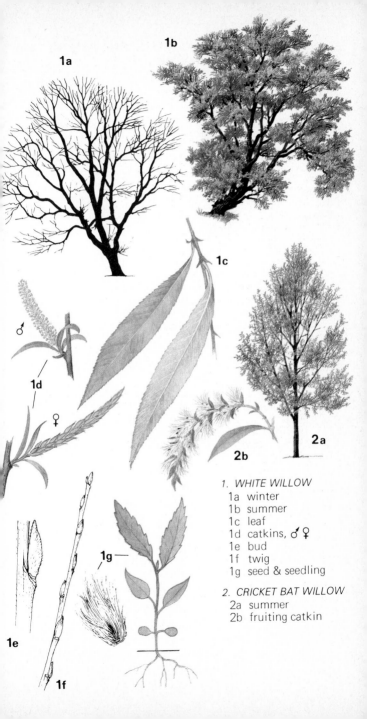

1. *WHITE WILLOW*
   1a winter
   1b summer
   1c leaf
   1d catkins, ♂♀
   1e bud
   1f twig
   1g seed & seedling

2. *CRICKET BAT WILLOW*
   2a summer
   2b fruiting catkin

WILLOWS II: POLLARDS, WEEPING WILLOWS AND OSIERS

SALIX genus   SALICACEAE

Most riverside trees growing as pollards prove to be willows. A pollard **looks like a bush on a pole**. This odd growth habit is achieved by **beheading** a normal tree about 2 m (6 ft) above ground. Trees respond by sending out a mop of side shoots, safely above the reach of browsing cattle. Cut back every seven years, they yield a perpetual supply of brushwood, firewood, small stakes, and material for making hurdles or rough baskets. Pollards were planted as big living stakes called 'truncheons', alongside miles of English rivers. Rarely cropped today, their boles are slowly decaying; yet they still provide picturesque scenery.

Weeping willows too are easily known by form. They ascend so far, then bend branches over in graceful arcs; if water is present, they grow more strongly towards it, to place their foliage in reflected sunlight. Twigs are very slender, buds fine and pointed. **Leaves always hang down**; those on ascending twigs have bent stalks. Weeping willows commonly open these narrow leaves **ahead of all other trees**; also the **last leaves to fade and fall**. Bright yellowish-green in spring, mid-green later, finally pale yellow.

Weeping willows may be *Salix babylonica*, a reputedly Chinese tree long cultivated in Asia, first brought to England by Mr Vernon, circa 1730, from famed Biblical 'waters of Babylon'; or else the cultivar 'Tristis' meaning 'the sad one', of white willow, *S. alba*, Other weeping willows are hybrids propagated by nurserymen, more concerned with future trade prospects than past ancestries. Commonest in Europe is golden-twigged *S. × chrysocoma*, a cross between the two foregoing. Popular in America is red-twigged *S. × elegantissima*, or Thurlow willow, a cross between *S. babylonica* and crack willow, *S. fragilis*.

The name 'osier' can be **applied to nearly any willow**, regardless of species, that is cultivated by cutting a main stem back to ground level, so that the tree sprouts or coppices from a stool. Commercially, this is done annually, to obtain long, thin, supple shoots called 'wands', basic material for willow basketry of all kinds. Many country districts were once self-supporting in osiers, but today most of them are imported from South America. Any osier can be propagated by cuttings; some are varieties of white willow, selected for suppleness or attractive bark colour. Others are derived from wild shrub willows, particularly basket willow or common osier, *S. viminalis*, illustrated here. This bears **exceptionally long narrow leaves**, commonly twelve times as long as wide, around $7 \cdot 5 \times 0 \cdot 6$ cm ($3 \times \frac{1}{4}$ in.) with inrolled edges and shining silvery undersides. Now naturalized over wide areas in North America.

1. POLLARD WILLOW
1a winter
1b summer

2. WEEPING WILLOW
2a spring
2b leaves

3. OSIER
3a summer
3b leaf

WILLOWS III: BLACK, CRACK AND GOAT WILLOWS

SALIX genus   SALICACEAE

Black willow, *Salix nigra*, so-called because of thick, heavily-ridged, **dark brown to black bark**, is commonest tree willow throughout eastern United States, and southern Canada. Pacific willow, *S. lasiandra*, which grows further west, is distinguished only by minor points—greyer leaf undersides, yellow twigs, glands at leaf bases. Both differ markedly from white willow in bearing leafy stipules at base of leaf-stalks, in having sickle-shaped leaves, one side longer than the other; both have **green leaf undersides**, not white ones. Black willow forms a large waterside tree with a spreading crown, and a trunk large enough for commercial timber cutting. Used for boxes and polo balls; also for coconut shies, being too light to dislodge many coconuts!

Crack willow, *S. fragilis*, native to Europe, is now naturalized over a wide extent of North America. Distinguished by an odd feature—pull a twig back and it breaks from a brittle joint with a sharp 'crack'! Spreading, untidy crown of long, slender, upswept branches shows **warm orange-brown branch colour** in winter. Yellow shoots, stouter than white willows, bear oval pointed buds. Leaf tends to **hang** on more distinct stalk; **rich glossy-green above, pale grey-green below**; about five times longer than broad, tapering towards base and more gradually towards pointed tip; edges bear distinct teeth. Bark thick, deeply ridged. Tree often pollarded.

The name 'pussy willow' is loosely applied to a group of shrub and small tree willows that bear **short hairy catkins** or **pussies**. The word 'catkin', derived from this catkin type, means 'little cat'; German equivalent *Kätzchen* and French *châton* both mean 'kitten' too. Most pussy willows have **broad leaves**, usually oval, with a network of interlinked veins. Hairiness makes it **hard to tell male catkins from females**; the latter appear on separate trees. Males show **yellow stamens** above the 'fur'; females have **green pistils**, lacking yellow tints. Catkins open ahead of leaves, and are often gathered for decoration. Fruit catkins mature rapidly after fertilization, split open in early summer, release dense white clouds of hairy seeds.

Goat willow, *S. caprea*, so-called because goats relish early spring foliage, is a typical European 'pussy'. A shrub or small tree very common beside ponds or on waste land. Bears bluntly pointed oval leaves, gay golden male catkins, and silvery female catkins that mature, towards midsummer, into oblong fruit catkins.

Commonest American kind is the pussy willow, *S. discolor*, a hardy shrub-like tree found over northern United States, and most of Canada. In spring it bears soft, silky catkins, with a silvery-blue tinge, before its long-oval, pointed, light green leaves appear.

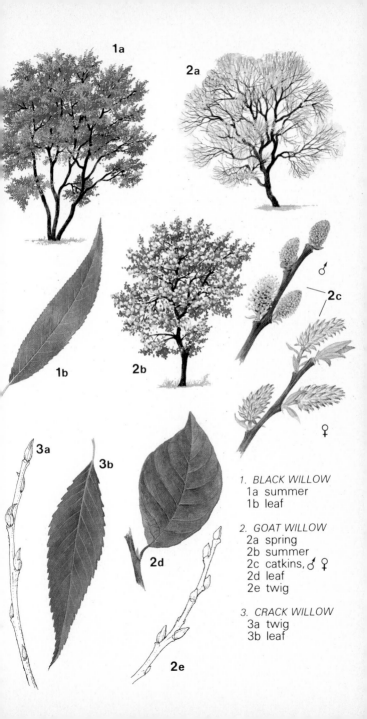

1. BLACK WILLOW
   1a summer
   1b leaf

2. GOAT WILLOW
   2a spring
   2b summer
   2c catkins, ♂ ♀
   2d leaf
   2e twig

3. CRACK WILLOW
   3a twig
   3b leaf

POPLARS I: WHITE POPLAR

POPULUS ALBA   SALICACEAE

Poplars or cottonwoods, of the big genus *Populus*, show a marked group of characters, rather than a single striking one. **Branching is random**, and often a huge poplar looks like a branch stuck in the ground, rather than a well-balanced tree. Shoots are usually vigorous, with pointed many-scaled buds set far apart at random angles. **Leaves**, always simple though occasionally lobed, **stand on long stalks**. In many poplars, especially aspens, these stalks are flattened, and this enables the leaf to flutter in the slightest breeze. The name 'poplar' is distantly derived from the Greek root *papaillo*, to shake, and poplars may often be identified from afar by **constant leaf motion**. This aids transpiration of water, and poplars grow typically on well-watered ground. Their very light, open-pored wood is adapted to rapid sap transport.

A constant feature of poplar leaves is **random venation**, with no symmetrical or regular pattern of veins. Flowers are always borne in separate male and female catkins, nearly always on separate trees.

White poplar, *Populus alba*, illustrates the main characters of the genus. Native to Europe, it is widely planted, and locally naturalized, in North America. It bears smooth **white bark**, tinged with greenish grey; but bark eventually becomes rugged and dark grey near the foot of the sturdy trunk; higher up it may be black-spotted. Leaves are dark green above, but **white below**; they retain that colour even when their green side has faded to yellow. On vigorous shoots they are **five-lobed** like those of maples, but slower-growing shoots bear **roundish** leaves with wavy edges. They stand on long stalks at random angles, following the pattern of the small oval orange-brown buds. **Soft white down** covers young shoots, buds, and unfolding leaves, making both sides appear white. It persists along veins on the leaf's otherwise shiny green upper surface.

Catkins open early in spring, before the leaves. The short-lived male ones, crimson and grey, hang down like wavy lambs' tails. Their central stalk carries numerous simple flowers, basically groups of red stamens shedding yellow pollen. Female catkins, on separate trees, have a long drooping stalk bearing pale green female flowers, each a single pistil topped by a stigma to catch pollen from the wind. After fertilization they mature rapidly to fruit catkins, ripe by midsummer. The seed capsules then break to release myriads of tiny black seeds, each bearing a tuft of fine white hairs, or 'cotton'. Seeds that alight on wet soil sprout promptly, sending up a shoot that bears two oval seed-leaves, followed by lobed true leaves.

White poplar also increases by root suckers, forming dense thickets that can give welcome shelter on sea-coasts, where it resists salt winds. Its light, white wood has no regular market. It is grown only for ornament or as a windbreak.

WHITE POPLAR

a winter
b summer
c sucker coppice,
  autumn
d catkin ♂
e leaf
f catkin ♀
g fruiting catkin
h seed & seedling

POPLARS II: ASPENS, GREY POPLAR

POPULUS genus   SALICACEAE

Aspens thrive further north than any other poplars, and higher up the mountains. They flourish typically along muddy streamsides, both in the tundras of North America and Eurasia, and in upland valleys further south. An aspen rarely grows alone; it is soon **surrounded by a thicket of sucker shoots**. Each round, wavy-edged leaf stands on a long, **very flat stalk**, which allows **incessant motion** in the slightest breeze. Two folk-names, Welsh *coed tafod merched*, French *langue de femme*, aptly express this. Both mean 'tree of the woman's tongue'. Aspen leaves open late in spring. Coppery-brown at first, they become rich green above, pale green below; they turn brilliant yellow before falling late in autumn. Bark, **grey-green and smooth**, develops odd **diamond-shaped hollows**. Slender, randomly-set winter buds are brownish-yellow.

Aspen catkins open in spring, before the leaves, as long dangling 'lambs' tails'; males, greyish-brown in general colour, are thicker than the grey-green female catkins, which appear on separate trees. Both are **densely clad in long white hairs**, like pussy fur. Fruit catkins burst before midsummer, to release fluffy masses of white cotton— the hair around the tiny black seeds. On average, **eight million** cleaned seeds weigh one pound. These tiny morsels of tree life only sprout if they alight on warm damp mud within a few weeks of ripening.

Aspens yield the world's best wood for making matches and match boxes. Like other poplar timbers, which compete closely, it is soft and supple, holds together when cut on a rotary peeling machine into the thin sheets from which matches are sliced out, and does not splinter or break when struck. Heavy when harvested, because its cells hold much water, it becomes very light after drying, and the emptied cells take up paraffin wax well. Other uses are light 'chip' baskets for holding fruit and vegetables, joinery, and paper pulp. Both heartwood and sapwood are white or very pale cream.

Common European 'trembling' aspen is aptly called *Populus tremula*. North American 'quaking' aspen, *P. tremuloides*, is very similar, but leaves have pointed tips. American big-tooth aspen, *P. grandidentata*, bears leaves with rounded tips and prominent teeth.

Grey poplar, *P. canescens*, is a vigorous, massively branched, tall tree intermediate in character between white poplar and common aspen. Possibly a natural hybrid, its features vary widely. Shoots are slightly downy, leaves may be round like aspen, or lobed like vigorous white poplar; white or very pale beneath, they **lack white down**. Bark, grey-green and smooth at first, develops diamond-shaped pits, then becomes **thick, coarsely rugged and grey**.

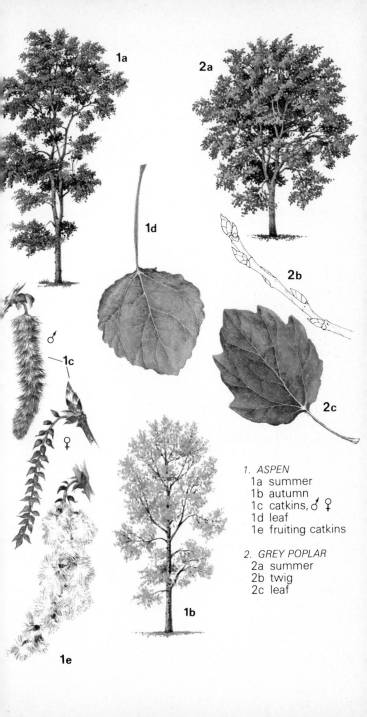

1. *ASPEN*
   1a summer
   1b autumn
   1c catkins, ♂ ♀
   1d leaf
   1e fruiting catkins

2. *GREY POPLAR*
   2a summer
   2b twig
   2c leaf

POPLARS III: BLACK AND HYBRID POPLARS

POPULUS genus   SALICACEAE

European black poplar, *Populus nigra*, grows wild in lowland marshes. Its American counterpart, eastern cottonwood, *P. deltoides*, grows in similar situations, from Quebec south to the Gulf of Mexico. Early in the eighteenth century the latter tree was introduced into Europe, and somewhere in France, about 1750, it hybridized with the European kind. The result of this and subsequent interbreedings has been a whole swarm of hybrids, most of which grow faster than either parent.

Nowadays the original, somewhat variable and relatively slow-growing wild black poplars are rarely planted. Everybody prefers cuttings of known hybrid clones or cultivars, guaranteed true to form and rate of growth. You will find them established—nearly always **in straight lines** like soldiers, as shelterbelts or screens, or to fill in odd patches of waste marshland. They yield timber fast, but their most profitable use is as overhead shelter from sun and wind, on camping sites, especially in France. Only specialists can hope to identify the scores of known hybrids. The description that follows is based on *Populus* 'Serotina', the commonest kind, curiously misnamed 'black Italian poplar'.

This typical hybrid has sturdy, smooth, pale brown twigs bearing **shallow ridges** leading to pointed many-scaled buds, bright brown and slightly resinous. They stand out at a constant sharp angle from branches, and gradually build up a broad, open, **fan-shaped crown**. This is never symmetrical, but **inclines sideways**, giving a 'branch stuck in the ground' effect. Pale grey bark splits early, due to rapid growth, exposing **sinuous vertical pink fissures**. Dark grey ribs develop between these, and become very thick and rugged.

Leaves open very late in spring; the name *serotina* means 'late (leafing)'. They are **coppery bronze** at first, then grey-green; later their upper surfaces darken and the whole leaf becomes pale yellow in autumn. Long-stalked, they are shaped like an **equilateral triangle, with a rounded base and a pointed tip**; edges are shallowly toothed. Male catkins, opening shortly before leaves, carry bright red stamens that shed golden pollen. As this hybrid is **always male**, female catkins and seeds never appear.

European black poplar, *P. nigra*, forms an even more rugged bole, bearing curious swellings. Its trunk is more erect, but the branches are irregular in size, form and direction. Leaves, triangular to diamond-shaped, unfold in yellowish brown shades, becoming pale green later, fading pale yellow. Male catkins are crimson, female catkins greyish white. Eastern cottonwood, *P. deltoides*, is almost identical, but bears more triangular leaves on longer leaf stalks.

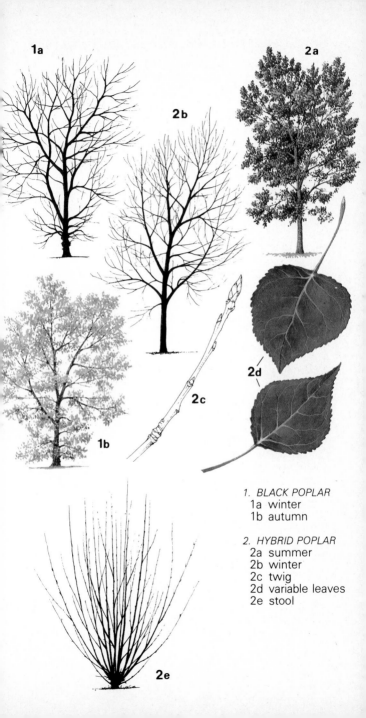

1. *BLACK POPLAR*
   1a winter
   1b autumn

2. *HYBRID POPLAR*
   2a summer
   2b winter
   2c twig
   2d variable leaves
   2e stool

POPLARS IV: LOMBARDY AND BALSAM POPLARS

POPULUS genus   SALICACEAE

Lombardy poplar is not easily confused with any other tree, for its crown waves like a **plume of feathers** over the landscape. This growth habit is called **fastigiate**, from a Latin word meaning a sweeping broom. On most trees the upmost shoot alone takes the lead, and lower ones form side branches. But on fastigiate trees every shoot tries to be leader, and grows upwards in competition with its fellows. The resulting trunk is worthless as timber, because every persistent side shoot forms a rib and a knot. But Lombardy poplar makes a fine scenic feature, and can be used to form narrow windscreens or sight-screens along very narrow plots.

Botanically, Lombardy poplar ranks only as a variety of European black poplar, being named *Populus nigra* cultivar 'Italica'. Most trees are male, and occasionally bear deep red catkins; a female cultivar called 'Foemina', with a broader crown, which bears green catkins, is sometimes seen. First noticed on the plains of northern Italy, Lombardy poplar was introduced to England by the British ambassador, the Earl of Rochford, in 1758. Easily propagated by cuttings, it has now been spread to all countries with temperate climates.

Balsam poplars are so-called because their buds, when they open in spring, are covered in a sticky brown wax or balsam, possibly a protection against insect attack. This substance is **delightfully fragrant**, but only remains so for a few weeks, until bud-scales fade and fall. **Vivid yellow-green** leaves emerge, and gradually become **dark green above, white below**. They are **long-oval** in shape, with shallow-toothed edges and a **long drawn-out tip**. In autumn they fade through yellow to brown, but retain white undersides. Balsam poplar bark is thinner and less deeply fissured than that of other kinds. Male catkins and seeds are similar. Female catkins have more dispersed flowers and seed-pods.

Common balsam poplar, *P. tacamahaca*, is found right across North America from Alaska to Newfoundland and south through the northern United States; it is occasionally cultivated in Europe. Western balsam poplar, *P. trichocarpa* or black cottonwood, grows along the Pacific slope from British Columbia to California. Introduced to England, it grows faster than any other tree, achieving 30 m (90 ft) in only 15 years. Used, in North America, for timber and paper pulp.

Oddly-named 'Balm of Gilead poplar', also called 'Ontario balsam poplar' and *Populus × candicans*, is apparently a hybrid, unknown in the wilds. Distinguished by **stout red-brown shoots and buds**, and **large yellow green leaves**, it has become established over neglected gardens and wastelands in both Britain and America. It suckers vigorously and becomes almost impossible to root out. Don't let it in!

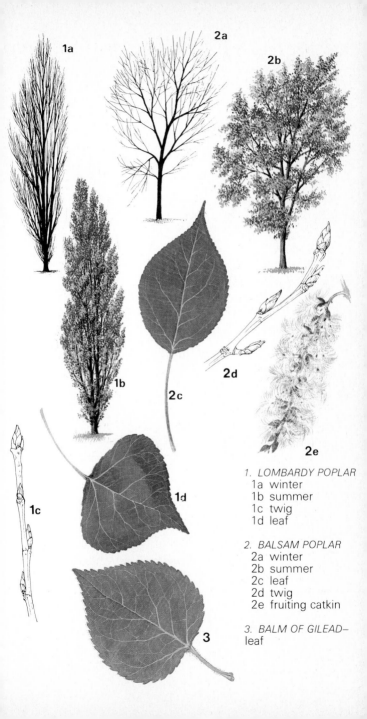

1. *LOMBARDY POPLAR*
 1a winter
 1b summer
 1c twig
 1d leaf

2. *BALSAM POPLAR*
 2a winter
 2b summer
 2c leaf
 2d twig
 2e fruiting catkin

3. *BALM OF GILEAD*–
 leaf

WALNUTS

JUGLANS genus   JUGLANDACEAE

A walnut tree can be known by its pale grey bark, **deeply fissured in an irregular network pattern** and showing **metallic lustre** on the ribs. It branches boldly in an irregular way, with a maze of stout twigs at the top. Pluck a twig and note big leaf scars, each with many vein traces from the compound leaf. Cut the twig across on the slant, to reveal **chambered pith**, looking like little ladder rungs, within. Twigs bend repeatedly, bearing a single large brown bud at every angle.

Walnut leaves, which open **very late**, are compound, with about seven leaflets, each a smooth-edged, short-stalked oblong set along a central stalk. Outer leaflets are commonly **larger** than inner ones. Crush a leaf, and a **strong aromatic odour** proves unmistakeable. **Brown leaf juice** will stain your fingers. Walnut leaves turn dull brown in autumn, breaking into leaflets when they fall.

Male walnut flowers open late in spring, along with the leaves. They are born in large wavy hanging catkins with many bracts, and scatter yellow pollen on the winds. Female catkins, on same tree, project in upright groups of two or three. They are green in colour and **flask-shaped, with two large curved stigmas pointing opposite ways**.

Following wind pollination, these flowers enlarge enormously to form, by late summer, **oval glossy green fruits like plums**, which people gather to make into savoury pickled walnuts. During further ripening the green outer husk falls away, to expose the **pale brown crinkly-shelled nut**, with its odd raised 'rim', familiar to everyone. When you crack a walnut you find within it two **wrinkled yellow seed-leaves** which form the 'flesh' or 'kernel', both delicious and full of nourishment. An odd **brown parchment tissue** runs across the centre of each nut. If it is sown, the seed-leaves remain hidden within the nutshell. The shoot that emerges bears, at first, small leaves with fewer-than-normal leaflets.

Walnut timber is very attractive and valuable. Heartwood shows lovely mottled effects, with **brown, chocolate, black, and pale purplish colours intermingling**. Strong and naturally durable: used for furniture, gun stocks, ornamental carving and wooden bowls.

The commonly cultivated walnut is *Juglans regia*, native to Asia Minor but grown since Roman times throughout Europe, more recently in America. The American native black walnut, *J. nigra*, has a larger leaf with more numerous pointed leaflets, and rugged bark. Its nuts are less tasty, and have rougher shells. Valuable timber, coloured **dark brown or purple to almost black**, has long been used by craftsmen for furniture and ornaments.

EUROPEAN WALNUT
a   winter
b   summer
c   flowers,♂ ♀
d   leaf
e   fruit
f   autumn
g   twig
h   nut and seedling

HICKORIES, PECAN

CARYA genus   JUGLANDACEAE

All hickories originate in North America; a few are grown in Europe.

Shagbark hickory, *Carya ovata*, forms a tall, narrow-crowned tree bearing the **rough, grey, shredding bark** that provides its name. **Stout, purple-brown shoots** bear large shield-shaped leaf scars **and large, oval, pointed, red-brown buds.** Distinctive leaf is large, around 25 cm (10 in.) long overall, and compound. Long main stalk bears **five short-stalked long-oval pointed leaflets. Terminal leaflet largest, closely matched by next pair down; basal pair distinctly smaller.** Leaflets are yellowish-green, thick and oily; turn bright gold in autumn.

Male flowers open when leaves do, at twig tips. Each **main catkin stalk branches into three catkins.** Each long, slender, drooping yellowish-green catkin is crowded with little male flowers, which release golden pollen. Female flowers arise at twig tips in **groups of three on a short central stalk.** Each flower is flask-shaped, green, with spreading bracts and a central feathery style.

Nuts, borne in pairs or threes on short stalks, ripen through soft green stage. Ripe nut has **round woody protective husk, dark reddish-brown, four-ribbed**, 5 cm (2 in.) across, 1 cm ($\frac{1}{2}$ in.) thick. This splits along four ribs and reveals **inner, round, pale-brown, four-ribbed, pointed nut**, with smooth, tough, hard shell and sweet edible white kernel.

Nuts sprout readily in spring. The two seed-leaves remain in the husk; the sturdy shoot bears first scale leaves, then trifoliate leaves, then normal leaves with five leaflets.

Hickory logs have white sapwood and red-brown heartwood, holding conspicuous pores—seen as streaks on longitudinal surfaces. Very tough, hard, heavy, the world's best wood for tool handles subject to shock, wheel spokes, ladder rungs and sports goods like lacrosse sticks and baseball bats.

Pecan, *Carya illinoensis*, native to southern United States, is cultivated in orchards for nuts. Becomes huge tree, 45 m (140 ft) tall and 1·3 m (4 ft) in diameter, with grey-brown, ridged, scaly bark. Stout, hairy twigs, bear large, sharp-pointed, yellow buds with yellow hairs on scales that meet, but do not overlap. **Huge leaf, up to 50 cm (20 in.) long bears nine to seventeen slender oval leaflets, progressively larger towards tip.**

Oblong nuts develop in thin dark-brown, prominently four-ribbed woody husks, which split to base on ripening. Nuts themselves are red-brown, smooth except for four ribs. Holds delicious white kernel. Sprouting seedling retains seed-leaves within husk; shoot bears scale-leaves first, followed by compound leaves with fewer leaflets than adult leaf type.

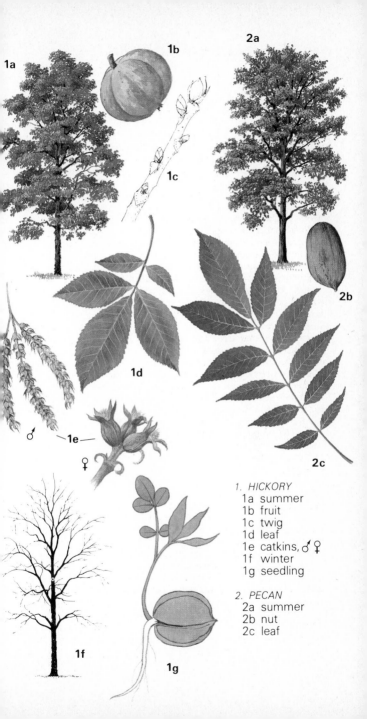

1. *HICKORY*
  1a summer
  1b fruit
  1c twig
  1d leaf
  1e catkins, ♂ ♀
  1f winter
  1g seedling

2. *PECAN*
  2a summer
  2b nut
  2c leaf

BIRCHES I : SILVER BIRCH

BETULA PENDULA   BETULACEAE

White bark is key sign of birch genus, *Betula*; but a few American birches bear brown or purplish-grey bark. Young shoots are brown or grey; black bark may develop at base of trunk. In between the trunk develops a **smooth white surface**, marked with **crosswise clusters of pale yellow, dark brown or black breathing pores**. Possibly white bark keeps trunk cool under 24-hour exposure to far northern sunshine. Birches are very hardy, growing **farther north** towards the Arctic, and **higher up mountains**, than any other tree. Following descriptions apply particularly to silver birch, *Betula pendula,* commonest species in Europe, frequently planted in North America.

Silver birch **twigs, very thin, whip-like, hang down in a graceful veil** from **slender** arching branches; whole crown has a **delicate appearance**. Twigs carry **rough raised whitish warts**. Buds, small, and slender, are pointed and diverge from twigs. In spring, when brown twigs are clad in purplish bloom, bud-scales become resinous, pleasantly fragrant. Leaves, very small, are set singly on thin stalks, have toothed edges, end in a point. Shapes vary from triangles through diamonds to ovals, even within same species or on same tree. Pale green, dull green later, then orange-yellow. White trunk usually develops **black horizontal bands, obliquely vertical marks below branch unions, diamond-shaped patches**, also **black buttresses** at base.

Male catkins develop in autumn, remain unopened but upright and **obvious through winter as purple-brown cylindrical structures**. In spring, when leaves open, catkins enlarge, markedly to 2·5 cm (1 in.) long and hang down. Their bracts open, revealing masses of simple yellow flowers grouped in threes. Each has a cluster of tiny green petals and four stamens, which scatter abundant pollen on the wind. Female catkins are **dark green, curved cylinders, initially carried erect**. They are rough to the touch, because numerous bracts and flower styles project all along them; each bract supports three simple two-styled flowers, without petals.

Pollinated female catkins expand markedly as they ripen in early autumn. They **hang down** as greenish brown structures shaped like gherkins. Soon they shatter. Bracts fall away from central stalk. Thousands of **tiny seeds, little nuts each bearing two oval side wings**, are scattered by autumn breezes. When a seed sprouts next spring, it raises two rounded-oval seeds, followed by **three-lobed primary leaves**, before normal leaves appear; whole tiny plant is densely hairy.

Birch timber is uniform dull pale brown, dense, hard, moderately strong. Useful for furniture, handles, broom-heads, and the thin veneer used in birch-faced plywood. Excellent firewood.

SILVER BIRCH
a winter
b summer
c autumn
d catkins, ♂ ♀
e leaves & fruit
f twig
g seed & seedling

BIRCHES II: OTHER BIRCHES

BETULA genus   BETULACEAE

Silver birches, individually, vary widely in form, but few cultivated kinds are recognized. Loveliest is Dalecarlian birch, *Betula pendula* 'Dalecarlica', discovered in 1767 in Swedish province of that name. Forms a slender tree with graceful drooping branches bearing pretty leaves broken into delicate fine-toothed lobes.

Downy birch, *B. pubescens*, is a northern species, common in the Scottish Highlands, with **hairy twigs and leaf stalks** and a round-oval leaf bearing **rounded teeth**.

Dwarf birch, *B. nana*, is a shrubby Arctic tree that survives from the Ice Age on high European mountains, including the Grampians around Glen Clova in Scotland. Quaint **round leaves** bear **large round teeth**, and seed has **very narrow wings**. Similar birches grow across northern Scandinavia, Siberia and Canada; they provide browse for reindeer.

Paper birch, *B. papyrifera*, also called canoe birch, is most northerly New World tree form; found from Alaska to Newfoundland, and south over the northern United States. Similar in general characters to silver birch, but bears **larger, more oval leaves**. Distinctive **bark peels away in papery strips with curled ends**. Brown or bronzy on young trees, it matures to clear white, later develops black fissures near ground. Tree forms tall trunk with irregular rounded crown. Following fires or fellings, paper birch invades bare land by self-sown seeds. It also sprouts from burnt stumps. Bark can be peeled away, especially in spring, in large, tough, waterproof strips, used by Red Indians to make light, portable birch-bark canoes.

Yellow birch, *B. alleghaniensis*, found in eastern Canada, the Lake States, New England, and the Alleghanies, is so-called for its **bronzy-yellow peeling bark**. **Long leaves** have **heart-shaped base** and tufts of fine hairs in leaf axils on underside. **Oval fruit catkins remain erect**, shed seed slowly. Bark is oily, flammable even when wet, useful for starting camp fires. Twigs smell of oil of wintergreen, which is in fact distilled from birch branches.

River birch, *B. nigra*, grows as waterside trees throughout eastern United States. **Bark, never white, matures from reddish brown through grey to black, becomes scaly.** Tall tree with irregular spreading crown. Large, irregularly oval, coarsely toothed dark green leaves have hairy veins underneath. **Globular fruit catkins remain erect**; they mature in late spring, when floods recede from mudbanks, providing places for seeds to sprout.

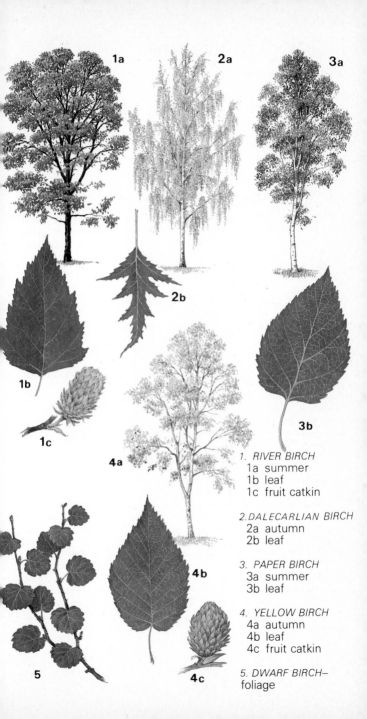

1. *RIVER BIRCH*
   1a summer
   1b leaf
   1c fruit catkin

2. *DALECARLIAN BIRCH*
   2a autumn
   2b leaf

3. *PAPER BIRCH*
   3a summer
   3b leaf

4. *YELLOW BIRCH*
   4a autumn
   4b leaf
   4c fruit catkin

5. *DWARF BIRCH*–
   foliage

ALDERS

ALNUS genus   BETULACEAE

Alders grow typically **along streams** or lakesides, or on marshy ground. They are easily known as the only **broadleaved trees that bear cones**, usually visible all the year round. Their broad leaves in summer and twiggy branches in winter combine with the absence of resin or needle-shaped leaves to distinguish them from true conifers.

In winter alders are also easily known by purplish-brown **club-shaped buds**, narrowed at the base, set alternately along dark brown twigs. They usually carry drooping oblong brown male catkins, which open in spring to shed yellow wind-born pollen. Female catkins are then seen as short-stalked dull red objects with rough protruding scales, held more or less erect. After pollination they develop into **soft green round cones**, which mature and turn **brown and woody** in autumn. Their scales then open, but spent cones hang on the tree for a year or more.

Each seed that falls from cones is a minute grain with two floats which help it to remain afloat on water. Seeds sprout on wet mud, raising two small oblong seed leaves, followed by toothed early leaves, then normal foliage. They only grow well on soil that holds a bacterium, *Schinzia alni*, which enables alders to fix atmospheric nitrogen. This eventually enriches marshland soils where many grow.

Many alders appear bushy because they are repeatedly cut back, either to harvest their poles or to clear river banks for drainage machinery. Exceptionally they become tall trees. Bark is dark grey, almost black, with a plated texture. If it is stripped from a newly-felled tree a **bright orange colour** develops. Stems have pale brown sapwood and darker red-brown heartwood, which lacks durability. Relatively soft and easily worked, alder wood is used for broom heads and cheap tool handles. Formerly it was carved to make soles for wooden shoes called clogs. Alder charcoal was widely used to make gunpowder.

Common alder, *Alnus glutinosa*, bears short-stalked round leaves with **flat** tops and toothed edges. Dark green in summer, they fade to **black** in late autumn. Native to Europe, common alder has been introduced to eastern Canada and the north-eastern United States. There it has become thoroughly naturalized and, along with native shrubby alders, invades abandoned damp pastures. Other European trees are grey alder, *A. incana*, a northern and mountain species with grey bark and pale green leaves, and Italian alder, *A. cordata* with glossy, dark-green heart-shaped ones. Oregon or red alder, *A. rubra*, distinguished by red shoots, is a leading species in western North America.

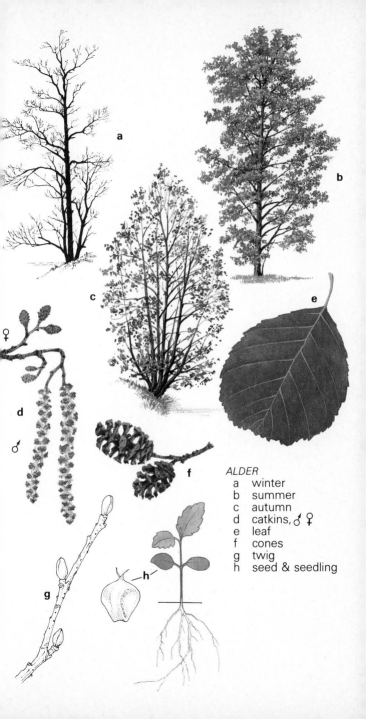

ALDER
a winter
b summer
c autumn
d catkins, ♂ ♀
e leaf
f cones
g twig
h seed & seedling

HORNBEAMS

CARPINUS genus   BETULACEAE

Hornbeam trees have the general aspect of the better known beeches, but a closer look shows clear points of difference. The slender, solitary buds **bend inwards towards the twigs**, and the oval leaves have **strong parallel veins** and **clearly toothed edges**. The trunk, seldom truly round, **bears protruding ribs** called flutes. The smooth beech-like grey bark usually shows **wandering veins of bright metallic silver shades.**

Hornbeam's male catkins, which open in spring, hang down like lambs' tails, and have a general greenish hue. Each central stalk bears numerous flowers, each being a dull red bract bearing many yellow stamens. The smaller female catkins, which also hang down, resemble leafy buds. Each component flower has a green bract-like cupule and a two-celled ovary. Following pollination by wind, these female catkins ripen, by autumn, to unmistakeable fruit catkins. Each becomes a hanging cluster of **green, papery three-pointed wings**. At the base of each wing you will find one or two **tiny, triangular, hard green** ridged nuts, the hornbeam seeds. When these sprout, in the **second** spring following ripening, each bears two oval seed-leaves with concave bases, followed by normal foliage.

Hornbeam draws its name from the **hard horn-like** character of its heavy uniform pale brown wood. This was used in the past for ox-yokes and the cogs of watermills and windmills. Today its main uses are as butcher's chopping blocks and the 'hammers' within pianos. First-rate firewood.

Because they hold attractive pale brown dead leaves, **all through winter**, though only on low branches, hornbeams are often used as **hedges**. They also occur as **coppice**, formerly cut over for branchwood—good kindling—especially in south-east England. The **pollard** hornbeams of Epping Forest near London were lopped at head height for centuries. European hornbeam, *Carpinus betulus*, is occasionally planted in America. The native American hornbeam, *C. caroliniana*, is also called 'blue beech' from its silvery bark.

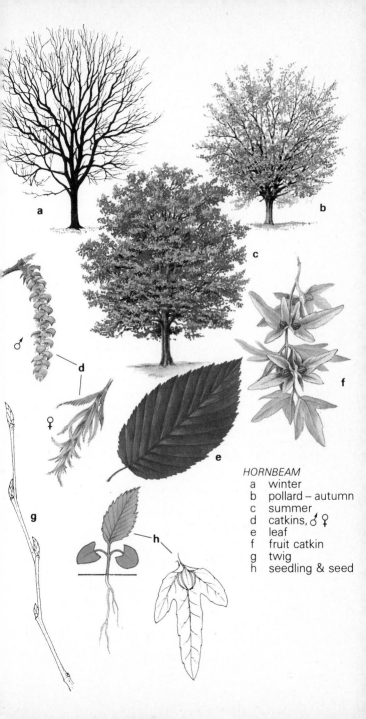

HORNBEAM
  a winter
  b pollard – autumn
  c summer
  d catkins, ♂ ♀
  e leaf
  f fruit catkin
  g twig
  h seedling & seed

HAZELS

CORYLUS genus   CORYLACEAE

Hazels grow wild as **straggling bushes,** occasionally becoming small woody-stemmed trees, on fertile patches of low-lying land, often near water. In England they have been artificially planted over large expanses of land, including high-lying chalk downs, to provide continuing large supplies of **coppice rods.** If cut back every seven years or so, hazel sends up vigorous shoots from a rootstock that endures for scores or even hundreds of years. This growth form aids identification, for few other trees are ever grown as **thin-stemmed shoot clusters.** The rods were formerly used, in round or cleft form, for making interwoven fences, hurdles, baskets, or wattles for wattle-and-daub buildings, or as spars for holding thatch to house roofs or corn ricks. Hazel also provided firewood, kindling, plant stakes, bean rods, pea sticks and clothes props. Today most coppices are neglected, or tended only as coverts for game.

In winter hazel can be told by thin **much-branched stems,** showing **prominent breathing pores** and **mottled grey and brown smooth bark** low down. Male catkins, formed the previous autumn, are already clearly seen as grey-brown oblong objects clustered near twig tips. Very early in spring (February in England) they expand to **dangling lamb's tail** structures that open to release clouds of yellow wind-borne pollen. Female catkins, now visible for the first time, are very small **green bud-shaped objects, with tufts of protruding crimson stigmas,** placed right at twig tips.

After fertilization, each female catkin expands during summer to ripen in autumn as a cluster of **hard round pale brown nuts each enclosed within leafy bracts.** In the common European hazel, *Corylus avellana,* and the American hazel, *C. americana,* the nuts are round and the bracts short. In the filberts, such as giant filbert, *C. maxima,* native to south-east Europe, larger nuts are partially hidden by longer bracts. Beaked hazel, *C. cornuta,* native to eastern Canada and eastern United States, and Californian hazel, *C. cornuta* variety *californica,* have nuts fully enclosed within a leafy husk. Varieties of several species are cultivated commercially to provide delicious edible nuts for dessert, confectionery and nut chocolate.

Hazel leaves, borne singly on short stalks, may be **round, broadly oval, or heart-shaped,** with **doubly-toothed edges** and a short-pointed tip. Winter twigs bear glandular bristles and pale brown or greenish, alternately-set oval buds. When seeds sprout, the seed-leaves remain in the husk. The first young shoot bears very small slender leaves, then normal foliage.

HAZEL

a	winter
b	'tree-form' summer
c	autumn
d	catkins, ♂ ♀
e	leaf
f	common hazel
g	beaked hazel
h	filbert
i	twig
j	seed & seedling

BEECHES

FAGUS and *NOTHOFAGUS* genus   FAGACEAE

Long, slender, pale brown pointed buds mark beech trees out from all others. Set singly on the twigs, they produce a light airy branching pattern that contrasts with a sturdy trunk bearing **smooth, metallic grey** bark. Leaves are **nearly perfect ovals**, short-stalked with well-marked veins and undulating edges, slightly hairy when young. Colour range: emerald green, mid-green, bright orange brown, dull brown; on young trees, **retained through winter** to height of six feet.

Male flowers are curious **tassels** of pollen-bearing stamens. Female flowers, less conspicuous, are bud-like. They ripen to egg-shaped green husks, bearing **soft brown spines**, which split to release two **triangular brown nuts**. Remarkable seedlings bear, above ground, two large, fleshy, oblong seed-leaves, dark green above, pale green below. A shoot carrying first a **pair** of leaves, of normal shape but opposite, springs up between them; then alternate leaves follow.

Timber has a uniform pale brown colour, shot through with **red-brown flecks** of ray tissue. Strong, working smoothly in any direction, it is used for furniture, especially school desks and work benches, in tools such as carpenters' planes, and for any job that needs a sturdy piece of wood. Not durable out of doors.

Beech casts dense shade and no green plants can live in pure beech-woods. The soil is bare or covered in brown faded leaves decaying to form leaf-mould. Natural beech-woods form major timber resources usually on low hills or foothills of mountain ranges. Widely planted as shelter belts or specimen trees. If grown as a hedge **retains faded brown leaves right through winter**.

European beech, *Fagus sylvatica*, is native from the English Midlands and southern Sweden to the Mediterranean. American beech, *F. grandifolia*, grows naturally in the eastern United States and southern Canada; it is distinguished by larger leaves.

Curiosities: copper beech, *F. sylvatica* 'Purpurea', has green leaf colour masked by copper-purple pigments; fern-leaved beech, 'Laciniata', has finely divided leaf blades.

The southern beeches, which form the genus *Nothofagus*, are native to Chile and Australasia. Differ from true beeches in having more oblong **leaves with clear parallel veins, toothed edges, male flowers few (2–3) per cluster, female flowers with 3-celled ovary, nuts three per fruit**. Rauli beech, *N. procera*, from Chile, is planted on a small scale for timber in British forests.

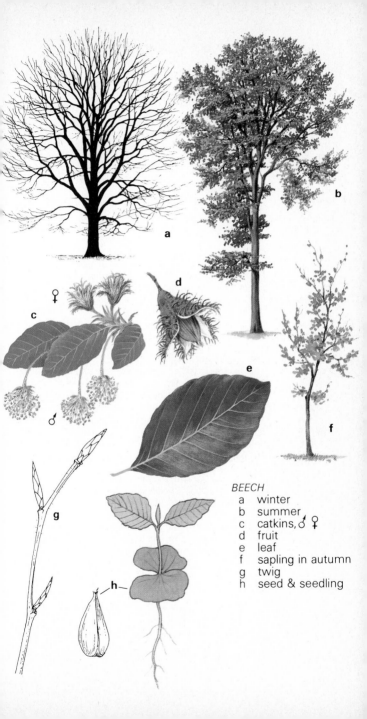

BEECH
a   winter
b   summer
c   catkins, ♂ ♀
d   fruit
e   leaf
f   sapling in autumn
g   twig
h   seed & seedling

SWEET CHESTNUTS

CASTANEA genus   FAGACEAE

Remarkably large oblong leaves, with saw-tooth edges, distinguish sweet chestnut during summer. Typical dimensions are 6 in. (15 cm) long by 2 in. (5 cm) broad. Each leaf has a short stout stalk, a pointed tip, and well-marked **parallel veins, each ending in a 'saw-tooth'**. Summer colour: green above, paler below. Autumn colour: bright orange-gold. Winter twigs are reddish brown and sturdy, with **longitudinal ridges running out to projections** bearing oval buds, set singly.

Catkins do not open until late summer; they are then seen as **beautiful yellow lacework** spreading over dark green foliage. The longer catkins, purely male, resemble **slender yellow caterpillars**. Each consists of a long stalk bearing numerous simple flowers, each a cluster of bracts and pollen-bearing stamens. Somewhat shorter catkins are bisexual, with male flowers towards their tip and **bud-shaped green female flowers near their base**. Though largely wind-pollinated, sweet chestnut flowers also attract bees and reward them with nectar; they have a musky fragrance.

Each female flower ripens by mid-autumn to a distinctive **oval green fruit bearing criss-crossed yellow spines** on its outer side; the inner surface of the husk is **white, soft and velvety**. Within this four-lobed husk, which splits when the fruit falls, stand from one to three large oval nuts—the familiar edible chestnuts. Each has a bright brown, shiny tough skin, and a pointed tip bearing **six black hairs**, the remains of the flower's stigma. Below the skin lies the **white, wrinkled, edible flesh**, actually two seed-leaves modified to store nutrients. When a nut germinates, these seed leaves remain within it, and a simple shoot arises. This bears scale leaves first, then normal leaves **in pairs or a whorl of four**, and next normal leaves set alternately.

Chestnut forms a large sturdy tree with a strongly fissured brown-grey bark, which typically shows a **strong spiral pattern**. Its trunk holds dark yellow-brown, durable heartwood, surrounded by a **very narrow band of non-durable, pale yellow sapwood**. The wood is strong, but often marred by splits called 'shakes', which restrict its use in large sizes. Smaller poles, grown as coppice in south-east England, are used for durable fencing, often as 'cleft-pale fencing' after hand cleaving.

The chestnut's delicious and nutritious fruit led the Romans, around A.D. 100, to take the tree north of the Alps and establish it across northern Europe, including Britain. It is now widely naturalized. This European species, *Castanea sativa*, is also grown in America. Native American chestnut, *C. dentata*, has been almost wiped out by the blight fungus, *Endothia parasitica*, accidentally introduced from China on Chinese chestnut, *C. mollisima*.

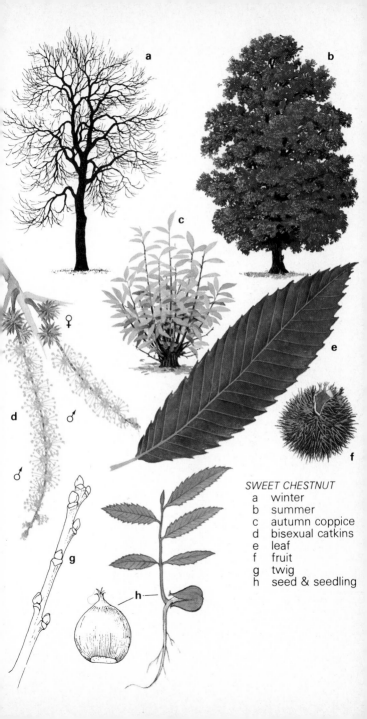

SWEET CHESTNUT
a   winter
b   summer
c   autumn coppice
d   bisexual catkins
e   leaf
f   fruit
g   twig
h   seed & seedling

OAKS I: PEDUNCULATE OAK

QUERCUS ROBUR   FAGACEAE

The best feature for identification of **any oak** as such is the **cluster of buds at the twig tip**. It governs the branch pattern of the tree, always rugged and sinuous. Another key feature is the seed or nut, the familiar **acorn nestling in its round cup**. The word 'acorn' is derived from old Danish *ek korn*, 'oak seed-grain', and recalls its value as mast for fattening pigs.

Pedunculate oak, *Quercus robur*, is so called because its female flowers and acorns are borne on long stalks or **peduncles**. Its leaves, by contrast, are **stalkless**. Native throughout Europe, as far north as Norway, it is England's commonest tree. Introduced by the Pilgrim Fathers, it has been grown in North America since early seventeenth century. Usually distinguished from other oaks by the **irregular lobing** of its leaf, which has an **entire, untoothed edge**, and bears two little lobes, called **auricles**, at its base. Remarkable late-season or 'Lammas' growth occurs after midsummer, when rapidly expanding shoots bear **young leaves, coloured bright crimson**.

Pedunculate oak has stout winter twigs, with pointed, many-scaled, pale brown oval buds. These are set singly along twigs, with the distinctive cluster at the tip, plus a large terminal bud. Leaves are reddish brown when they unfold in spring, then bright green, rich dark green later, golden-orange before they fall in autumn.

Oaks bear separate male and female catkins, usually on same tree; they open late in spring. Short-lived male catkins arise in profuse bunches near twig tips. Each is a **long hanging stalk bearing clusters of vivid yellow-green flowers**, which consist only of short-stalked stamens and minute bracts. Female catkins, much less obvious, consist of two or three green flowers set on long stalks near twig tips. Each flower is surrounded by bracts, and bears two styles on a squat pistil. After wind pollination, each female flower ripens one large bright brown oval acorn, within a woody, grey-green, rough-surfaced cup, which develops from basal bracts. Acorns fall from cups and sprout next spring. Oak seedlings keep their seed-leaves within the husk, and send up sturdy shoots bearing first scale-leaves, then typical leaves.

Pedunculate oak bark is **mid grey, thick, tough, rugged and broken both ways into irregular patches by deep fissures**. Timber logs show pale yellow outer sapwood and golden-brown inner heartwood, naturally very durable. **Distinct bright yellow rays** run radially through both zones. Very strong, hard, yet readily worked, oak is used for building, shipbuilding, fencing, furniture, roofing-shingles, barrel staves, ladder rungs, and as veneer. Bark yields tannins for treating hides to make leather.

PEDUNCULATE OAK
a winter
b autumn
c summer
d catkins, ♂ ♀
e leaf
f fruit
g twig
h seed & seedling

OAKS II: OTHER DECIDUOUS OAKS

QUERCUS genus   FAGACEAE

Sessile oak, *Quercus petraea*, has the same European range as
pedunculate oak; the two interbreed and hybrids of intermediate
character are common. Typical sessile oak has **long-stalked
leaves, wedge-shaped at base**, without lobes, **unstalked female
flowers and acorns**, short **conical acorns**, and forms a straighter,
more persistent main trunk.

Downy oak, *Q. pubescens*, resembles sessile oak but has densely
hairy shoots, and hairy leaf undersides, a protection against drying
out on arid sites in southern Europe. It has dark-grey bark and
holds faded leaves right through winter.

Hungarian oak, *Q. frainetto*, native to eastern Europe and
southern Italy, is planted as a vigorous ornamental tree in
parklands. It bears a large leaf, **broader towards the tip, deeply
divided into numerous irregular lobes**, which themselves bear
minor sub-lobes. Average 20 cm (8 in.) long by 10 cm (4 in.)
broad, rich green above, grey and hairy beneath. Acorn cup, sessile
on twig, is clad in downy scales, and holds a large brown seed.
Grey bark, broken by network of fissures into elliptical islands,
looks like snake's skin. Wood strong, heartwood durable.

The tree known in Europe as Turkey oak, *Quercus cerris*, is
distinct from American Turkey oak, which is *Q. laevis*, a south-
eastern species with deep-cut, narrow-lobed leaves. The Turkey
oak of the Balkans is, however, grown as an ornamental tree in
America and most of Europe; naturalized in Britain. Easily known
by **long persistent whiskers** (botanically, stipules) **surrounding
every bud**. Leaves **deeply cut with jagged, saw-tooth, irregular
lobes** rough to the tough on upper surface. Acorn borne in a **mossy
cup, clad in long, soft, pale green scales**, some pointing forwards, others bent back. Very thick, rugged grey bark, shows
lines of bright tangerine orange colour, deep in fissures.
Timber highly esteemed in Turkey, but as grown in Britain shrinks
and warps unduly, so proves worthless.

White oak, *Q. alba*, produces finest timber of any American
kind, used for furniture, joinery, building, shipbuilding, ladder
rungs, wheel spokes and barrels for sherry and whisky. Distinctive
deep green leaf, which fades through purple to brown, is large:
15 cm (6 in.) long by 7·5 cm (3 in.) wide. It is **deeply divided into
irregular lobes in a blunt saw-tooth** fashion; **some lobes often
bear lesser sub-lobes**. Oblong brown acorns are borne directly on
twigs in bowl-like cups covered in warty-scales. Grey bark
becomes very thick and rugged, broken by deep fissures into
irregular fragments. Related California white oak, *Q. lobata*, has
exceptionally slim acorns, 6 cm (2·5 in.) long.

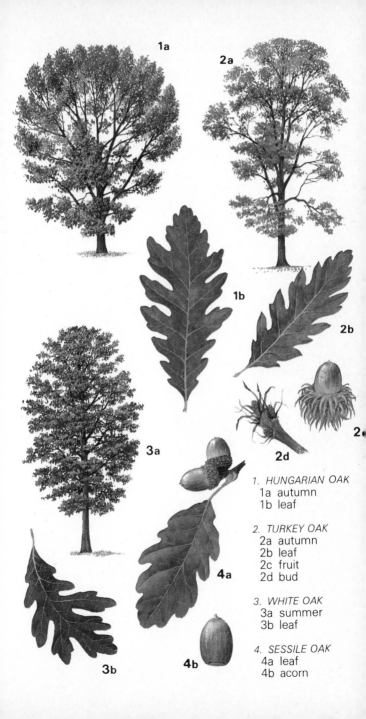

1. *HUNGARIAN OAK*
   1a autumn
   1b leaf

2. *TURKEY OAK*
   2a autumn
   2b leaf
   2c fruit
   2d bud

3. *WHITE OAK*
   3a summer
   3b leaf

4. *SESSILE OAK*
   4a leaf
   4b acorn

OAKS III: RED, BLACK AND BLUE OAKS

QUERCUS genus   FAGACEAE

American botanists use both terms 'red' and 'black' to cover a group of oaks that bear, for the most part, **red-tinged foliage** above trunks with **black bark**. All lose their leaves in winter. **Their seeds take two years to ripen**, so **immature acorns may be found all year round**. Those kinds with lobed leaves **bear bristles** extending beyond the points of the lobes. Some kinds, including 'blue' oaks, that live in dry places have another pattern of foliage better adapted to resist drought; their leaves have no lobes, and may resemble those of true evergreen oaks, laurel, holly or willow. All yield timbers that serve well enough for building or furniture where only moderate strength is needed, but none rivals white oak, *Quercus alba*, or its allies. Several kinds with attractive red autumn foliage are nowadays widely planted in Europe, though mainly for ornament, rarely for timber.

Northern red oak, *Quercus borealis* (= *rubra*) common throughout the eastern United States and Canada, bears **broad-lobed flame-shaped leaves**, which open reddish-brown, on golden shoots, become dark green with reddish veins, and change to warm crimson in autumn. Large acorns, 2·5 cm (1 in.), **bulge towards tip**, sit in **flat cups**. Scarlet oak, *Q. coccinea*, has **more deeply cut leaves** with narrower, sharper lobes, and brighter autumn colour; acorns are **short squat** hemispheres. In pin oak, *Q. palustris*, lobes are narrower still, with every point bearing a **long bristle or 'pin'**.

California black oak, *Q. kellogii*, has black, heavily ridged bark, and leaves shaped like those of red oak but **golden-green** throughout summer. Its ellipse-shaped acorns, set in deep cups and 2·5 cm (1 in.) long, were once a staple food for Red Indians. California blue oak, *Q. douglasii*, bears shallow-lobed, dark green leaves, whose blue tinge is associated with drought resistance. Long, cylindrical, pointed acorns sit on shallow cups, mature in one year. Bark grey-brown, scaly. Crown spreading, with drooping, sinuous branches.

Blackjack oak, *Q. marilandica*, found in the warm south, bears leaves **markedly broader towards tips, only slightly lobed**. Dark green above; **undersurface brown and hairy**. Acorns conical, half enclosed in deep, thick, scaly, bowl-shaped cup. Bark thick, black, in deep plates. Willow oak, *Q. phellos*, also southern, bears **narrow unlobed leaves**, each tipped with a bristle; they are light-green above, paler below. Squat round acorns sit on thin, saucer-shaped cups. Bark grey-black with irregular furrows.

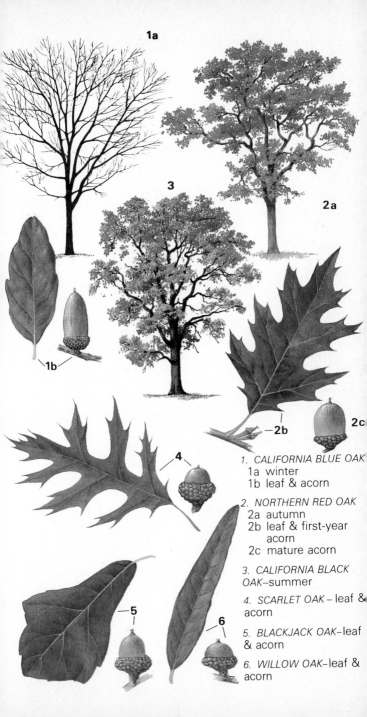

1. *CALIFORNIA BLUE OAK*
   1a winter
   1b leaf & acorn

2. *NORTHERN RED OAK*
   2a autumn
   2b leaf & first-year
      acorn
   2c mature acorn

3. *CALIFORNIA BLACK
OAK*–summer

4. *SCARLET OAK* – leaf &
acorn

5. *BLACKJACK OAK*–leaf
& acorn

6. *WILLOW OAK*–leaf &
acorn

OAKS IV: EVERGREEN OAKS

QUERCUS genus   FAGACEAE

Evergreen or live oaks bear leaves modified to resist drought, with **thick texture, waxy dark green upper surfaces, paler undersurfaces**. Usually have **hairy coating** to slow air movement through breathing pores. Bark thick, black or corky grey-brown. **Crowns appear dark, heavy, gloomy**; foliage casts deep shade. Timbers exceptionally dense, hard, heavy. Most wood goes for fuel; some used for tools.

Holm oak, *Q. ilex*, native to Mediterranean zone, is often planted farther north in Europe and America for decoration or seaside shelter, since it resists salt-laden gales. **Bark black, broken into small squares**. Crown low, spreading. Leaves open **white**, mature through yellow to dark green with hairy fawn-coloured undersides. Turn grey and fall after four years. Leaves, on woolly shoots, vary in shape, sometimes spiny, usually oval with toothed edges; **conspicuous male catkins**, around midsummer, change from pink-and-green to golden hue of stamens. Acorn oval, light green, half-enclosed in cup clad in **regular fawn-coloured felted scales**.

Chermes oak, *Q. coccifera*, also Mediterranean, is shrubby, with holly-like **spiny leaves, smooth on both sides**. Host plant of scale insect, *Kermes vermilio*, which when crushed yields brilliant red dye, used since Roman times. Oval acorns, in deep cups, take two years to mature.

Live oak, *Q. virginiana*, native to southern United States, forms huge wide-spreading crown, often festooned with epiphytic plant called Spanish moss, *Tillandsia usneoides*. Trunk usually short. Bark dark reddish-brown, scaly, fissured. **Leaves oval, with rounded ends**. Cylindrical acorn, broader towards tip, matures green, brown, black.

Cork oak, *Q. suber*, native to Mediterranean, is usually known by **thick, fawny-grey, rough textured bark**, source of commercial cork. Once every ten years outer bark is stripped from living trees, about midsummer, exposing **bright reddish-orange bast beneath**. Rough 'virgin cork', harvested first, used for floats or insulation, is succeeded by finer-textured 'female bark' suitable for bottle-stoppers; one tree yields 800 corks! Cork, developed to check water loss, also stops passage of alcoholic spirits, provided breathing pores run *across* bottle top. Bark stripping is effected by making horizontal cuts at base and top of unbranched trunk, next vertical cuts, then prizing off curved segments of outer bark.

Leaves like those of evergreen oak, less crowded, with fine-toothed edges. Acorn cups have **inverted cone shape**, with neat flat scales at base, **longer thong-like scales** towards broad upper rim. Acorn, somewhat oblique, is conical, **tapering markedly towards tip**. Needs two years to ripen. Seedling retains seed-leaves in husk, bears typical leaves of increasing sizes.

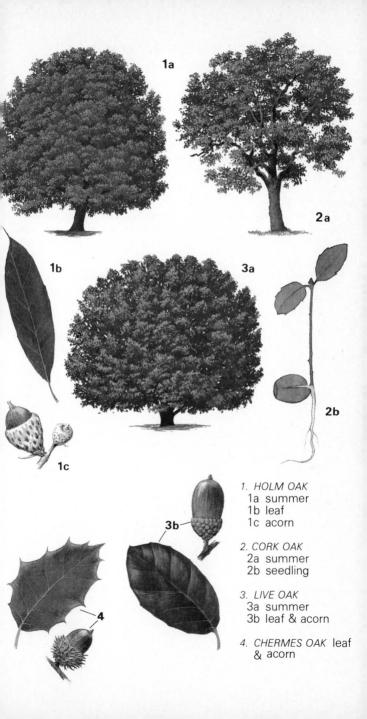

1. *HOLM OAK*
   1a summer
   1b leaf
   1c acorn

2. *CORK OAK*
   2a summer
   2b seedling

3. *LIVE OAK*
   3a summer
   3b leaf & acorn

4. *CHERMES OAK* leaf
   & acorn

ELMS I: WYCH ELM

ULMUS GLABRA   ULMACEAE

All elms, members of large genus *Ulmus*, show a curious key
character on their leaves: **leaf-base is always oblique or one-
sided**. Other constant leaf features are an oval shape with a toothed
edge and a blunt-pointed tip, a strong central vein with prominent
side veins, and a short stalk. Many kinds, including the misnamed
U. glabra ('glabra' is Latin for smooth) have **rough leaf surfaces**.
Elm foliage is mid-green to dark green, but becomes gold or russet-
orange in autumn. Bark is often **corky**, especially on young stems.

There are many species, varieties, and hybrids of elms, both in
Europe and North America; no two authorities agree on best ways
to sort them out! Here wych or Scots elm, *U. glabra*, represents
general characters of genus. Native to northern and central Europe,
including British Isles, and commonest kind in Scotland. Often
planted as specimen tree in North America.

Wych elm shows more resistance than most kinds to serious,
usually fatal, Dutch elm disease. This is caused by inconspicuous
fungus *Ceratocystis ulmi*, which is carried from dying trees to fresh
victims by elm bark beetles, such as *Scolytus scolytus*. Though
scientists now know chemicals that kill both fungus and insect, they
are clumsy and costly to apply. The discovery and propagation of
resistant strains of elm offers the best hope of these beautiful trees'
salvation.

Wych elm forms a short trunk that divides low down into stout
branches that make up a broad, vase-shaped crown. Despite this
poor timber form, its supple wood is valued for boatbuilding and
furniture making. It has rich brown heartwood and pale brown
sapwood, with an interlocked pattern of grain. Thick grey bark
carries networks of ridges and furrows. Sturdy shoots bear, singly,
stout, oval chestnut brown buds with pointed tips. Wych elm
leaves are broad, often broader towards tip, and **shouldered**. Elms
flower late in winter (February, March) ahead of their new leaves.
Both flowers and flower-clusters are small; they look like a
reddish-purple haze high up on bare branches. Each flower in a
cluster of two or so has a little basal bract, a calyx of five sepals,
four or five stamens, and a central pistil with a feathery style.

After pollination by wind, elm flowers rapidly ripen **conspicuous winged seeds**, seen as bright yellow-green 'petals'
before darker green foliage in early summer, and often mistaken for
flowers. Each seed in a cluster of about twenty has a short stalk and
a **circular pale yellow-green wing around the round, darker
brown grain**. Wind-dispersed seed sprouts in same summer. Each
seedling raises two crescentic-oval seed-leaves, with convex outer
surfaces, concave or notched bases. A **pair** of opposite, long-oval
deeply-toothed and pointed juvenile leaves follows, succeeded by
normal alternate-leaved foliage. The seed coat remains **stuck to the
ground**.

WYCH ELM
a winter
b summer
c weeping form
   'Camperdown' –
   spring
d flowers
e fruit
f leaf
g twig
h seed & seedling

ELMS II: OTHER ELMS

ULMUS genus   ULMACEAE

American white elm, *Ulmus americana*, found throughout eastern States and southern Canada, forms a magnificent dark-foliaged tree with a broad spreading crown, highly valued for shade in streets and gardens. It has suffered sadly from Dutch elm disease, but recent observations show that, in some districts at least, some resistant trees survive. Leaves are oval, with very oblique bases, and shining bright-green. Seed wings have a **notch at their tip**, a key feature.

Rock-elm, *U. thomasii*, found in Great Lakes region of the United States and Canada, shows in contrast a far more persistent main trunk. **Twigs have corky ribs.** Timber, exceptionally hard, strong, and tough, is exported world-wide for exacting work in boatbuilding, engineering, tool handles, machinery parts, and dockside work.

Slippery elm, *U. fulva*, found across the eastern States and southern Canada, owes its name to a sticky aromatic substance found in its inner bark. This was once chewed as a cough cure. Slippery elm has slender, oval leaves and **fuzzy winter buds**. Resembles white elm in general form.

Certain regions have elms of remarkable shapes that lend a particular character to local scenery; these exceptional kinds are naturally used for landscape planting elsewhere. Guernsey, in the Channel Islands, is the home of Guernsey elm, *U. carpinifolia* variety *sarniensis*, also called Jersey or Wheatley elm, which forms a **graceful, narrow, spire-topped crown**. Like most elms, it is completely resistant to salt sea winds—it has to be to thrive on such small exposed islands. Cornish elm, *U. carpinifolia* variety *cornubiensis*, has a similar narrow crown, but **broadens out towards the top**.

English elm, *U. procera*, grandest of all elms, is usually known from afar by its **billowing, cloud-shaped crown**, set on a sturdy, erect, persistent main trunk. It rarely sets seed, but renews its kind by vigorous sucker shoots from its roots. Leaves, small for so large a tree, are very oblique; twigs make an intricate 'bent' foliage pattern. Distinctive **grey bark cracked into small squares. Huge limbs**, apt to fall after gales. Wood, very tough and **hard to split**, traditionally used for chair seats, wooden rollers, heads of mallets, partitions in cowsheds, coffins, water pipes and pumps; more recently for cable drums, and packing cases for metal or machinery. Unfortunately this magnificent tree has proved exceptionally susceptible to the latest, 1970s, wave of Dutch elm disease; future hopes are pinned on rare survivors.

In Britain elms are typically **hedgerow trees**. They spring up from suckers in the protection of the hedge, and help provide the characteristic lowland landscapes of sunny fields and shady-trees, immortalized by the painter Constable.

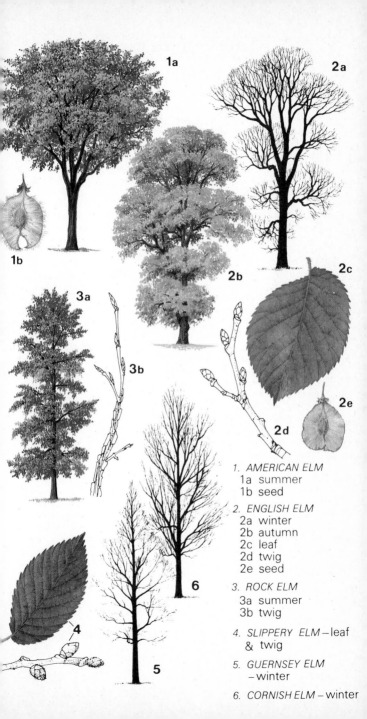

1. *AMERICAN ELM*
   1a summer
   1b seed

2. *ENGLISH ELM*
   2a winter
   2b autumn
   2c leaf
   2d twig
   2e seed

3. *ROCK ELM*
   3a summer
   3b twig

4. *SLIPPERY ELM* – leaf
   & twig

5. *GUERNSEY ELM*
   – winter

6. *CORNISH ELM* – winter

MULBERRIES

MORUS genus   MORACEAE

Mulberries are usually seen as small branchy trees of irregular form, bearing **rough scaly pinkish-brown bark. Winter buds are neat, glossy dark brown, pointed ovals. Leaves are heart-shaped or occasionally lobed, with toothed edges, pointed tips and rough surfaces**. Colours: pale green, dark green, golden. The fruit, **like a raspberry**, is built up of many fruitlets, each an oval mass of bright reddish-pink, crimson or white pulp holding one seed. Mulberries are good to eat, but have a **sharp, acid taste**, and are gathered mainly for making jellies or pies. When fully ripe, they change colour to dark crimson and become sweeter, but by then most have been plucked by the birds. Once they were more highly esteemed, and this explains why mulberries are often found on the lawns of old country houses, particularly rectories.

Mulberry flowers are green catkins, pollinated by wind. Usually a tree bears only male, or only female, catkins; the latter can ripen fruit without fertilization. Male catkins, which open early in summer, are short-stalked cylindrical structures, built up of four bracts and four stamens apiece. Female catkins are oval and **bristly**, since two styles project from the ovary of every component flower.

Seedlings expand two oval seed-leaves above ground, then open broad-oval juvenile leaves with wavy edges; adult lobed leaves follow.

Mulberry trunks have deep yellow heartwood and pale yellow sapwood, both hard, strong, firm, and capable of taking a fine polish. Used by craftsmen in the east for decorative carving, inlay and musical instruments, but too small for ordinary use.

Black mulberry, *Morus nigra*, with dark ripe fruits, is the species usually grown for berries. White mulberry, *M. alba*, with white fruits, is preferred for silkworm fodder. Both are considered native to Central Asia, but have been cultivated for centuries in India, China and Italy, and their true origins are unknown. Red mulberry, *A. rubra*, with cylindrical red berries that ripen through red to purple, is native to eastern and mid-western United States.

The growing of mulberry leaves as food for silkworms is an ancient practice in Japan and China. It has been pursued, with greater or less commercial success, in the south of France from the Middle Ages to the present day. The trees are either coppiced or pollarded so as to gain the greatest possible weight of foliage from any given extent of land. An attempt by King James I, circa 1600, to establish silkworm culture in England, failed as the climate proved unkind.

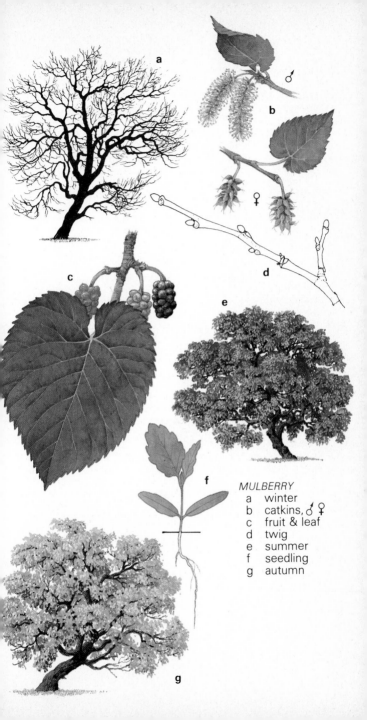

MULBERRY
a winter
b catkins, ♂ ♀
c fruit & leaf
d twig
e summer
f seedling
g autumn

FIG

FICUS CARICA   MORACEAE

Fig trees can be told in winter by their **smooth but leathery textured mid-grey bark, resembling elephant hide**. They form low, spreading trees with **stout branches that bend down, then sweep up**, often knobbly. **Shoots very stout**, ribbed, dark green, with big leaf scars. **Terminal bud cone-shaped, sharp-pointed, pale green.** Side buds are single, squat, purplish or reddish brown. In Britain, fig trees flourish as such only in the warm south; elsewhere they can be raised as climbers against south-facing walls.

Fig leaves are **exceptionally variable in shape, even at same time on same tree**. The **conventional fig leaf**, used in design, sculpture, and standard textbooks, has five lobes—a big blunt middle one, two long blunt side ones, and two basal bulges. **Unconventional fig leaves** may have more deeply cut, pointed lobes, or none at all, being oval in outline. All fig leaves are placed alternately on twigs, have long stalks and five radiating main veins. Dark green, very large—up to 30 cm (12 in.) long by 25 cm (10 in.) across. Thick and leathery, rough-surfaced with hairs above, they look evergreen, but fall each autumn.

The **globe-shaped fig** fruit is actually a flowering and fruiting stem, modified for pollination by specialized gall wasps. What we see from outside is the outer surface of a cup-shaped flower-head, bent over until its surfaces **almost meet in a small round hole at the tip**. Cut it across, and it proves to be a **hollow globe**, lined with flowers at one stage, and fruits holding seeds at another. The hole is the point of entry for the gall wasp, *Blastophaga psenes*, which breeds in female flowers at the base of the hollow fig. To reach them, or to proceed to those of another fig, the wasp must pass a group of male flowers that develop round the hole; here it is dusted with pollen, and this assures fertilization.

Wild figs, and some choice varieties of cultivated fig, only ripen after cross-pollination. In 1899 Walter T. Swingle of the United States Department of Agriculture introduced gall wasps, within figs, from Algiers to California, to ensure success for local orchards. British and Northern growers plant Adriatic figs, which ripen fruit, and set fertile seeds, without fertilization. Such fruit-ripening is called **parthenocarpy**; self-fertilization is **parthenogenesis**.

Wild figs are spread by birds, who relish their purplish-brown juicy, sweet-flavoured fruits. Flat, hard, yellow seeds are very small, very numerous. A sprouting seed raises two blunt, broad seed-leaves, followed by paired, oval, true leaves. Typical lobed leaves, set singly, develop later.

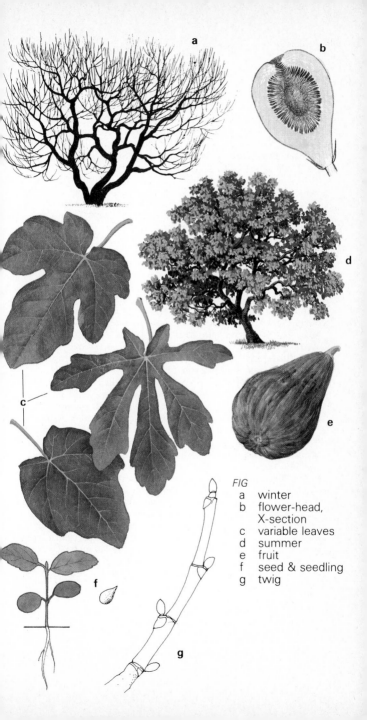

FIG
a   winter
b   flower-head,
     X-section
c   variable leaves
d   summer
e   fruit
f   seed & seedling
g   twig

MAGNOLIAS

MAGNOLIA genus   MAGNOLIACEAE

The melodious word 'Magnolia' commemorates Pierre Magnol (1638–1715) of Montpellier. Showy flowers, with gay-coloured, numerous petals, open to reveal **mop of numerous golden-headed stamens** surrounding central **cucumber-shaped green pistil**, composed of many seed-bearing units called **carpels**. This pistil ripens to unique fruit, brown or red oval cone-like structure, with individual carpels visible. These carpels split lengthwise and one or two **round crimson seeds emerge from each and hang down, on long slender threads**. Bark and leaves fragrant when crushed. Winter buds, set singly projecting from stout brown twigs, are green, oval, and **pinched-in at base**; protected by oval sheath which falls in one piece, leaving **circular scar**.

Soulange magnolia, *Magnolia × soulangeana*, is named after Monsieur Soulange, who bred it by crossing Chinese species, *M. denudata* and *M. liliflora*. Opens large goblet-shaped flowers, like giant lilies, ten centimetres (4 in.) across, on bare branches in spring. First specimens were pink; cultivars include white 'Alba' and luxurious 'Lennei', with tulip-shaped flowers rose-purple outside, white within. Flowers lack apparent green sepals, hence appear **naked**. Large mid-green, glossy oval leaves turn yellow in autumn, then fall. Usually spreading shrub, occasionally small tree with thin grey bark. Sets fertile seed. Usually propagated by layering to keep varieties true to name.

Evergreen magnolia, *M. grandiflora*, called bull bay in its homeland, southern States of America, becomes tall timber tree, 25 metres (78 ft) high—1 metre (3 ft) thick, with smooth to scaly brownish-grey bark. Strong yellowish-brown timber valued for furniture and box-making. In northern States and Europe evergreen magnolia is grown as ornamental tree, often as climber trained against a south-facing wall.

Fawn-coloured **shoots clad in dense, long, rust-coloured hairs**; large **glossy-green, oval, blunt-pointed leaves**. These short-stalked alternately-set leaves, with inrolled edges, reach 15 centimetres (6 in.) long by 10 centimetres (4 in.) broad; **clad underneath with rust-brown hairs**. Flowers open from midsummer to mid-winter. Each has three green sepals, six thick white petals spreading from a cone to a bowl, often 25 cm (10 in.) across. Cone-shaped, short-stalked fruits, 10 cm (4 in.) long, half as broad, are red-brown, **hairy**, carry dangling red seeds. Seeds have hard grey stones covered by soft oily flesh; spread by birds. Seedlings raise two long-oval seed-leaves, with distinct midribs; these fall after one season. Paired evergreen leaves, small at first, succeed them; solitary leaves follow.

1. SOULANGE
MAGNOLIA
   1a spring
   1b flower
   1c leaf
   1d twig

2. EVERGREEN
MAGNOLIA
   2a wall climber
   2b free-standing
   2c fruit
   2d seedling
   2e flower and leaves

TULIP TREE

LIRIODENDRON TULIPIFERA   MAGNOLIACEAE

This magnificent tree never quite lives up to the promise of its names, especially the Latin one which means 'lily tree bearing tulips'. Easily known in winter by **flat, club-shaped buds, each with a 'stalk' at its base**, set singly along chocolate-brown shoots. Major buds are enclosed within **reddish-brown stipules**, but the lesser buds, which appear later, are enclosed within **green leafy stipules**.

Tulip tree is unmistakeable in summer because every **four-lobed broad leaf** ends in a **broad right-angled notch**, as though 'cut-out' with scissors. Leaves are conventionally called **saddle-shaped**. Colours: pale green, light green, clear gold.

Flowers, borne freely high in crowns of tall trees early in summer, are greenish-yellow, with golden stamens. Cup-shaped, they expand later and look less like tulips, more like lilies. Each has three large green sepals, which soon droop downwards. Within stand six waxy oval petals, blue-green at base, bearing an orange middle zone, then pale yellowish-green tops. Within these comes a circle of numerous, erect, slender, cream-coloured stamens. The central ovary, also cream-coloured but having a green tip, is made up of numerous distinct, female seed-bearing organs called carpels, each tipped with a dark stigma.

This ovary ripens into an odd **long-egg-shaped, hard, pale brown fruit** which breaks up in late winter, starting at its tip, into long seed-wings, each with a brown oval seed at its base. A central stalk remains. Seedlings, next spring, raise two slender oblong seed-leaves, and then bear a few rectangular, unlobed juvenile leaves. Normal lobed leaves follow. The seed-coat remains stuck to the ground.

Tulip tree bark, at first smooth, green and aromatic, becomes thick, brown and closely furrowed into long rough ridges. The timber is a remarkable shade of greenish-yellow, with slightly darker heartwood. Trade-names are 'yellow poplar' and 'canary whitewood'. Strong and very stable, it is used in America, and exported elsewhere, for making furniture and engineering patterns.

Tulip tree is native to the central and eastern states of the USA, where it is often known as 'yellow poplar'. It thrives best on fertile soil in river valleys, spreading downstream by floating seeds. In Europe it is grown only as an ornamental specimen, deservedly planted in many parks and large gardens.

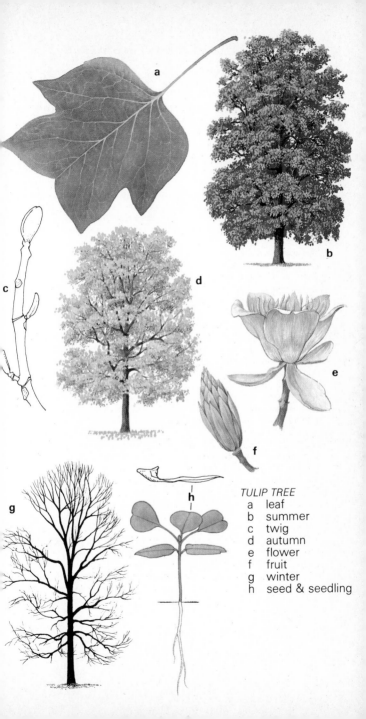

TULIP TREE
a leaf
b summer
c twig
d autumn
e flower
f fruit
g winter
h seed & seedling

TRUE LAUREL AND SASSAFRAS

LAURUS and *SASSAFRAS* genera   LAURACEAE

True laurel, *L. nobilis*, bears leathery leaves, glossy dark green above, paler below, with crinkled edges, blunt points, short reddish-green stalks. It can easily be told from similar trees by its **sharp, piquant aroma**. Crush a leaf to test this. It accounts for laurel's common use as a spice in cookery, and as a flavouring in tins of Portuguese sardines! Laurel is also called 'sweet bay', a name derived from its scent and French *baie*, meaning 'berry'.

Laurels grow wild in Mediterranean lands as shrubby trees, with black bark bearing paler cracks on older trunks. They constantly send up root suckers, producing thickets. Cultivated in cottage gardens for spicy leaves. Also grown in tubs, and trained into cones or balls, as the only evergreen to stand such harsh treatment, especially in smoky cities.

Small flowers, borne in leaf axils in spring, are all male on some trees, all female on others. Both appear in clusters, and have four sepals plus four petals, all yellowish-white. Males bear twelve stamens, females a single-celled pistil. The one-seeded berry that develops from the latter, after insect pollination, is green at first, then black; an odd swelling at its base represents remains of former flower parts. Sprouting seedlings raise a thin young shoot that bears small scale leaves, then typical leaves, small at first, becoming progressively larger; the seed-leaves remain within the hard seed-coat.

The sassafras tree, *Sassafras albidum*, of the eastern United States and southern Canada is closely related. Grown occasionally in European botanical collections. Key character is again scent: a strong sweet **aroma of oranges and vanilla**. It runs through leaves, bark, twigs and roots, and is the source of oil of sassafras used to scent soaps, and tonic sassafras tea, made by boiling bark.

Sassafras bears deciduous bright green leaves that turn bright yellow or orange before they fall in autumn. Their **variable shape**—simple, two-lobed, or three-lobed on the same twig, is a handy recognition point. Yellowish-green flowers, all male or all female, appear in loose, green-stalked, bunches. Males have six stamens. When blue-black berries ripen in autumn, stalk colour has become red. Each berry has a marked green swelling below its base, and holds soft flesh around a hard, round, ridged seed, which sprouts as does laurel.

Brown bark is finely ridged. Winter buds are plump and greenish. Timber has orange-brown, durable heartwood, yellowish-white sapwood. Used today for fence posts or fuel. The Indians found it excellent for dug-out canoes—it was soft enough to be hollowed out, light, yet lasting.

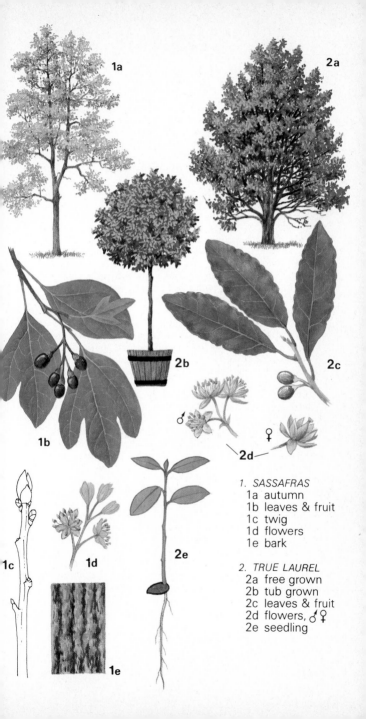

1. *SASSAFRAS*
   1a autumn
   1b leaves & fruit
   1c twig
   1d flowers
   1e bark

2. *TRUE LAUREL*
   2a free grown
   2b tub grown
   2c leaves & fruit
   2d flowers, ♂♀
   2e seedling

SWEET GUM

LIQUIDAMBAR STYRACIFLUA HAMAMELIDACEAE

The **star-shaped leaf** of this lovely tree marks it out in summer. Long-stalked, bright green, with reddish tinges along veins, it has five lobes, each with a toothed edge and a bold point. Buds and leaves are set **singly** along twigs; this helps to avoid confusion with paired lobed leaves of maples. In autumn sweet gum leaves display a dazzling **range of colour** that varies from tree to tree, branch to branch, and one day to another. Bright golden yellows, gay orange shades, gleaming scarlets, deep crimsons and lustrous purples all appear, in turn or side by side until early frosts cause the fall of these brilliant, glowing stars.

Winter twigs bear conical brown buds. Corky outgrowths usually develop on older ones. Bark, pale grey at first, becomes dark grey and fissured into oblongs, rough, with network of thick ridges. Timber, with red-brown heartwood, creamy white sapwood, is a leading commercial hardwood in the United States; used for furniture, building, veneers, joinery and wooden household ware. Selected logs imported to England were marketed as 'satin walnut'; cheaper ones were cut into blocks to pave the streets of London! The sweet gum, or storax, that oozes from cut stems and gives the tree its name, is used in perfumes and drugs. Sweet gum forms forests from New York State south to Mexico and Nicaragua. Extensively planted for ornament outside this range, also in Europe; hardy in southern England, not farther north.

Yellowish-green flowers open when leaves do, in separate male and female catkins, often side by side. Male flowers, individually minute, form long, crowded oval clusters. They have no sepals or petals, being simply bundles of stamens that spread yellow, wind-borne pollen. Female flowers make up a smaller, short-stalked ball. Each individual is tiny, with a ring of short, undeveloped sepals and petals, and a pistil with two projecting stigmas.

Burr-like fruit catkins, about 3 cm (1¼ in.) across, ripen from female catkins, becoming brown, hard and long-stalked by autumn. Each round head is built up of many small pods, tipped with remains of paired stigmas, which open like birds' beaks. Two seeds escape from each pod. They are light brown, oval, angular, about 1 cm (⅓ in.) long, and bear an oval wing of equal length. The wind disperses them. Empty fruits hang on trees through winter. Seedlings, which do not sprout until second spring after ripening, raise two oval seed-leaves. The first true leaves have broad blades with toothed edges, but only three obscure lobes and points. Five-lobed, five-pointed leaves come later. Sweet gum also grows vigorously from root suckers.

SWEET GUM

a winter
b autumn
c summer
d flowers, ♂ ♀
e fruit
f leaf
g twig
h seed & seedling

PLANE, AMERICAN SYCAMORE

PLATANUS genus   PLATANACEAE

The *Platanus* genus trees, known in Europe as 'planes', were called
'sycamore' by early American settlers because their broad,
palmately lobed leaf looks like that of the Biblical 'sycamore',
actually the fig-mulberry, *Ficus sycomorus*. Planes share this leaf-
shape with the maples, including European sycamore, *Acer
pseudoplatanus*, but three features fix plane's identity. **Plane
buds, shoots and leaves are always separate and alternate,**
never in pairs. **Plane buds have only one visible external scale,
shaped like a pointed dunce's cap.** Plane leaves have a **deep
hollow at the base of the stalk, which completely encircles next
year's bud, making it invisible until the leaf falls**. Leaf colours:
pale green, mid-green, pale brown.

As a plane trunk enlarges the bark remains smooth but **flakes
away in patches,** revealing younger bark within. This results in a
dappled jig-saw effect, with irregular patches of dark olive brown,
dull olive green, pale green, and pale yellow mingled at random. In
smoky cities this bark-shedding habit helps the tree trunk to
breathe.

Planes produce, in late spring, characteristic 'bobbles' or
round-ball catkins, hence they are sometimes called buttonwoods.
These **catkins hang down on long, green flexible stalks** that
appear to pass through them, though actually side-tracked, with
two or three balls per stalk. Each catkin holds only male or only
female flowers; both appear on same tree. In both sexes, tiny green
cup-shaped flowers are packed round the ball, surface. Male
bobbles appear yellowish-green, females crimson-green. Tiny male
flowers have three or four stamens, equally small female flowers a
single pistil. Fertilized female catkins ripen by autumn to brown
fruit catkins. Later they break up, untidily, freeing numerous
**round brown oval seeds, very small, each tipped with brown
hairs,** which some people find irritating. Some bobbles hang on
trees all winter through.

Seedlings raise two curious slender curved seed-leaves, called
sickle-shaped; a few unlobed juvenile leaves follow, then come
normal lobed leaves.

Pale brown, uniform timber, shows a beautiful 'lacewood'
pattern when specially cut in a tangential plane; used thus for
decorative veneer. Solid plane, a strong stable wood, is used for
furniture and high-grade joinery.

American plane, native to eastern States, botanically *Platanus
occidentalis*, has smooth leaf lobes. The common plane of south-east
Europe, *P. orientalis*, has toothed or indented leaf lobes. About the
year 1650, these two planes met, probably in a Spanish garden, and
produced hybrid 'London plane', *P.* × *hispanica*. This shows
exceptional hybrid vigour, and has become, deservedly, a
favourite city street and shade tree both in Europe and America.

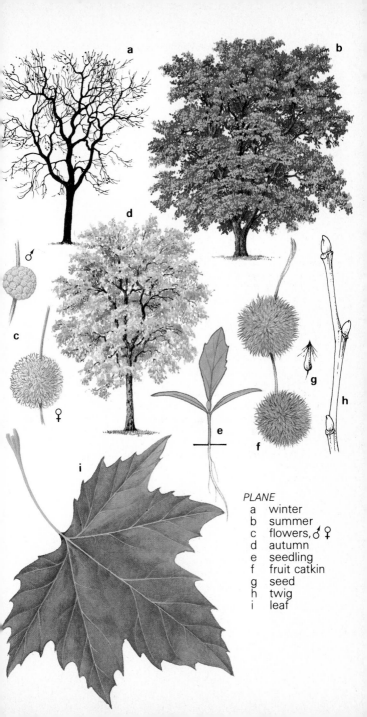

PLANE
a winter
b summer
c flowers, ♂ ♀
d autumn
e seedling
f fruit catkin
g seed
h twig
i leaf

HAWTHORNS

CRATAEGUS genus   ROSACEAE

All hawthorns have alternate, **conspicuously toothed, sharply cut or lobed leaves**. All bear clusters of showy white, pink or red blossoms in early summer—hence often called 'May trees'. Oval, attractive berries or haws are clearly tipped with five sepals remaining from the earlier green calyx; usually scarlet, crimson or orange, but some species bear dark blue, black or yellow berries. Pulp within leathery coat is usually yellow, soft and **mealy**, unattractive to humans though birds eat it greedily. Seeds within may be solitary, or two or three together; they are dark brown, oval, hard, ridged, stone-like; many pass unharmed through alimentary canals of birds, who carry them long distances in their flight.

In such ways hawthorns quickly colonize bare ground, such as abandoned pastures. Some seeds sprout in spring after ripening, others two or three years later. Each seedling raises a hard seed-coat which splits and allows two fleshy oval seed-leaves within to spread. Typical lobed leaves follow on an unarmed shoot; spines develop later.

Hawthorn spines, always single, are really modified shoots; they spring from leaf axils. Bark, smooth and greenish-brown on branches and young trunks, becomes grey-brown with age, breaks up into **small, thin, squarish flaking plates. Trunks** of mature trees often **fluted with ribs that become buttresses at their bases**. Wood within is hard, heavy, strong, with rusty-brown heartwood, creamy-white sapwood. Used mainly for fence stakes or fuel.

Typical hawthorn flower has five sepals, five petals, many stamens, and a central pistil bearing one to three stigmas. Double flowers, with stamens modified into petals, are common in garden varieties; being sterile, these are propagated by grafting. Only untrimmed trees flower. Winter buds are scaly, very small.

Hawthorns make ideal hedges or **living fences**. Two common species, used for hedging in Europe, have been introduced and become naturalized in North America. Both have deeply-cut leaves and crimson berries. Midland hawthorn, *Crataegus laevigata*, has two or three seeds in each berry. Common English hawthorn, *C. monogyna*, has only one. Most striking American species is aptly-named cockspur hawthorn, *C. crus-galli*, which bears sharp curved spines often 7·5 cm (3 in.) long. It has an oval leaf with a tapered base, widest and most clearly toothed above its middle. Scarlet fruits, about 1·5 cm ($\frac{1}{2}$ in.) long, ripens in clusters in autumn, when leaves turn bright orange.

Usual hawthorn leaf colours: bright emerald in spring, dull green in summer, golden in autumn: Twig colours: green, but **crimson** on sunlit sides.

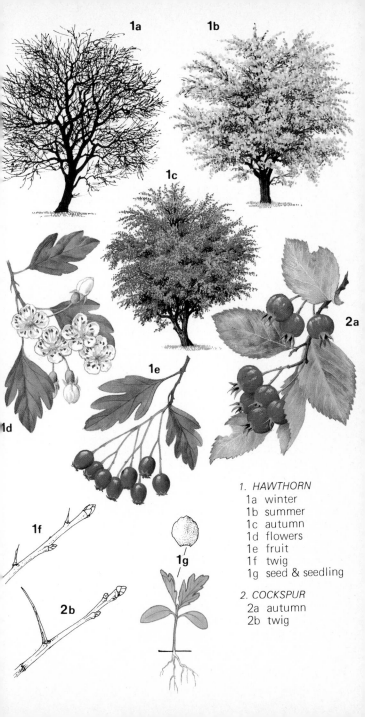

1. *HAWTHORN*
   1a winter
   1b summer
   1c autumn
   1d flowers
   1e fruit
   1f twig
   1g seed & seedling

2. *COCKSPUR*
   2a autumn
   2b twig

MOUNTAIN ASH TREES

SORBUS AUCUPARIA and   ROSACEAE
S. AMERICANA

The pinnately-compound leaves of mountain ash can be distinguished by their **reddish-green midribs**, compared with the pale green of true ash which is unrelated botanically; they are set alternately on twigs—true ash, leaves arise in pairs. Mountain ash leaflets have clearly toothed edges; on true ash teeth are much shallower. Mountain ash trees are also called 'rowans', a Scottish name derived from both Gaelic *ruadh-an*, or 'red one' and Norse *røn*.

American mountain ash, *Sorbus americana*, native to eastern Canada, New England, Appalachians, is almost identical with European mountain ash, *S. aucuparia*. Pointed leaflets distinguish American kind; on average they are twice as large, at 7·5 cm (3 in.) long, as European kind; latter has blunt-ended leaflets. European mountain ash is widely planted, for ornament and a source of wildlife food, in North America, and has become naturalized. American mountain ash is occasionally grown in Europe.

Both mountain ashes are upland trees, growing as high as any. They often spring from seeds dropped by birds in rock crevices, even on sheer cliff faces. Silvery **blue-grey bark** carries **clear horizontal breathing pores**, it is otherwise smooth until, on old trees, a network of thin scaly ridges develops. Tough, strong timber has purplish-brown heartwood, pale yellow sapwood; used for fence stakes, tool handles, small carved or turned objects. **Remarkably large purplish-brown buds** stand on **short stalks** or narrowed bases which bear distinct leaf scars. Bud-scales have white hairy edges.

Typical mountain ash leaf has short stalk, then eight pairs of oval unstalked leaflets, finally a terminal leaflet (17 in all); all show toothed edges. Pale green in spring, rich green later, yellow, orange, or brilliant scarlet in autumn.

Creamy-white flowers open in late spring in much-branched, flat-topped clusters. Each blossom has five sepals, five petals, many stamens, and a central ovary that ripens to a soft berry holding two seeds. Berry develops through green and yellow stages to orange, then scarlet by early autumn. Promptly devoured by birds, especially thrushes, who scatter seeds. Too sour for people to eat, but make tasty jelly—a seasoning for game.

Each hard brown rough-coated seed is pear-shaped, with **curved tip**. Most seeds lie dormant until second spring after ripening. Sprouting seedling bears first two oval, opposite seed-leaves, then true leaves with only three leaflets; eventually larger leaves, with numerous leaflets, appear.

MOUNTAIN ASH

a   autumn
b   winter
c   spring
d   leaf
e   fruit
f   flowers
g   twig
h   seedling & seed
i   American leaflet

WHITEBEAMS, WILD SERVICE TREE

SORBUS ARIA, S. INTERMEDIA,   ROSACEAE
S. TORMINALIS

Whitebeam is so-called from **white undersides of its leaves**. 'Beam', meaning 'tree' or 'timber' perpetuates Anglo-Saxon *beam*, cognate to German *Baum*. This beautiful tree is only common in wilds on chalk and limestone rocks. Varieties and hybrids are grown in gardens, both in Europe and North America, or as street trees.

Lovely foliage breaks from **large green stalked buds** in mid-spring. Unfolding leaves stand upright at first in cup-shaped formations, displaying **white under-surfaces like petals of giant lilies or tulips**. Then their stalks bend, and only dark green upper surfaces are seen. In autumn the leaves fade to golden-brown, still showing white undersides. Whiteness is due to coating of felty hairs, which check water loss—helpful on dry limestone soils. Leaves are oval, pointed, have toothed edges.

Whitebeam bark is greenish-grey and remains smooth. Very old trees show thin scaly plates. Timber has yellowish-brown heartwood, pale yellow sapwood; sometimes used for carving, turnery, or tool handles; burns well.

Whitebeam flowers expand in spring in flat-topped clusters, with creamy white petals and a structure resembling those of mountain ash. Berries, ripe by early autumn, mature from green through yellow to bright red. Too sour to eat; relished by birds. Small, hard, irregularly pear-shaped, yellow seeds, two per berry. Seedlings raise two oval seed-leaves with smooth edges; normal oval leaves, with toothed edges, follow.

Swedish whitebeam, *S. intermedia*, is natural hybrid between common whitebeam which has simple leaves, and mountain ash, which has compound ones. Its own leaves, as Latin name suggests, are *intermediate*, that is, lobed on a *pinnate* plan, with toothed edges. A vigorous, smoke-resistant tree, often planted in town streets and gardens. Seeds oval, yellow, smooth.

Wild service tree, *S. torminalis*, is a rarity found scattered through ancient woods in southern England and western Europe. It bears a **broad lobed leaf like a maple, but alternately set**. Bark is broken into squares like hawthorn. It has white flowers like whitebeam. The dull red berries are just sweet enough to be eaten raw.

WHITEBEAM
a winter
b autumn
c spring leaves
d leaf & flowers
e fruit
f autumn leaf
g Swedish
   Whitebeam
h Wild Service tree
i seed & seedling

APPLE

MALUS genus   ROSACEAE

Wild crab apple, *Malus sylvestris*, is one of the ancestors of many
kinds of apple cultivated today as *eaters, cookers, cider apples* or
ornamental crabs, in all countries of temperate climate. Many of
these are hybrids, raised by crossing with other species. All are
propagated by grafting.

'Crab' comes from Norse *skrab*, meaning scrubby. Wild trees,
common along European hedgerows, naturalized in North
America, spring from pips, discarded by people or birds. Short-
boled, branchy, they bear **rosy-purple-grey bark**, first smooth,
then wrinkled, finally **shedding loose scales. Purple-brown
shoots**, which may be spiny or not, are of two kinds. Long slender
ones extend tree's crown. **Short, stout ones, wrinkled with scars**
from fallen leaves and fruit, bear blossom and, later, apples. These
spurs are naturally retained by fruit growers when they prune
orchards. Winter buds, set singly, are oval, with **purple-brown,
pointed scales, fringed with grey hairs**.

Apple leaves are oval to round, bluntly-pointed, long-stalked,
have toothed edges. Colours: pale green, mid-green, grey-brown.
Leaf stalks often tinted red. Flowers, opening on short stalks in
spring just after leaves, appear **rose-pink** at first, the outside colour
of their petals; later they look white, the inside colour. They have
five green sepals, five petals, many stamens, and a central five-
celled pistil. They bear abundant nectar, and attract many bees
who effect pollination, and gather much honey.

The fleshy, roundish apple fruit, technically a pome (from
French *pomme*, meaning apple) is really the swollen flower stalk,
holding the deep-seated ovary and thus the seeds. **Withered black
pointed sepals at tip of fruit** indicate an apple or close ally.
Deeply indented base where stalk is attached is apple's key
feature. Tip is indented in some kinds, not all. Wild crab apples are
small, round, yellow, with hard, intensely bitter flesh. This
softens later, becoming just sweet enough to eat. **Small, oval,
pointed, hard brown seeds** or pips are **encased in paper cells.**
Hungry birds disperse them, either scattering them or swallowing
them, later voiding them unharmed. A sprouting apple pip raises
two oval seed-leaves. A shoot emerges between them, bearing
normal foliage.

Apple logs, harvested when old orchards are cleared, have rich
red-brown heartwood contrasting with white sapwood. First-rate
firewood. Known as fruitwood, apple is used for bowls, decorative
carving and mathematical drawing instruments. Countrymen
select tough knotty butts for mallet heads, knowing it resists
splitting under stress.

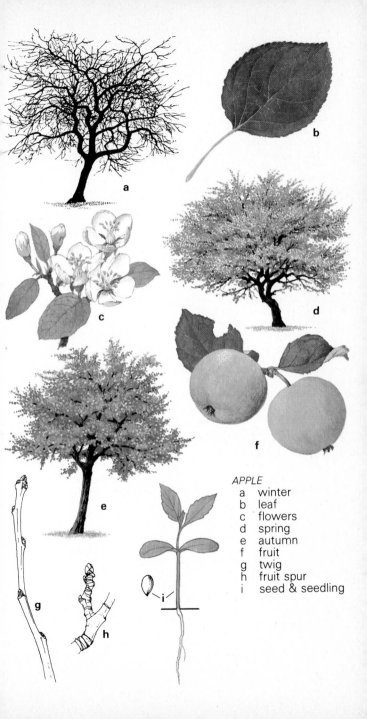

APPLE
a   winter
b   leaf
c   flowers
d   spring
e   autumn
f   fruit
g   twig
h   fruit spur
i   seed & seedling

PEAR, QUINCE AND MEDLAR

PYRUS, CYDONIA and *MESPILUS*   ROSACEAE

Three commonly-grown trees resemble apples in foliage, flowers and fruit, and have similar seedlings. Wild pear, *Pyrus communis*, an ancestor of most cultivated kinds, grows in European hedgerows as a slender small tree with **grey bark broken into many small** squares. Unlike orchard varieties, it usually bears **long, sharp, brown spines on its twigs**. Buds are brown, short, broadly conical, sharp pointed. **Leaves have exceptionally long stalks**, one-and-a-half times length of blade. They are oval, pointed, and have toothed edges. Pale green; gold, then black in autumn. Tree form is slender, spire-like. Many flowering spurs spring from longer, main shoots.

Flowers open just before leaves, in crowded clusters springing from short spurs. They are **white throughout**, not tinged with pink like apple blossom. Flower structure is similar, fruit quite different. **Pears have no hollow** at their junction with the stalk. Instead they start as **narrow cylinders that broaden out towards the tip** in the conventional pear shape. Tip carries a five-pointed, withered calyx cap.

Wild pears are **brown, hard and woody** when first ripe. Later they soften and attract soft-billed birds, such as blackbirds, which peck away pulp and scatter seeds. Pear timber, which has the same uses as apple, has a pleasing, even, pink-brown heartwood. Cultivated pears, like apples may be soft-fleshed yellow dessert pears, or harder greenish-brown cookers. Perry, an alcoholic drink, is made by gathering pears of particular strains after they have fallen, crushing them to get pear juice, and then fermenting it.

Quince, *Cydonia oblonga*, grows wild in southern Europe and is planted in northern orchards. Leaves short-stalked, smooth-edged **downy underneath**; turn yellow in autumn. Flowers, borne singly, have five **woolly reflexed, green sepals**, five pretty, pinkish-white petals. **Large woolly yellow fruit has battered oval shape**, with ribs on shoulders. **Strongly fragrant**, one quince can fill a room with fruity odour. Used in jams, jellies, and to strengthen flavour of apple pies. Too strongly tasting to be eaten raw. Small black, gritty seeds have irregular oblong outline.

Medlar, *Mespilus germanica*, grows wild in central and southern Europe and as an escape from cultivation in Britain and North America. Its downy leaf has a remarkable **long, blunt, oval shape**, broadening towards tip; fades to yellowish brown. Large, solitary flowers have **white, frilly petals, alternating with long green sepals. Round, downy, yellowish-brown fruit has deep hollow at its outer end, surrounded by large, leafy, faded brown sepals**. It remains hard until late autumn, then suddenly becomes soft, fleshy, delicious. Within a few days it decays. Birds attack it at short ripe stage, and scatter its large, flat, very hard, irregularly oblong seeds.

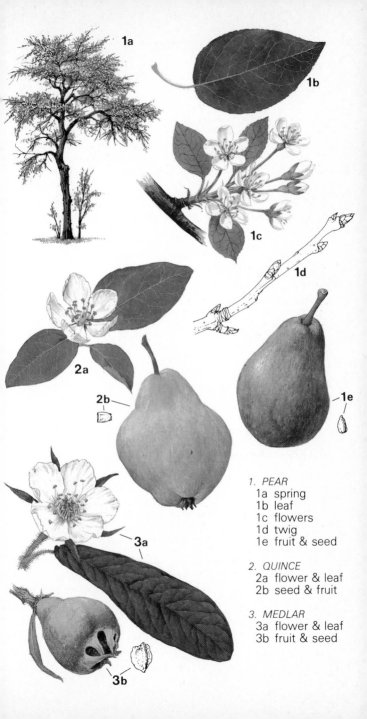

1. *PEAR*
   1a spring
   1b leaf
   1c flowers
   1d twig
   1e fruit & seed

2. *QUINCE*
   2a flower & leaf
   2b seed & fruit

3. *MEDLAR*
   3a flower & leaf
   3b fruit & seed

PLUMS

PRUNUS DOMESTICA, P. SPINOSA   ROSACEAE
and allies

Orchard plums, *Prunus domestica*, arose as hybrids between wild European blackthorn, *P. spinosa*, and Asiatic cherry-plum, *P. cerasifera*. Shoots have bluish-brown bark; finer ones are crimson above, green below. Fruit-bearing twigs, **rugged with scars**, carry **short spurs**. Purplish brown buds are conical, with distinct, pointed scales; oval, short-stalked leaves, have **regularly toothed edges and rounded tip**. **Distinct marginal veins** link ends of other veins near leaf edges, bounding a random network. Leaf-stalks crimson above, green below; leaf-blades dark green above, paler beneath.

Attractive white flowers have five green sepals, five showy white petals, many stamens with bright golden anthers, and central green pistil. They open in mid-spring. Fruit ripens rapidly towards late summer; red, black, green, purple or golden, according to variety: **silvery grey, waxy bloom** covers tough outer skin. Curious **crease** or long hollow runs from short stalk-base right around oval fruit. Greenish-yellow, sweet pulp surrounds oval, pale brown seed or stone, **flattened with ridges either side**.

Sprouting plum stones crack hard woody coat and expand two large, fleshy, oval seed-leaves, succeeded by normal foliage. Plums also renew their kind by vigorous root shoots—a plague to gardeners. Bark purplish-brown, smooth, becomes wrinkled later. If a trunk is damaged, a pale green, sweet-tasting translucent wound gum oozes through bark. Timber has purplish-brown heartwood, pale brown sapwood; used occasionally for decorative craft work.

Blackthorn or sloe, wild plum native in Europe, naturalized in North America, forms dense thickets on abandoned farmland by sending up root suckers. Has **black bark and shoots**, bearing **vicious spines. Small dark green, toothed-edged leaves** stand on short **crimson stalks**, set alternately. Tiny oval winter buds are purplish black.

White flowers open before or with leaves. Autumn fruit, a sloe, first green, then lustrous **deep blue-black, covered in silvery white waxy bloom**. Green flesh, bitterly acid at first, becomes sweet enough for eating after frost. Hard stone lies within. Used to make jelly, or flavour sloe gin.

Blackthorn stems, exceptionally strong and tough, have dark red-brown heartwood, golden brown sapwood. Too small and mis-shapen for general use, they are the traditional timber for the Irishman's knobbly cudgel or shillelagh.

American wild plum, *P. americana*, is a small brown-barked tree that bears white flowers with **red sepals**. Large round red fruit holds tart yellow flesh, grows in thickets on moist ground.

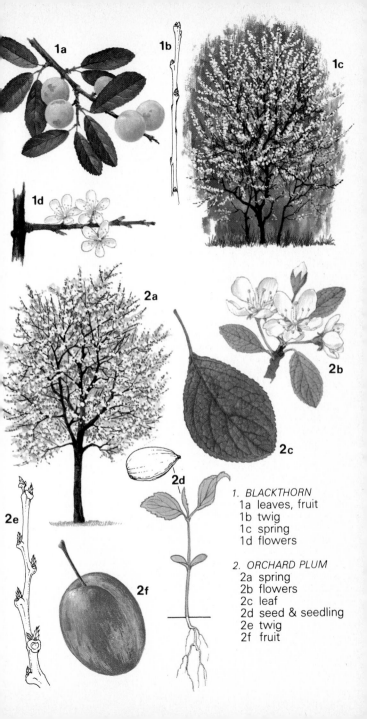

1. BLACKTHORN
1a leaves, fruit
1b twig
1c spring
1d flowers

2. ORCHARD PLUM
2a spring
2b flowers
2c leaf
2d seed & seedling
2e twig
2f fruit

PEACH AND ALMOND

PRUNUS PERSICA, P. AMYGDALUS   ROSACEAE

Peaches, *Prunus persica*, native to Persia, are grown for sweet, luscious pulp that surrounds their seeds; hard woody stone has a **thick, ridged shell**, with only a small kernel within. The almond, *P. amygdalus*, by contrast, has no sweet pulp, but only a **tough, grey-green, leathery skin, clad in dense hairs.** In autumn this splits revealing a *whitish* inner surface, then falls away from **smooth, pitted, pale brown stone.** Its value lies in the oval, mid-brown, rough-coated, ribbed kernel, obtained by cracking the stone. Under its brown coat this kernel holds white flesh which is both delicious to eat and a highly nutritious food, rich in fat and protein. 'Sweet' almonds used for dessert, are variety *dulcis*; bitter almonds, variety *amara*, are used for flavouring.

Both peach and almond grow as small, much-branched trees, often grafted on rootstocks of a less high-yielding strain. In Britain and northern North America, they are often grown for flowers, rather than fruit. Their bark is smooth and **dark purplish-grey to blue-black** with scattered horizontal, pale-grey breathing pores. On old stems it becomes rougher and scaly, and flakes away. Timber has a purplish-brown heartwood core, surrounded by white sapwood. Strong, tough, yet readily worked; occasionally used for carving or turning ornaments: burns well.

Young twigs are slender, but old twigs of both peach and almond are **stout, and ridged with rough scars left by fallen leaves. Purplish brown** except near tips, where they are dull red on sunlit surfaces, pale green elsewhere. Oval buds, clustered, or alternate, show many dark brown scales. Leaves are long-stalked, long, narrow, roughly six times as long as broad, end in gradual points. Glossy dark green above, paler below; show no bright autumn colour.

Lovely **bright pink flowers** open on bare branches **before the leaves,** in gay groups. Each blossom has a very short individual stalk, a dull red basal cup, five green sepals, five broad-oval pink frilly petals in single forms, many more in double ornamental kinds. There are many stamens, with golden antlers, ample nectar to attract early-flying bees, and a central green pistil. After fertilization this ripens a single-seeded fruit. On true peach this matures through green stage to become beautiful **yellow and red succulent fruit,** with a rough velvety skin. On the nectarine, a cultivated variety, skin is smooth, and fruit resembles a large crimson-and-orange plum.

When peach or almond stones sprout, their seed-leaves remain within the hard husk; the shoot bears typical leaves from the outset.

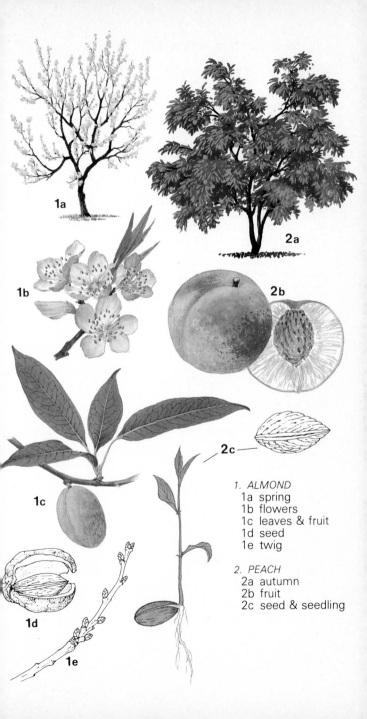

1. *ALMOND*
   1a spring
   1b flowers
   1c leaves & fruit
   1d seed
   1e twig

2. *PEACH*
   2a autumn
   2b fruit
   2c seed & seedling

CHERRIES

PRUNUS AVIUM, P. PADUS and allies   ROSACEAE

European wild cherry, *Prunus avium*, also called gean or mazzard, an ancestor of orchard kinds, is naturalized over wide areas of North America. In European woodlands it forms a tall tree with an exceptionally straight stem and open crown. Striking bark is **purplish brown with a metallic lustre**, smooth except for **prominent, corky, brown breathing pores in horizontal groups**. On old trunks it peels away in horizontal strips or becomes scaly with shallow fissures. Valuable timber has heartwood richly patterned in warm golden brown with greenish overtones, pale brown sapwood; used for finest furniture, often as veneer, wood sculpture and decorative turned or carved work.

Oval leaves have **long crimson stalks**, toothed edges, end in sharp points. Pale green at first, become mid-green later, blaze into bright orange and fiery red before falling in autumn. Shoots, red-brown above, fawn-grey beneath, carry large oval, pointed, red-brown winter buds.

White flowers burst from large buds just before leaves open in spring, forming a dazzling snowstorm of blossom over bare branches. Grouped in showy clusters, bunched three, four or five together, they have long stalks, five green sepals, five broad white petals, many stamens, and a central green pistil. Fruit ripens quickly, cherries changing through green to red and finally black by midsummer. Birds eat them greedily. People find their reddish pulp sweet, though only a thin layer surrounds the hard round pale brown stone.

When cherry seeds sprout the woody husk cracks open, to reveal two oval thick, fleshy seed-leaves. A shoot grows up between these and bears a pair of *opposite* true leaves; alternately-placed leaves follow.

Japanese cherries, planted for glorious bursts of blossom in spring, are mostly varieties of *Prunus serrulata*, chosen long ago by Japanese gardeners, and propagated by grafting. 'Kanzan', most popular cultivar, has lilac-pink double flowers, metallic purple bark with bulging orange-brown breathing pores; it is sterile and sets no seed or fruit.

Bird cherry, *Prunus padus*, native to upland Europe, including Britain, often planted elsewhere, is a small tree with **black, finely-grained bark** and long-oval pale-green leaves. White flowers open in midsummer, **crowded along spikes**, not bunched, fragrant. Cherries are small, round and black. American black cherry, *P. serotina*, is similar but bears larger flowers and cherries, and forms a taller tree; young bark reddish brown, smooth; old bark black, scaly. Aptly named choke cherry, *P. virginiana*, bears red cherries with astringent, bitter taste.

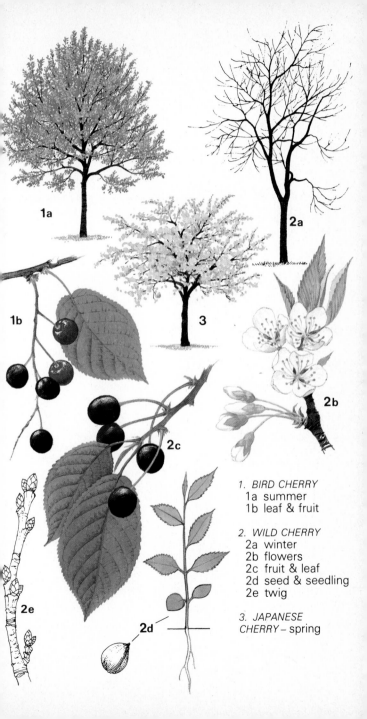

1. *BIRD CHERRY*
   1a summer
   1b leaf & fruit

2. *WILD CHERRY*
   2a winter
   2b flowers
   2c fruit & leaf
   2d seed & seedling
   2e twig

3. *JAPANESE CHERRY* – spring

CHERRY LAURELS

PRUNUS LAUROCERASUS, ROSACEAE
P. LUSITANICA

Two evergreen cherries, native to the Mediterranean region, have been widely planted in gardens in temperate-zone countries because of adaptability, hardiness, and attractive winter colour. Most broadleaved evergreen trees and shrubs look much alike. Cherry laurel, *Prunus laurocerasus,* can easily be told by crushing a leaf, whereupon it promptly gives out a **smell of bitter almonds or marzipan**. This is due to minute traces of prussic acid. Butterfly hunters use these leaves in 'killing bottles'; if a few are crushed and put in a closed glass bottle holding an insect, it is soon killed without damage.

Oblong in outline, short-stalked and blunt-ended, cherry laurel leaves are **glossy dark green** above, pale below. Soft and light green when they emerge from buds, set alternately along **green twigs**, they quickly harden and become leathery. After a few seasons of active life they fall without fading.

Cherry laurel bark is **jet black** with a finely textured surface, Large stems hold hard pale-brown timber, with no colour distinction between heartwood and sapwood. Few grow stout enough for use; only a firewood tree.

Upright flower spikes spring in early summer from branches of unclipped cherry laurels but not from clipped ones. Pale green stalk bears about twenty small, short-stalked blossoms, each having five green sepals, five creamy-white waxy petals, many stamens and a central pistil. Insects, attracted by ample nectar and strong **smell of bitter almonds**, as in the leaves, carry pollen from flower to flower.

Small black one-seeded cherries ripen in autumn. Too small for people to eat, these fleshy fruits attract birds, who spread seeds. Seedlings germinate by cracking their hard seed coat. A short stem bearing two broad fleshy seed-leaves, which fall after one season, develops. A shoot grows up between the seed-leaves and carries ordinary evergreen permanent leaves.

Portugal laurel, *P. lusitanica,* has similar flower and fruit characters, but its leaves are **glossy dark green, almost black**, above, mid-green below. They are more oval than those of cherry laurel, with longer stalks and pointed tips. **Dark crimson shade** of twigs and leaf-stalks is Portugal laurel's clearest key feature. Berries ripen through red to **reddish-purple**, rather than black. Looks like true laurel (*Laurus nobilis*) but leaf is *not* aromatic. Wood has a *purplish* tinge to its underlying brown hue.

1. *PORTUGAL LAUREL*
   1b flowers, leaves
   & fruit

2. *CHERRY LAUREL*
   2a summer
   2b flowers & leaves
   2c fruit
   2d seed & seedling

JUDAS TREE, REDBUD

CERCIS genus   LEGUMINOSEAE

The small, spreading trees of the genus *Cercis* are easily known by their **leaves**, which are almost **round, to kidney-shaped or heart-shaped**. On Judas trees leaves have **lobes that overlap** at the base. Leaves are set on long, reddish stalks, and spring singly from **crimson twigs**. They open very late, are **tinged at first with blue**, and finally fade to yellow.

Flowers, likewise autumn fruits, appear in **bunches on old branches**, as well as on young twigs. Botanists call this 'cauliflory', meaning 'stem-flowering'. Flowers **open early, ahead of leaves**. On common European Judas tree, *C. siliquastrum*, they are **bright lilac-purple**. California redbud, *C. occidentalis*, shows this colour too. On Eastern redbud, *C. canadensis*, native to eastern United States and Ontario, they are rosy-pink. The structure of each individual, short-stalked flower resembles that of laburnum. But in this *Cercis* genus the large upper petal, called the standard, lies within the two side wing petals, not behind them. Flowers have sharp acid taste and are sometimes eaten in salads. Below these petals comes a neat calyx-cup of five brown or deep-red sepals, on a stalk of same colour. Ten stamens surround a central pistil.

Fruits ripen by autumn as long, broad, **flat**, crimson pods, with short stalks and pointed tips. Each holds about twelve **flat black** seeds. The sprouting seedling raises its husk above ground; this splits and two opposite oval seed-leaves appear. Normal round to heart-shaped leaves follow.

Judas tree, hardy only in southern gardens, was apparently introduced from Israel to southern France by Crusaders, circa A.D. 1200, and called *arbre de Judée*, tree of Judea. This had become 'Judas tree' by the time it reached England, and the legend soon arose that Judas Iscariot, after betraying Christ, hanged himself from its branches.

Judas tree bark is dark grey, almost black, broken up into very regular small squarish islands. Redbuds bear reddish-brown scaly bark, sometimes divided into long narrow scaly ridges.

The timbers of Judas tree and redbuds, too small for practical use, are peculiar and attractive. They are grey, blotched or veined with black, green and yellow.

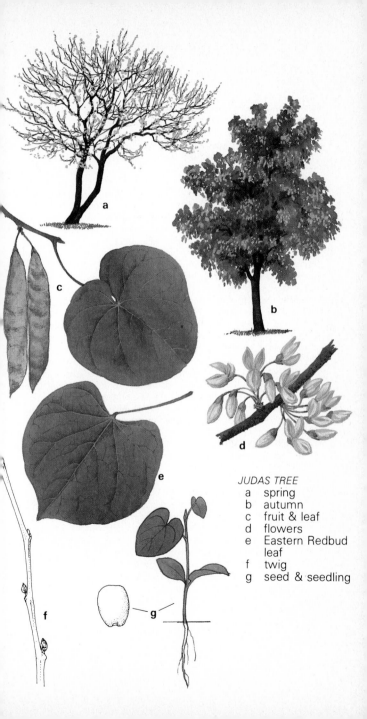

JUDAS TREE
a spring
b autumn
c fruit & leaf
d flowers
e Eastern Redbud leaf
f twig
g seed & seedling

HONEY LOCUST

GLEDITSIA TRIACANTHOS   Leguminoseae

The second word in this tree's scientific name is the clue to identity; *triacanthos* is Greek for 'three-spined'; honey locust is the only common timber tree to show this feature. Below most leaves or buds it bears **three spines**, central one longer than side ones. Old trunks are fiercely armed with an array of big three-spine groups, or even larger spine-branchlets.

Another exceptional feature is the **doubly compound leaf** found on vigorous shoots. An ordinary compound leaf carries many leaflets on a central stalk. In doubly compound form stalks that themselves bear minor leaflets arise from the central stalk instead. Sometimes only a sprinkling of major leaflets grow this way. Leaves are naturally large, often 15 cm (6 in.) long, and hold many elements—commonly thirty major leaflets of 150 minor leaflets! Terminal leaflets are seldom developed; side leaflets may be neatly paired, or not. Leaves open late in spring, in glossy bright yellowish-green shades; they turn gold in autumn.

In early summer honey locust bears small pale yellowish-green flowers, in large numbers on long stalks that spring from leaf axils. Males and females grow in separate spikes. Each male flower has five green sepals, five petals, ten stamens. Each female flower has a central pistil instead of stamens. After insect fertilization, this develops through a yellow-green stage to become, by autumn, a **distinctive seed pod; red-brown, flat, jointed, thick-edged, curved, often twisted**, and up to 40 cm (16 in.) long by 2·75 cm (1 in.) broad, though often shorter. Pods, which hang in groups on short stalks, hold up to twenty large dark brown oval seeds, about 2 cm (nearly 1 in.) long, embedded in the soft succulent pulp that explains honey locust's name. This pulp attracts animals that eat fruits and help scatter seeds. Cattle, deer, rabbits, squirrels and hares all devour pods greedily.

Seedlings raise two broad seed-leaves above ground. A shoot arises between these and bears simply compound leaves from the outset; eventually doubly compound leaves appear.

Honey locust's dark grey-brown or purplish bark forms narrow flat-topped plates, bounded by wandering wide shallow scaly ridges. Green winter twigs are zig-zag, with odd swellings at angles; buds are small, usually with three spines below them. Timber has red-brown, hard, durable heartwood, paler sapwood; used for posts, poles and firewood. Native to Mississippi basin, honey locust is widely planted in North America and Europe as a highly decorative shade tree. Spineless, podless cultivated varieties are preferred by tidy parks departments. In England it is hardy only in the south.

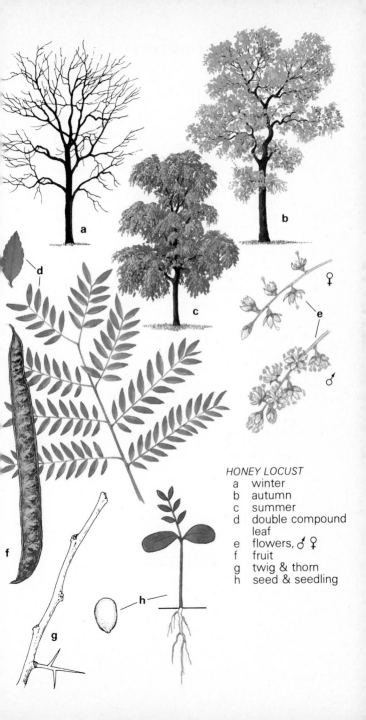

HONEY LOCUST
a   winter
b   autumn
c   summer
d   double compound
    leaf
e   flowers, ♂ ♀
f   fruit
g   twig & thorn
h   seed & seedling

LABURNUM

LABURNUM genus   LEGUMINOSEAE

Laburnum is easily known as the only common tree that has a **leaf with three leaflets**, in botanical terms *trifoliate*. Dark green, neatly oval, these leaflets stand on short stalks, set singly along blackish-green twigs. Winter buds have grey-green **pointed scales, fringed with white hairs**. Laburnum bark is a peculiar **rich dark olive-green to brown colour**, smooth but bearing black patches of breathing pores. Heartwood, strong, naturally durable, is **deep red-brown** and contrasts strongly with white sapwood. Too small for general use, but employed by craftsmen for decorative carving, inlaid work, and in musical instruments, including bagpipes. It gives a fine smooth finish and holds its shape well.

Yellow flowers, borne profusely in hanging chains, are another key character. Each chain consists of a central drooping stalk that carries, on individual short stalks, small blossoms built up in the typical pattern of the sweet-pea family or Leguminoseae. Inside the calyx of five green sepals comes a corolla of five variously shaped golden-yellow petals. Two at the front are infolded to form the *keel*, two at the sides stand out as *wings*, and one at the back stands up as the *standard*. Insects, attracted by the three outstanding petals, alight on the keel, which holds ten curved stamens and a pistil with a bent style. As they press inwards towards the central nectary, the insects brush pollen, collected from the stamens of one flower, on to the stigma of another, and so effect cross-fertilization.

Each pistil ripens by autumn to a **slender, thin, leathery and jointed black pod**. This holds several **hard black oval seeds**, which are poisonous. When a seedling sprouts, it raises two oval seed-leaves, then a few simple, undivided oval juvenile leaves; normal trifoliate leaves follow.

Common laburnum, *Laburnum anagyroides*, grows wild in the mountains of Central Europe, where it forms a small tree up to 10 m (30 ft) tall.

So-called Scotch laburnum, *L. alpinum*, native to southern Europe, has broader leaflets, longer flower-chains, and blooms two weeks later. Most garden trees are hybrids between these two species, chosen because they bear dazzling displays of brilliant blossoms, and propagated by grafting. One of the best is Voss's laburnum, *L. × vossii*; another is aptly called 'Golden Rain'.

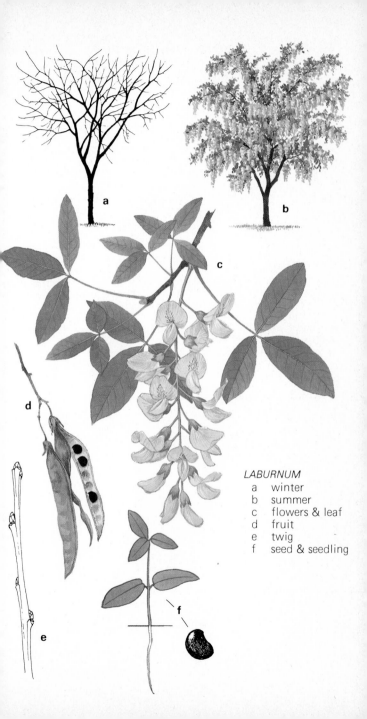

LABURNUM

- a winter
- b summer
- c flowers & leaf
- d fruit
- e twig
- f seed & seedling

ROBINIA, BLACK LOCUST

ROBINIA PSEUDOACACIA LEGUMINOSEAE

This easily-known tree was called 'locust' by early settlers in New England, because they mistook it for the biblical locust whose seeds sustained John the Baptist in the wilderness. **Long, slender, tough, hanging, jointed, black seed pods hold oval black seeds**, one per joint. Unfortunately seeds are no good to eat. Another name, 'false acacia', arises from confusion with spiny true acacia trees; robinia bears **sharp spines in pairs below every bud**. The name *Robinia* records Jean Robin, French botanist, associated with tree's introduction to Europe, circa 1636. 'Black' refers to seed-pods.

Robinia bark, pale grey-brown, is exceptionally thick and develops a **random meshwork of deep ridges and hollows**. Main trunk often bends; **branches are tortuous**, ending in **curly-wurly fine twigs**. Minute buds, set singly, have **large triangular scars** beneath them, and a spine on either side. Large compound leaves have long stiff midrib, **two ranks of paired oval, short-stalked leaflets**, either side, plus a terminal leaflet. Leaflets number, overall, from eleven to twenty-three. The two of each pair are almost opposite, not precisely so. Open very late, uncrumpling, as delicate pale greenish-yellow fronds. Later true green, finally golden. Break up as they fall.

Robinia's **conspicuous white flowers, shaped like sweat-pea blossoms**, open in midsummer in **hanging tapering clusters**. For flower structure *see* Laburnum. Dark red-brown or black seed pods ripen in autumn, hang on trees, split during winter, to reveal shiny, brown inner surfaces. They release hard seeds, then fall.

Seedling raises two oval seed leaves, next a few roughly oval simple leaves. Compound leaves follow, with three, five, seven, etc. leaflets until adult leaf quota, from eleven to twenty-three, is achieved.

Robinia timber has lovely, **golden-brown, lustrous, heart-wood with intricate lively grain**; sapwood somewhat paler. Strong, naturally durable, yet readily worked, it was soon applied by New England settlers to tough jobs—tool handles, cart shafts, wooden platters, kitchen spoons, fencing and sturdy yet attractive furniture. First-rate firewood too. Nowadays esteemed mainly for craft work; bendy stems don't suit modern machinery.

Introduced to Europe for ornament, timber and firewood. Almost indestructible. After felling, sprouts furiously and shoots up everywhere as root suckers. Spines make it vandal proof. Naturalized over much of Europe and North America.

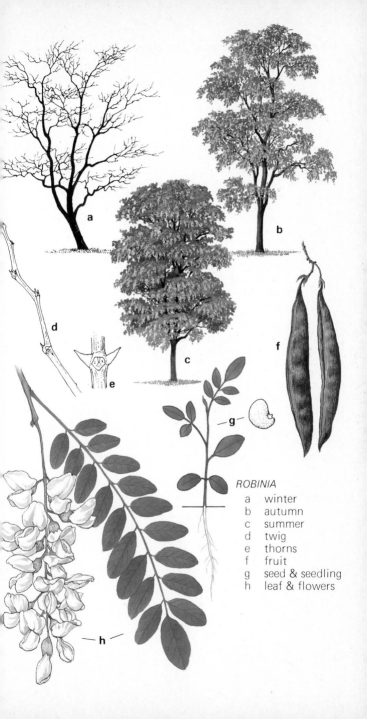

ROBINIA

a winter
b autumn
c summer
d twig
e thorns
f fruit
g seed & seedling
h leaf & flowers

TREE OF HEAVEN

AILANTHUS ALTISSIMA   SIMARUBACEAE

The imaginative name of this striking tree proves to be a simple translation of a Chinese phrase meaning 'very tall tree', though in fact it rarely reaches 30 m (100 ft). Introduced from North China in 1751; now widely planted in European and American streets and gardens, even in cities. In New England and eastern Canada it has become naturalized. It grows rampantly like a native tree, spreading by seed and **suckers** from underground roots. Timber is soft, pale brown, rarely used. Twigs have orange pith.

Tree of Heaven's key feature is its **enormous compound leaf**, often mistaken for a shoot. Ranging in length from 10 cm (4 in.) to 1 m (3 ft), it may bear from ten to forty leaflets. The stout central stem, green or dark red, may end in one or two leaflets. Every leaflet has its own short stalk and a broad base with a **swelling or gland on either side**. Oval in outline, each leaflet tapers to a pointed tip. The odd composite leaf, dark green above, pale and smooth beneath, opens very late, about June. It falls late, too, while still green, all in one piece. If crushed, it emits an unpleasant smell.

Tree of Heaven grows fast, even in smoky towns, forming an open-branched tree. Bark is smooth brown or grey, with characteristic **white angular streaks**, running more or less vertically. Twigs are very stout and angular, with numerous pale breathing pores. Scars left by fallen leaves large, with numerous vein-traces from equally numerous leaflets. A remarkably small round bud arises above each scar.

Each Tree of Heaven bears only male, or only female, flowers. Blossom consists of open panicles or bunches of countless small flowers, red in bud but cream-coloured when open in midsummer. Each flower has ten sepals and ten petals. The male flower, which has an unpleasant smell, has ten stamens; the female bears three to five carpels. In autumn each carpel ripens a single seed, crimson in colour, set at the centre of an oblong yellow wing that **tapers towards each end**. Massed displays of seeds then make many female trees appear decked by golden blossoms.

Seedlings first raise two seed-leaves, then a pair of three-lobed leaves. Typical compound leaves follow, with increasing sizes and numbers of leaflets. Gardeners sometimes cut back small Trees of Heaven to ground level. Next summer they send up huge decorative leaves, often tinged red.

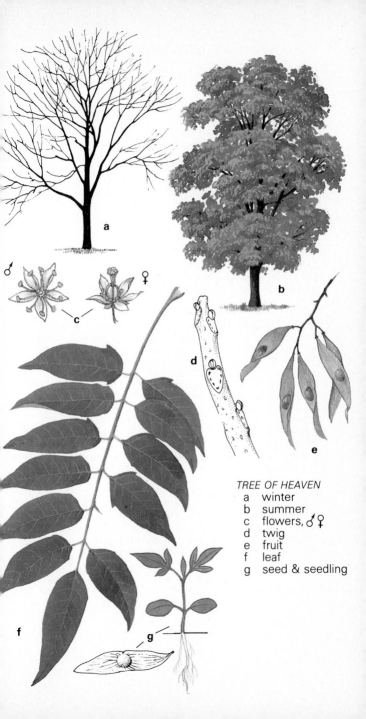

TREE OF HEAVEN
- a winter
- b summer
- c flowers, ♂ ♀
- d twig
- e fruit
- f leaf
- g seed & seedling

BOX

BUXUS SEMPERVIRENS   Buxaceae

Box trees are familiar to most people as low evergreen shrubs that can be clipped to make miniature hedges, or trained into quaint shapes like balls or castle battlements. These shrub forms are a variety, *suffruticosa*, of an elegant small tree that grows wild in central and eastern Europe, and at a few isolated places in England. Box is usually found on dry chalk or limestone soils, where its thick-skinned evergreen leaves enable it to resist drought. English native locations are Box Hill, a chalk down near Dorking in Surrey, Boxwell in Gloucestershire, Chequers in Buckinghamshire, and Boxley in Kent. Box stands shade and, aided by evergreen habit, can live as an undershrub below deciduous broadleaved trees. Shade tolerance also enables it to be grown as close low hedges, even though close-ranked leaves shade one another.

Opposite, oval, dark green leaves, somewhat paler below, with **inrolled edges**, are box's key character. They are **ranked in flat planes** along **squarish green twigs** that bear minute buds. Each leaf lives for about four years, then falls while still green. Bark, at first smooth and greenish grey, later develops a **chequerboard pattern of corky, pale yellow squares**. Boxwood is unique in being **bright golden-brown or yellow** right through. It is even-textured, very hard, and very heavy even when seasoned. Despite the tree's small size, its wood once enjoyed great demand for making rulers, and mathematical drawing instruments—now usually made of plastic. Still used for decorative wood sculpture and inlay. The best wood for fine wood engravings, cut on its hard *end grain*, a process invented by the great Northumbrian countryside artist John Bewick.

Flowers of box, little-known, open in leaf axils in early summer. Males and females are separate, but occur on same tree, sometimes in same cluster. Both are very small and have four sepals alternating with four petals, all yellowish-green. Male flowers have four stamens, female flowers a pistil holding three two-seeded cells, topped by three styles. After pollination each female flower ripens into a **pale grey papery seed pod, shaped like a Greek urn** and **topped by three odd bent-back horns**. Pod holds about six small hard black seeds. Box seedlings start life by raising two small, oval, pale green seed-leaves, which fall after one summer's existence. Normal evergreen foliage follows.

BOX
a wild tree
b newly-planted
   hedge
c flowers, ♂♀
d box topiary
e fruit
f leaf
g seed & seedling

STAGHORN SUMAC

RHUS TYPHINA   ANACARDIACEAE

Unmistakable in winter when bare branches stand out like a stag's antlers, tipped, on female trees, with **crimson plume-shaped fruit clusters**. Named also from the resemblance of **stiff, stout hairy shoots** to horns of a stag during their velvet growing stage in early summer. Break a shoot and **milky sap** flows out; central pith is **thick, yellowish brown**. Side buds small, round, **velvety**; no terminal bud. Bark dark brown, with prominent yellowish breathing pores; thin, smooth, becoming scaly with age. Light, soft, brittle wood, orange with broad greenish rays, sometimes used for decorative work.

Native to eastern Canada and United States, staghorn sumac often forms **thickets** from root shoots so is sometimes planted to check soil erosion. Commonly grown in Old World gardens as small ornamental tree; occasionally runs wild. Spreads widely by roots, which bear vigorous suckers. **Huge compound leaves**, commonly 0·5 m (1·5 ft) long, are placed alternately on twigs. Each resembles a shoot, bears from 11 to 31 stalkless, long-oval long-pointed leaflets, with toothed edges. **Central leaflets much longer than those at ends**. When leaves open they are clad in red hairs; become yellowish green, then mid-green through summer. In autumn they blaze into tints of orange, scarlet, crimson and purple before falling early in winter.

Male flowers, borne on separate trees from females, appear in spring in large branching clusters, 0·5 m (1·5 ft) long. These short-lived flower-heads look reddish green because of hairs growing amid numerous bracts. Very small individual male flowers have five sepals, five yellowish green petals, five stamens.

Female flowers, borne in shorter, more crowded clusters, also look reddish green, have five sepals, five petals, and a one-celled pistil that produces single hard brown round seed. As seeds mature, female flower-heads begin to look even more compact, through vigorous growth of crimson hairs. Resulting fruit heads persist on tree right through winter.

A sumac seed will not sprout until second spring after it has ripened. Then it bears two oval seed-leaves on a very long, thin stalk. First juvenile leaves that succeed these are **simple**, oval and pointed, with deeply-toothed edges. They are followed in turn by leaves with three or five leaflets, then fully-compound adult leaves. Staghorn sumac is increased by root cuttings or suckers; most gardeners demand picturesque female form, rather than plainer male.

Red Indians, who coined name *sumac*, used its hollowed-out, pithy stems for tubes and pipes. Settlers used such pipes for tapping sugar maples, also tannin-rich bark for tanning hides to make leather.

STAGHORN SUMAC
a winter
b summer
c flowers, ♂ ♀
d fruit
e autumn leaf
f seed & seedling
g twig

HOLLIES

ILEX genus   AQUIFOLIACEAE

Hollies are the only common trees bearing **thick tough, waxy, glossy, evergreen leaves with spiky edges**. These short-stalked leaves, set alternately on twigs, are dark green above and pale green below; they have a waxy surface that can burn fiercely, even on living trees. This foliage character restricts water loss and helps holly to thrive through summer droughts; its evergreen habit helps it to gain nourishment through mild wet winters; both these features are typical of Mediterranean climatic zone. Holly is favoured for Christmas decoration because it **does not wither** when cut. On growing tree, leaves age slowly, but finally fall, still green, after three or four years' life, and fade to greyish fawn on the soil, also becoming softer. Spiky leaves, which resist browsing by animals, only appear on lower branches. Leaves borne higher up, out of reach of beasts, are **oval, with pointed tips**.

Each holly tree is either male or female. In early summer both sexes bear clusters of **white, waxy flowers** on short stalks near twig tips. **No sepals** can be seen. The **four creamy-white oblong petals** have **purple tips**. A male flower bears **four** stamens with golden anthers. Each female flower has a squat egg-shaped pistil, with a very short-styled **four-lobed stigma** set on a **four-celled ovary**. Pollination is by insects, rewarded with ample nectar. Berries ripen in autumn, in familiar **scarlet clusters**. Each berry has tough skin around soft yellow pulp, holds **four** hard yellow, ribbed seeds. Birds eventually eat most berries, often swallowing and voiding seeds, which then sprout next spring. Otherwise seeds lie dormant in soil for eighteen months before sprouting. Holly seedlings bear, on a purple-tinged stem, two fleshy oblong dark green seed-leaves, which last only one year. Fleshy oval dark green and evergreen leaves, without spines, follow. Spiky evergreen leaves first appear in second season.

Holly shoots, **purplish green**, bear small **green** sharply-pointed winter buds. Bark **smooth and greenish grey**, only becoming fissured on very old trees. Wood uniformly **white**, exceptionally dense, burns well without seasoning. Used for firewood or decorative wood carving, inlay, or turnery. Though usually bushy, holly can form a tree up to 27 m (80 ft) tall, 2 m (6 ft) in girth. Because it stands dense shade, holly can be close-planted, then clipped to make an impenetrable hedge.

Common European holly, *Ilex aquifolium*, is widely cultivated in North America also; has countless varieties, bearing green, golden, variegated, spiky, or smooth foliage. Native American holly, *I. opaca*, resembles European holly closely, but has larger leaves, fewer berries.

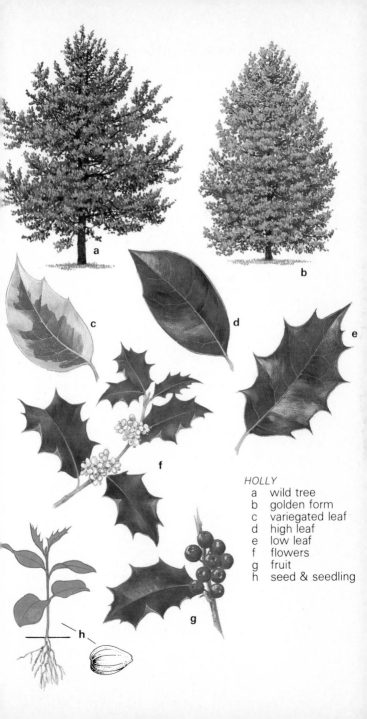

HOLLY
a   wild tree
b   golden form
c   variegated leaf
d   high leaf
e   low leaf
f   flowers
g   fruit
h   seed & seedling

SPINDLE TREE, WAHOO

EUONYMUS genus   CELASTRACEAE

Spindle trees are so called because their hard, greenish-white, horny wood is ideal for making spindles for spinning wool by hand. Spindles, invented in remote times, still used in eastern Europe, are straight, smooth-surfaced sticks, easily twirled by fingers of women, especially spinsters! Rough sheep's wool is fed into them and twisting motion, maintained by weight of stone spindle whorl, draws it into a strong fine thread.

Spindle shoots, at first round, soon become **square**, later round again as they expand further. Young shoots are **green**. Bark on old stems, at first smooth and grey, later becomes **crinkled, with pink-tinged fissures**. Leaves, in **opposite pairs**, are long-oval in outline, pointed, short-stalked, with **toothed edges**. Pale green in summer, become **purplish orange** in autumn.

Flowers open in small clusters in leaf axils early in summer. Textbooks assert that spindle trees are male or female, but some bear flowers with fertile organs of both sexes, male stamens becoming evident first. Each flower has four green sepals, four yellowish-green petals, four stamens and/or a central pistil with four-celled ovary.

Conspicuous, brightly coloured fruits develop through green summer stage, ripen in autumn. Four-lobed, they resemble a priest's biretta, hence French name *bonnet du prêtre*. Lobes become **pink** outside, then split into four parts, revealing four **orange** seed-coverings, technically called **arils**. Striking colour combination attracts birds, who scatter hard white seeds, with crinkled seed-coats, that lie within these orange coverings. A sprouting spindle seed raises two wing-like oval seed-leaves, with entire edges, on a slender stalk. Normal paired leaves, with toothed edges, follow.

Common European spindle, *Euonymus europaeus*, grows on lime-rich soils, rarely elsewhere, and forms a smallish tree; naturalized locally in eastern North America. Gardeners prefer more showy south European broadleaved spindle, *E. latifolius*, which bears larger leaves, bigger and brighter berries; flower parts and fruit elements are in **fives**, not fours. Warty spindle, *E. verrucosus*, also European, has warted twigs, yellow fruits, blood-red seed coverings, black seeds, flower parts in fours.

American spindle tree or eastern wahoo, *E. atropurpureus*, bears large leaves and distinctive flowers, 1·25 cm (0·5 in.) across, having **four purple petals**, four stamens and a fertile·pistil. Four-lobed **dark purple berries** open to reveal the **scarlet seed-coverings**, or arils, of four hard brown seeds. Sometimes called 'eastern burning bush' because of bright orange-red autumn leaf colour.

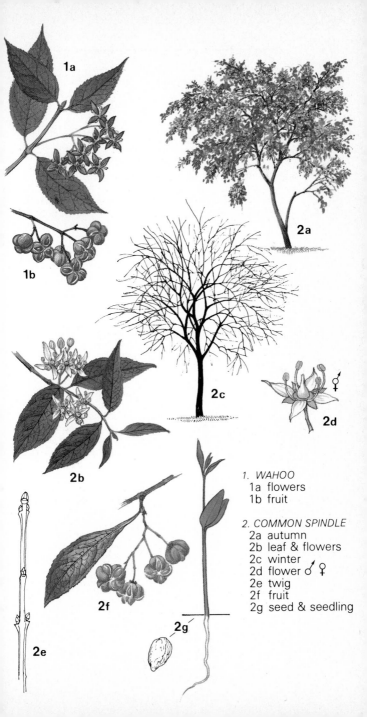

1. *WAHOO*
   1a flowers
   1b fruit

2. *COMMON SPINDLE*
   2a autumn
   2b leaf & flowers
   2c winter
   2d flower ♂ ♀
   2e twig
   2f fruit
   2g seed & seedling

MAPLES I: GREAT MAPLE, EUROPEAN SYCAMORE

ACER PSEUDOPLATANUS   Aceraceae

The large maple genus is known by **paired leaves and buds, broadly lobed leaves with palmately spreading veins**, and **winged seeds in opposite pairs**. Europe's largest maple, is known in Britain as 'sycamore', since leaf resembles that of *Ficus sycomorus*, biblical fig-mulberry. American sycamore, a 'plane tree' in genus *Platanus*, always bears leaves *singly*.

In winter sycamore is identified by **hard green buds, always paired** except for terminal bud at shoot tip. When buds break, oval green scales, **tinged rose red**, expand. Leaves, **purplish brown** at first, become mid-green; they fade in autumn to **drab grey-brown**, lacking bright autumn tints of other maples. They have **five broad lobes, rounded in outline** except for blunt tips. Long stalks are **tinged dark red** and have hollow bases where they partially encircle a bud. Purple sycamore, variety *purpureum*, has purplish-brown undersides to leaves, dark green above.

Maples vary widely in time and pattern of flowering. European sycamore flowers in early summer, after leaves have expanded, and blossoms are borne on **long hanging stalks, carrying many short side stalks**. Perfect flowers, found only near centre of panicle, have five green sepals, five greenish-yellow petals, **eight stamens**, a two-celled pistil topped by two stigmas, and central nectaries that attract insects that effect pollination. Flowers that open nearer base or tip of panicle are often imperfect, being male, female, or sterile.

Fertilized pistils ripen, by autumn, into fruits that consist of paired oval seeds, coloured green, grey-brown or red-brown, each bearing a grey-brown papery wing. The two wings make an angle of 90 degrees to one another. When seeds fall, they revolve like the rotors of a helicopter; slow falling aids dispersal by wind. Two seed leaves neatly folded within husk are **already green** with chlorophyll, ready to start growth. In spring seed-coat breaks, and these strap-shaped seed-leaves, raised by a **deep red stalk**, unfold and point in opposite directions. The first true leaves that follow are oval, pointed, unlobed; lobed leaves come later.

Sycamore forms a wind-resistant angular-branched broad-spreading domed crown, valued for hill farm or seaside shelter. Trunk often develops basal buttresses. Bark, at first smooth, greenish brown, becomes **bluish brown, breaks away in shallow scales**. Timber creamy yellow to white throughout, very strong, works smoothly. Used for furniture, flooring—especially dance halls, wooden rollers. Also as back, sides and stock of stringed instruments—their face must be spruce. Ornamental 'fiddle-back' veneers are peeled from wavy-grained stems. Introduced to Britain by the Romans, European sycamore is naturalized everywhere; planted and naturalized in North America too.

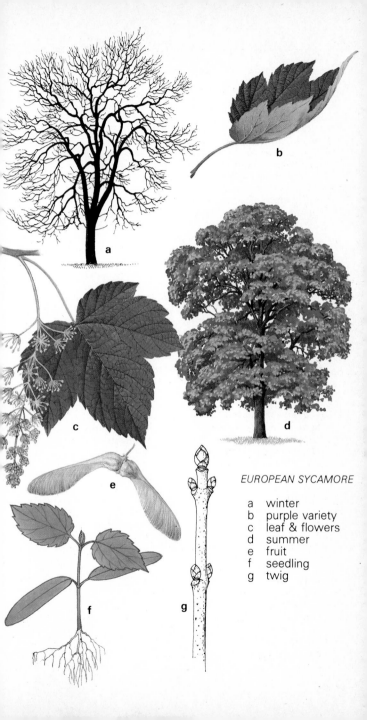

EUROPEAN SYCAMORE

a   winter
b   purple variety
c   leaf & flowers
d   summer
e   fruit
f   seedling
g   twig

MAPLES II: OTHER EUROPEAN MAPLES

ACER genus

ACERACEAE

Norway maple, *Acer platanoides*, is a smaller, neater tree than sycamore. Native to central and northern Europe, it has become naturalized in Britain, and is frequently planted for ornament in North America. Distinguishing features are smooth grey-brown bark, pinkish brown shoots, **red pointed buds**, and **sharply-cut and pointed leaf-lobes**, with tips prolonged into whiskers. Seeds and wings are yellow; wings make a **shallow angle** with one another. Leaves unfold pale green, fade to **brilliant yellow** shades in autumn.

Norway maple flowers **early in spring**, before leaves expand. Clusters of **upright** stalked broad-petalled flowers, of brilliant 'acid' **greenish-yellow**, unfold on bare twigs. Striking purple-leaved forms, increased by grafting, are planted in gardens, parks, or as street trees; one of the best is the cultivar 'Schwedleri'.

Field maple, *A. campestre*, is a small, remarkably pretty tree common along hedgerows and forest fringes in Britain and northern Europe. Bark grey-brown, **cracked into squares**. Twigs dark brown and smooth at first, later pale brown with **corky ribs**. Leaves **deeply cut** into five lobes with **sinuous margins forming sub-lobes**. Buds red-brown with grey, hairy tips. Leaves unfold first pink, then **bright red**, later bright green, dark green, finally **clear golden** in autumn. Clusters of small yellow flowers, **held erect** on branching stalks, otherwise like those of European sycamore, open just after leaves. Fruits are yellowish-green, stained crimson; their wings form a **straight line**, with no angle between them. Too small to yield timber.

Montpelier maple, *A. monspessulanum*, native to southern Europe, is occasionally planted for ornament. Its **three-lobed leaf, with untoothed oval lobes** each served by its central main vein, makes identification easy. Yellow flowers in June, each on its long individual stalk. Brown seeds on red-tinged green wings, set at sharp angle to each other.

Italian maple, *A. opalus*, has **three broad-spreading leaf-lobes, with toothed edges**. Large leaf, often 10 cm (4 in.) across, equally deep, stands on a long slender, red and green stalk, also measuring 10 cm (4 in.). Native to southern Italy. Occasionally planted for its gay display of large pale yellow flowers, in long hanging branches, which open with the leaves in spring.

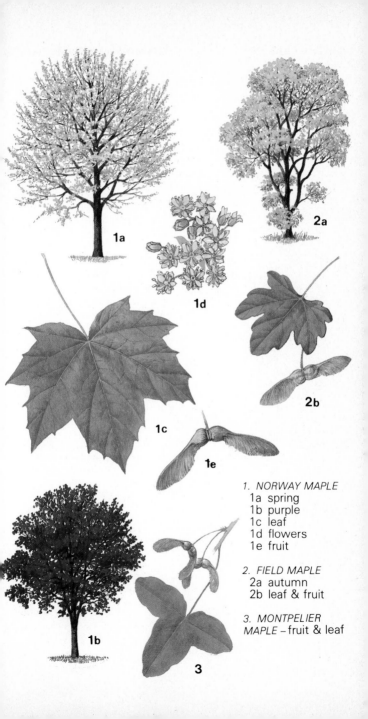

1. *NORWAY MAPLE*
   1a spring
   1b purple
   1c leaf
   1d flowers
   1e fruit

2. *FIELD MAPLE*
   2a autumn
   2b leaf & fruit

3. *MONTPELIER MAPLE* – fruit & leaf

MAPLES III: SUGAR, RED AND SILVER MAPLES

ACER genus   ACERACEAE

Sugar maple, *Acer saccharum*, native to north-east United States and south-east Canada, is the chief source of maple syrup and sugar, and one of the most colourful trees in the fall. Its leaf, familiar on the Canadian flag, distinguishes it from other kinds by its **sharply cut outline**, with three main lobes and about a dozen lesser lobes **ending in sharp points**; these lack the whiskers of Norway maple. Bark is firm and ridged, with ridges curling outwards along edges. Twigs reddish brown, shiny, hairless, carrying sharp-pointed, many-scaled reddish-brown buds, set in pairs close to twig. Flowers open with the leaves, in tassels; about fifteen blossoms spring from a bud, on long individual stalks. They have no petals; each is a yellowish green bunch of sepals and stamens around a pistil. Fruits ripen in autumn, hanging on long slender stalks; brown seeds are plump, wings grey-brown, almost **parallel with each other**.

Sugar maple is tapped in spring, when free-flowing sap, which holds much sugar, stored through winter in roots and wood, moves upwards to nourish expanding leaves. A hole is bored into the sapwood of the trunk, and sap is diverted through a spout into a cup. After daily collection, it is concentrated, by boiling in a pan, into syrup, from which sugar can by crystallized out. Heavy, hard, strong, yellowish-brown timber, known commercially as 'hard maple', is valued for furniture, flooring, farm tools, turnery, bobbins, veneer, plywood, and engineering patterns. Autumn leaf colours range from brilliant yellow through orange to vivid scarlet.

Red maple, *Acer rubrum*, has a wider range from Quebec south to Florida. Leaf, with more rounded shape, less sharp-cut outline, has **very long red stalk and red veins**. Reddish-brown twigs bear red buds, also clusters of flower buds ringing the twigs. Male flowers, with short stalks, open in **separate clusters** from **long-stalked** female ones, early in spring. Both bear **small red petals**. Autumn colour is **brilliant scarlet**. Often planted for ornament. Light brown timber, classed as a 'soft maple', used for purposes where great strength and hardness are not essential.

Silver maple, *A. saccharinum*, another eastern American species, has **very deeply-lobed, repeatedly sharp-pointed** long-stalked leaves, with **silver undersides**. Light green above, they turn pale yellow in autumn, remaining silver below. Flowers, open before leaves, resemble those of red maple, but have no petals; males are short-stalked, females, separate, long-stalked. Seeds mature same spring on long stalks; ribbed, thick, and swollen, on scimitar-shaped, elliptical wings; one of each pair often fails to develop. Grey-brown bark flakes away, making trunk look **shaggy**. Silver maple makes a vigorous tree with brown spreading crown; often planted for ornament in Europe. Seed-leaves remain within seed even when it sprouts.

1. *SUGAR MAPLE*
   1a autumn
   1b flowers, leaf
   & fruit

2. *RED MAPLE*
   2a autumn
   2b flowers, leaf
   & fruit

3. *SILVER MAPLE*
   3a summer
   3b leaf & fruit

MAPLES IV: JAPANESE, BIGLEAF, ASH-LEAVED AND STRIPED MAPLES

ACER genus   ACERACEAE

Two small maples that grow wild in Japan are ancestors of cultivated varieties now widely planted in gardens for beauty of autumn colour. Downy Japanese maple, *Acer japonicum*, is easily known by large number of lobes, **seven to eleven**, on its broad, fan-shaped leaf, which when young bears soft hairs. Usually grown as cultivar 'Vitifolium', for striking parade of leaf colour in the fall—from green through pink and yellow to scarlet and gold, ending deep ruby red. The other species, *A. palmatum*, or smooth Japanese maple, has **fan-shaped leaves** cut half-way into oval lobes, **five to seven in number**. Its numerous cultivars include 'Atropurpureum' with dark purple foliage, even in summer, 'Osakazuki' with leaves that change from green to bright scarlet, and others with finely divided foliage, usually called 'Dissectum'. Seeds very small, neat, in facing pairs that look like a fly.

Big-leaf maple, *A. macrophyllum*, native to western North America from Vancouver south to California, is easily known by deeply-lobed **giant leaves**, averaging 25 cm (10 in.) across. Yellow flowers open when leaves do, in hanging bunches; each blossom holds both male stamens and a female pistil. Seed is hairy; the two wings of each pair diverge only slightly from each other.

Ash-leaved maple, *A. negundo*, bears **compound leaves, made up of five leaflets**, but all other characters fit its maple clan. Often called 'box-elder', because leaves also resemble those of elder, somehow confused with box tree. Native to southern Canada and most of United States, wild ash-leafed maple forms a small green-foliaged tree. Each individual is male or female; yellow flowers open before leaves in spring; brown seeds, with **inturned wings**, ripen early. Planted frequently in streets and gardens in its female variegated form 'Variegatum'; first noticed at Toulouse, France, in 1845. An untidy little tree, with **blotchy white-and-green leaves**, which usually **reverts** later to green-leaved pattern but often falls over! Fruit ripens as leaves fade, at first bright green with **cream-and-pink wings**, later pale grey.

Striped maple, *A. pensylvanicum*, is so-called because of conspicuously **striped bark**; brilliant white vertical stripes develop in a greyish green background. In its native New England forests it is called **moosewood**, because leaves and tender shoots are a favourite food for moose deer. The leaf, pale green in summer, turns yellow in autumn; it is **heart-shaped with three prominent points**. Remarkable **yellow flowers, in long narrow hanging chains**, open after leaves; males and females are separate. Brown wings on green seeds make a shallow angle with one another.

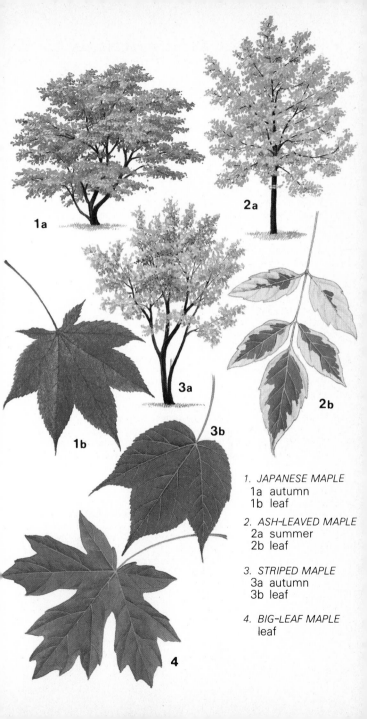

1. *JAPANESE MAPLE*
   1a autumn
   1b leaf

2. *ASH-LEAVED MAPLE*
   2a summer
   2b leaf

3. *STRIPED MAPLE*
   3a autumn
   3b leaf

4. *BIG-LEAF MAPLE*
   leaf

HORSE CHESTNUTS, BUCKEYES

AESCULUS genus   HIPPOCASTANACEAE

Horse chestnuts draw their curious name from the resemblance of their seeds to real chestnuts, *Castanea*, and their use by the Turks, at Istanbul in the sixteenth century, to cure broken-winded horses. Bark is still used in veterinary medicine, but only hungry deer relish the nuts. Buckeye, the American name, arises from resemblance of the nut, with its **pale brown patch** on a **dark brown ground**, to the eye of a deer.

The **stout** winter twig of horse chestnut bears large **shield-shaped scars** with a 'horse-shoe' arrangement of old vein traces, like **horse-shoe nails. Big** brown buds, in opposite pairs, become **sticky** in spring, then burst and expose **soft pale brown felted hairs** within. The remarkable palmately compound leaf unfolds about seven **leaflets radiating from a stout central stalk**; up to 12·5 cm (5 in.) across. Each stalkless leaflet broadens towards its tip, then narrows abruptly to a blunt point; prominent veins, shallow-toothed edges. Colours: pale green, deep green, **rusty orange**. Disintegrate when they fall.

Flowers, opening around May, give **magnificent displays** of white or red. Each main stalk resembles a **candelabra**, carrying many short-stalked blossoms. Individual flowers are **asymmetrical**, larger towards their base. Each has five green sepals, five wavy petals, five to eight (usually six) stamens, bent downwards then upwards, and a pistil bearing a long style, likewise curved. Crimson honey-guide markings at petal bases direct pollinating bees, which alight on stamens, to a central nectary.

Fruits, relatively few to each main stalk, have **hard leathery husks, bearing stiff brown spines**; they change from green to brown, but remain white within. They ripen in autumn, then split to release solitary seeds. Each nut is **large, glossy brown with a paler patch, hard, heavy and lop-sided**. Used by schoolboys to play 'conkers'. When these seeds sprout in spring their seed-leaves remain within the husk; the stout upright shoot bears compound leaves from the outset.

Horse chestnut bark is dark **rusty-brown** and breaks away gradually in shallow flakes. Bole often fluted at base, branch pattern irregular; often downswept, then upcurved. Uniform pale brown wood, showing no darker heartwood, has low strength and is used only for toys, trays, or the like. Trees are therefore planted for ornament rather than use. Common white horse chestnut, *Aesculus hippocastanum*, comes from the Balkans and Asia Minor. Red horse chestnut, *A.* × *carnea*, is a hybrid with an American red buckeye, *A. pavia*.

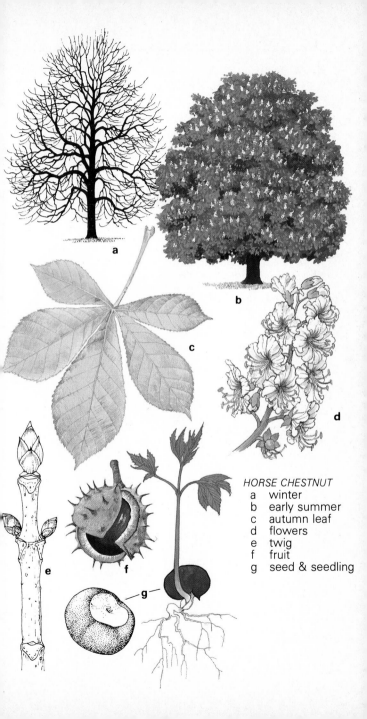

HORSE CHESTNUT
a winter
b early summer
c autumn leaf
d flowers
e twig
f fruit
g seed & seedling

BUCKTHORNS

RHAMNUS and *FRANGULA* genus   RHAMNACEAE

Most buckthorns are spineless. Group takes its name from purging buckthorn, *Rhamnus catharticus*, common tree on dry lime-rich soils in Europe, naturalized locally, as 'European buckthorn', in United States and Canada. This buckthorn bears three kinds of shoots—long ones that extend its branches, short ones modified into spines and short spurs that bear leaves, flowers and berries. Leaf-scars at base of short shoots give them a corrugated appearance, remarkably like pearling at base of a roe-buck's antlers. Hence *buck's horn tree*, later corrupted to buckthorn.

Purging buckthorn becomes a small, black-barked tree up to 10 m (30 ft) tall, with close, wandering branches. **Oval leaves**, clustered on short shoots, have **regularly toothed edges**, unique for a spiny tree. Autumn leaf colour: bright yellow. Small green flowers open in spring in small clusters in leaf axils. Individual trees bear male flowers or female flowers. Both sexes have **four sepals, no petals**. Males bear **four** stamens, females a pistil with a **four-armed** stigma and a **four-celled** ovary. Berries ripen in autumn; blue-black, fleshy, holding **four hard yellow seeds**, oval, with ridged edges. A sprouting seedling raises two broad, lobed seed-leaves, followed by normal adult foliage.

The name purging buckthorn arises from the use of the berries as a strong purgative in herbal medicine. Birds gobble them greedily, with no harmful after-effects.

Cascara buckthorn, *R. purshiana*, native to America's Pacific coastline from British Columbia south to California, is similar but spineless. Its oval leaf is larger, more blunt-ended, has **toothless edges**. Small greenish-yellow flowers are succeeded by black, indented berries. Young bark, smooth, dark green, often with yellow stripes, is source of purgative drug *cascara*. Timber, of no commercial value, is yellowish brown, tinged red. Winter buds are **naked, lacking scales**, ending with pointed leaves.

Alder buckthorn, *Frangula alnus*, is so-called because it grows on damp ground amidst alders. Common in marshy woodlands throughout Europe; naturalized in North America. Spineless **black twigs** bear brown breathing pores and **opposite oval leaves** with blunt points or rounded ends. Rich pale gold autumn leaf colour. Inconspicuous flowers ripen beautiful berries, first green, next yellow, then red, finally glossy black. Pretty, thin bark, carries **purplish zones** that gradually form a network; it has purgative properties like cascara. Thin stems hold yellow sapwood, red-brown heartwood. This timber yields a fine-grained charcoal better than any other for making gunpowder; still used for slow fuses.

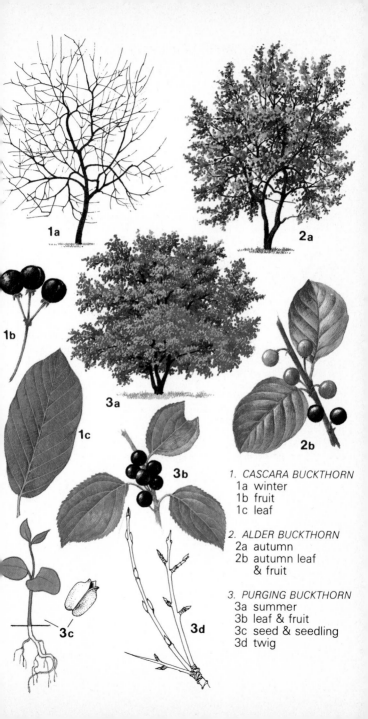

1. *CASCARA BUCKTHORN*
   1a winter
   1b fruit
   1c leaf

2. *ALDER BUCKTHORN*
   2a autumn
   2b autumn leaf
      & fruit

3. *PURGING BUCKTHORN*
   3a summer
   3b leaf & fruit
   3c seed & seedling
   3d twig

LIMES, LINDENS, AND BASSWOODS

TILIA genus   TILIACEAE

'Linden' an old English name for lime trees, is applied to
ornamental specimens in North America, though forest trees, and
their timber, are often called 'basswoods'. This word originates in
the tough fibrous *bast* that lies just below the shallowly-ridged
bark. It was once used for brooms and coarse ropes.

All lime trees have curious buds, with only **two visible outer
scales, one larger than the other**. Buds and leaves are set singly
along **reddish** twigs. Each long-stalked leaf has the shape of a
conventional **playing-card heart**, though it may be lop-sided near
its base; its edge is toothed, its tip pointed. Colours: pale green,
deep green, bright gold.

Lime flower clusters, which open in early summer, have a long
main stalk that carries an **oblong papery bract**. Two, three, or
more side stalks diverge from this, each bearing a blossom. Each
flower holds five green sepals, five white petals, numerous stamens
and a central pistil. Fragrant, it yields ample nectar and attracts
many bees. It ripens to a hard brown round pod, holding a single
seed. The fruit group, still attached to the brown bract, is
unmistakable. Seedlings expand two seed leaves, each **divided
into fingers like a hand**. The uniform, pale yellow-brown timber
is very stable, and ideal for carving or pattern making. Typical
uses: piano keys, shoe trees and wood-carving, including the
masterpieces of Grinling Gibbons.

The lime usually planted as a street avenue or garden tree is the
common one, *Tilia* × *vulgaris* (synonym × *europaea*) a hybrid
between two European species, namely small-leaved lime, *T.
cordata* and large-leaved lime, *T. platyphyllos*. A curious feature,
which aids identification of old specimens, is the **outgrowth of
bushy side-stems near its base**. American linden, *T. americana*,
bears bright-red buds. Silver-leaved lime, *T. petiolaris*, from eastern
Europe, is widely planted for the beauty of its lower leaf surface.
Limes have light airy crowns, and commonly outgrow other
broadleaved trees.

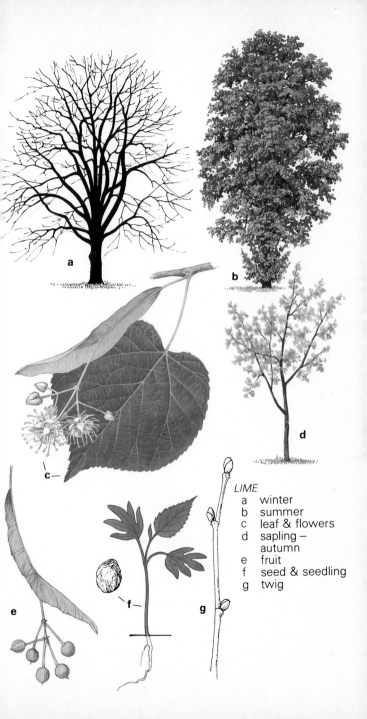

LIME

a winter
b summer
c leaf & flowers
d sapling –
   autumn
e fruit
f seed & seedling
g twig

TAMARISKS

TAMARIX genus   TAMARICACEAE

Though tamarisks are often grown as garden shrubs, they can attain tree size and form. They are used to shade promenades on exposed sea fronts at many southern European resorts. Tamarisks originate in sandy, salty deserts, and show marked resistance to salt-laden sea breezes; hence they are often planted as windscreens for seaside gardens. Tamarisks have become naturalized locally on sandy or salty waste ground, both in Britain and the United States. They colonize newly-formed sand dunes and freshly-exposed shingle beds in rivers.

Tamarisk foliage resembles that of certain conifers, such as junipers, but is quite distinct from that of all other broadleaved trees. It is made up of very **small, slender leaves like blades of grass**, which often **overlap** their neighbours at their tips. Because of the leaves' small surface area, tamarisks lose little water by evaporation, and can therefore thrive in dry semi-desert places, even below a burning sun. Tamarisk foliage is evergreen, or partially so, persisting on the twigs until midwinter. Colours are pale green, dull green, golden-brown. Young shoots, **tinged red**, are **very slender**. The supple branches are narrow and whip-like. Dried tamarisk branches can be used as brooms and are imported as such to England. The name 'tamarisk' comes from *tamaris*, a Hebrew word for sweeping broom.

Tamarisk bark, dull brown in colour, has a distinctive pattern of ribs and hollows, that bend around former branch bases. It is fibrous, with a rough surface. The trunk is usually curved, rather than straight, suggesting a struggle with the elements. Tamarisk wood is pale brown and very hard.

Minute pink flowers open in midsummer, in **plume-like clusters** along young shoots. Each separate flower has four to five green sepals, pink petals, five stamens, and a central pistil. Petals persist until the fruits ripen in autumn, forming **woody boxes** along stems. Each fruit is a hard brown capsule holding many tiny brown oval seeds, each bearing a tuft of hairs. Seedlings raise two seed-leaves; normal narrow leaves follow.

Four common species are distinguished mainly by small botanical details, English tamarisk, *Tamarix anglica*, is most frequent in south and east England. French tamarisk, *T. gallica*, more tree-like, is commonly planted in southern Europe. Small-flowered tamarisk, *T. parviflora*, and five-stamened tamarisk, *T. pentandra*, are planted in both English and American gardens.

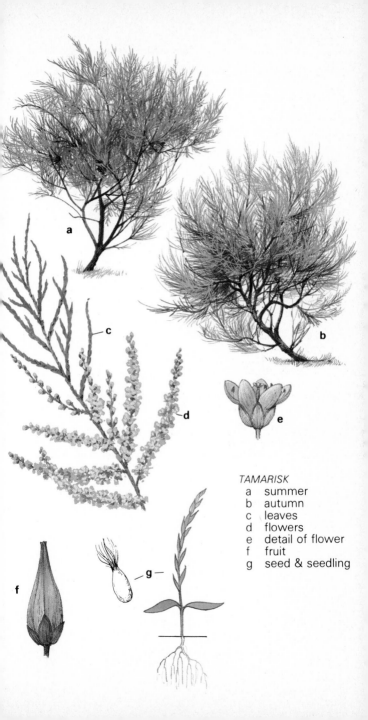

TAMARISK
  a summer
  b autumn
  c leaves
  d flowers
  e detail of flower
  f fruit
  g seed & seedling

TUPELO

NYSSA SYLVATICA   NYSSACEAE

Black tupelo, *Nyssa sylvatica*, is the commonest of six similar species native to eastern North America; its range extends from Ontario south to Florida, east to Texas. It is frequently planted outside this native territory, both in America and Europe, for the splendour of its autumn foliage colours—orange, scarlet, and crimson.

A medium-sized tree found in lowland woods, with rich soil, often near rivers, tupelo may be spotted in winter by its **much-branched, very twiggy crown**. Trunks develop deeply ridged-and-furrowed thick grey bark. Twigs are reddish grey, with pointed, oval buds; twigs cut across on the slant show **pith with hard greenish bars**.

Long-stalked leaves, which open very late, are sometimes solitary, sometimes clustered near shoot tips. Broadly oval in outline—sometimes broader towards tip, sometimes broader towards base, bluntly pointed. **Glossy surface** is distinctive. Pale green in spring, dull green later, with whitish green undersides. Turn to brilliant orange, scarlet and finally deep red autumn colours very early in fall, when other trees are still green.

Male flowers, yellowish green, open in club-shaped catkins, on long stalks in spring. Bees carry pollen. Female flowers develop apart from males, **grouped in threes** at tips of long slender stalks; flask-shaped, green, with protruding yellow styles, tipped purple. Blue-black fruits ripen in autumn in long-stalked **clusters of two or three**. Each fruit holds a single oval, ridged seed, with a thick light brown or white husk. Birds and beasts, eating the fruit's bitter pulp, disperse the seeds.

A sprouting tupelo seedling opens two large, irregularly oblong seed-leaves, followed by normal foliage.

Tupelo's mid-brown timber has only minor uses, for boxes, crates, and furniture construction. Being soft, smooth, stable, and easily curved, it has also been used for hatters blocks, pistol grips, and wooden rollers.

Other common names for black tupelo are: blackgum, sourgum, and pepperidge.

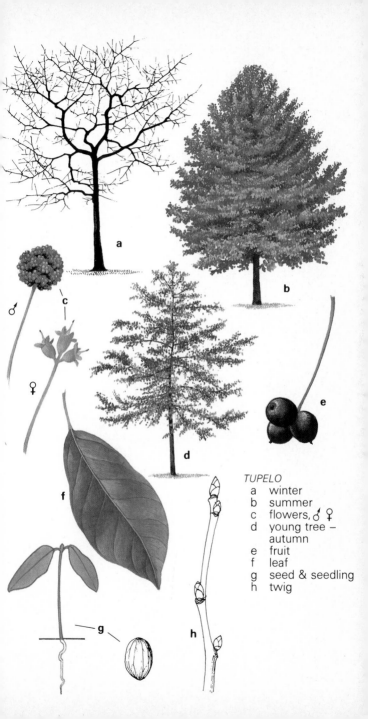

TUPELO

a winter
b summer
c flowers, ♂ ♀
d young tree –
 autumn
e fruit
f leaf
g seed & seedling
h twig

EUCALYPTUS

EUCALYPTUS genus   EUPHORBIACEAE

All eucalyptus trees are native to Australia. Grown in plantations for timber or foliage in southern Europe, Africa, California and Florida. In the British Isles hardy kinds are grown in mild coastal districts as decorative trees; not fully frost-hardy. Called 'gum trees' because of red resin that occasionally oozes from trunk.

Eucalyptus trees are known by evergreen, **blue-green** broad leaves that exude unmistakable **'oil of eucalyptus' smell when crushed**. Commercial oil, used in cold cures, is distilled from leaves. Young trees bear **round unstalked juvenile leaves in opposite pairs**, with bases clasping them. Older ones carry **adult leaves, set singly on short stalks**, long, slender, sickle-shaped. Adult leaves hang downwards, with **one edge directed up towards sunlight**. Sunlight filters through foliage, hence trees **cast little shade**. Leaf thus keeps cooler, loses little water; the oil also helps in water-retention.

Eucalyptus trunks carry **blue-grey bark** that constantly **peels away in strips, exposing irregular yellow patches**. Timbers vary from one species to another. Some yield only firewood or pulpwood, others building, furniture, flooring and tool handle-wood. Sydney blue gum, *Eucalyptus saligna*, has reddish brown, moderately durable heartwood, pale yellow sapwood. Eucalyptus stumps sprout vigorously when a tree is felled; coppice is cultivated for foliage, firewood, and pulpwood. Eucalyptus trees form no winter resting buds; growth continues year-round except for cold spells. May grow 3 m (9 ft) taller each year in temperate zones, 10 m (30 ft) in tropics.

Flowers open from inverted cone-shaped buds, **grouped in threes** on short-stalks. Each bud is topped by a **round cap**, the **calyptus** that gives group its name. It is part of the calyx; no distinct sepals or petals appear. When cap falls off, a showy, **fluffy mass of numerous white or red stamens** spreads out, and this attracts pollinating bees; eucalyptus flowers yield much nectar for honey. A central style rises above a deep-seated ovary. The round, top-shaped, hard woody pod, or capsule, that develops opens by three to six flaps, or valves, releasing very numerous seeds.

Each tiny seed is hard, black, and wedge-shaped, with ridges at angles. A sprouting seedling raises two small kidney-shaped seed-leaves on a slender stem. Paired-leaf juvenile foliage follows, adult leaves, set singly, about four years later.

Tasmanian blue gum *E. globulus*, known by long (25 cm or 10 in.) deep blue-green leaf and large (2·5 cm or 1 in.) blue-black pod, is hardy in Cornwall and Ireland. Widely planted and naturalized in California. Tasmanian cider gum, *E. gunnii*, reckoned hardiest kind, has smaller adult leaves on yellow stalks, and tiny pods, less than 5 mm (0·25 in.) long. Name derives from scent of sap.

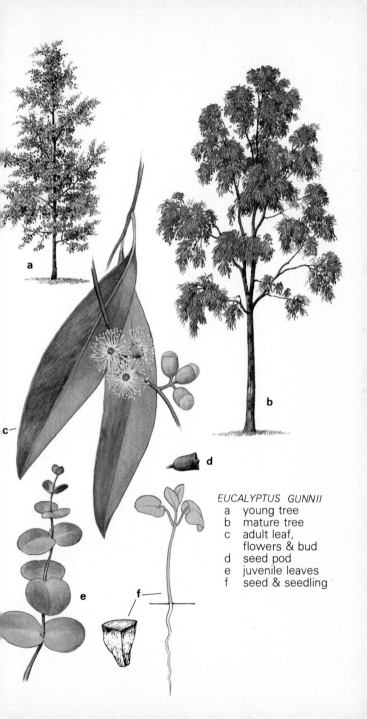

EUCALYPTUS GUNNII
- a young tree
- b mature tree
- c adult leaf, flowers & bud
- d seed pod
- e juvenile leaves
- f seed & seedling

DOGWOODS

CORNUS genus   CORNACEAE

Dogwoods owe their odd name to the use of their wood for 'dogs', or skewers, in the Middle Ages. This word survives in 'dagger' and the timberman's 'dogs', which are strong, sharp, iron spikes used to grip logs. The Latin name, *Cornus*, implies a horny-textured wood.

Dogwoods have **leaves and buds in pairs**, except for the terminal bud of each twig. Their leaves are simple, long-stalked, pointed ovals, with **main veins curving upwards along margins**. Pull the tip of a leaf gently and you find that tiny threads in veins hold together after the blade breaks. Flowers, white or pink, are borne in dense **terminal clusters**, and ripen to a **bunch of berries**, each holding one hard seed. Each flower has **four** sepals, four petals, four stamens, plus a central pistil.

Common dogwood, *Cornus sanguinea*, grows as a tall shrub or small tree on lime-rich soils throughout Europe. Its **blood-red shoots, bloodshot leaves** and **crimson autumn leaf colour** combine with **red buds** to justify its specific name *sanguinea*, which means 'bloody'. Creamy-white, fragrant flowers, midsummer; blue-black berries in autumn. Bird-sown berries quickly colonize abandoned chalk downland pastures in southern England. Shoots grow vigorously from stumps if the tree is cut back, American red-osier dogwood, *C. stolonifera*, found along streamsides, is similar.

Flowering dogwood, *C. florida*, native to the eastern United States, gives a magnificent display of pinkish-white blossom in early summer. Its gay **'flower-petals', grouped in fours**, are actually bracts that grow out from the base of each cluster of small greenish flowers. They serve, like real petals, to attract pollinating insects.

In autumn flowering dogwood may be known by **red, bottle-shaped, black-tipped** berries packed on a central stalk. In winter you can tell it by **round, green turban-shaped flower buds** at tips of fertile twigs. Dark-brown bark is broken up by fissures into small, irregular oblongs. Flowering dogwood, a small tree in America, is often cultivated as a decorative shrub in milder parts of Europe, including southern England.

Cornelian cherry, *C. mas*, from southern Europe, is grown in British and American gardens for its delicate yellow blossoms, which open in little clusters on bare, leafless branches late in winter. There are **four yellowish-green boat-shaped bracts** at the base of every flower head. The autumn fruit that gives the tree its name is bright red, with a hard stone. Pleasantly flavoured, good to eat, and makes excellent jam.

When dogwood seedlings sprout they raise two large irregular oval seed-leaves on a slender stalk; the seed coat falls away. Normal foliage, with leaves in pairs, follows.

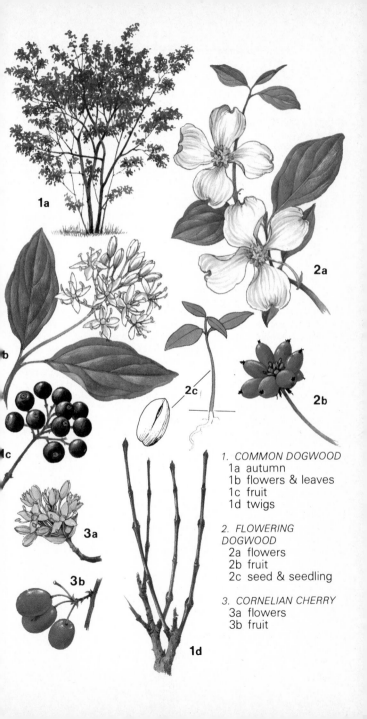

1. *COMMON DOGWOOD*
   1a autumn
   1b flowers & leaves
   1c fruit
   1d twigs

2. *FLOWERING DOGWOOD*
   2a flowers
   2b fruit
   2c seed & seedling

3. *CORNELIAN CHERRY*
   3a flowers
   3b fruit

STRAWBERRY TREE, MADRONE

ARBUTUS genus   ERICACEAE

The strawberry tree, *Arbutus unedo*, of southern Ireland and southern Europe closely resembles its American cousin, the Pacific madrone (or madrona), *A. menziesii*, native from British Columbia south to California. Both are cultivated as garden trees in other regions of mild climate. Madrone has the larger leaf, commonly 10 cm (4 in.) long, against strawberry tree's 5 cm (2 in.). Strawberry tree leaves have **toothed edges**; those of madrone are **toothless**.

Both *Arbutus* trees bear evergreen, tough, leathery leaves characteristic of the Mediterranean-type climatic zone of wet mild winters, hot dry summers. Leaves are oval, blunt-pointed, glossy, **very dark green** above, pale green below. They grow singly, on short red leaf-stalks, springing from **dark red shoots** that end in minute purplish-red buds. Characteristic bark is thin, **rust-red**, and **scales away in thin strips**. Typical trees are short-boled, bushy, much branched. Hard red-brown wood is used only for fuel, or carving tourist souvenirs, as at Killarney in south-west Ireland.

Pretty white flowers, like lilies-of-the-valley, open in **autumn** in long branching clusters at tips of outer shoots. Each flower, about 1 cm (0·4 in.) long, is shaped like a bell. It has five small green sepals at its base, then five pinkish-white petals united to form the 'bell', but with points free. Within stand ten stamens and a pistil with a five-celled ovary.

Strawberry-like fruits take a whole year to ripen, so are seen side-by-side with flowers. Each 'strawberry' changes colour through yellow to orange or bright red as it ripens; **rough surface** due to countless close projections is unique. Yellow mealy flesh within is eatable but unpalatable. Latin name *unedo* means 'eat one only'. Birds relish it and help spread seeds. At heart of berry lie five cells, each holding many tiny, brown, pear-shaped, hard, ridged seeds.

Quaint seedlings sprout in first spring after seeds ripen. Two small oblong seed-leaves, green with reddish rims, appear above ground with their tips still in the seed coat, which soon falls. A hairy shoot arises between these seed leaves, bearing small shiny green primary leaves, fringed with long hairs. Seed-leaves fall after one summer. Normal adult foliage appears in following spring.

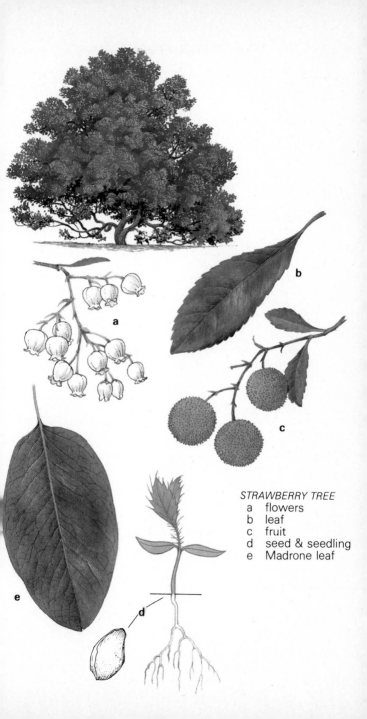

STRAWBERRY TREE
a   flowers
b   leaf
c   fruit
d   seed & seedling
e   Madrone leaf

PERSIMMON

DIOSPYROS VIRGINIANA EBENACEAE

Persimmon trees, native to eastern and southern United States, from New York south to Florida and east to Texas, are valued both for hard timber and luscious fruits. In Europe they are only occasionally seen, usually in botanical collections. A tall upstanding tree with **black or dark grey bark, cracked vertically and horizontally into irregular squares**. Branches end in markedly zig-zag twigs, because **shoots lack well-defined terminal buds**. Side buds are small, pressed close to twigs, pointed, cone-shaped, yellowish green.

Oval, leathery, glossy, pointed leaves stand on long green leaf-stalks. First yellow, then bright green, finally fade to golden brown.

Every persimmon tree is wholly male or wholly female; both bear bell-shaped four-petalled flowers, opening in spring. Male flowers, in long-stalked clusters, are whitish and hold four fertile stamens; pollen is carried by insects. Female flowers, solitary on twigs and more yellow in colour, ripen to round fruits with a prickle—the former style—at the tip. Remnants of petals may also be carried on tip. Withered **four-lobed calyx persists at base**. From four to eight flattened seeds ripen within each fruit. Unless harvested, fruits hang on tree all through winter. Fruits are usually yellow-skinned, sometimes red or purple. Soft pulp within is delicious.

When a persimmon seed sprouts it raises its husk on an upright stem, then discards it. Two long-oval seed-leaves emerge, normal leaves succeed them.

Persimmon wood, grey-brown in colour, is exceptionally hard, stable and resistant to shock. It is therefore chosen for golf club heads, plane stocks and shoe lasts. Also made into shuttles used in weaving looms in textile mills, which must be shot short distances under exacting conditions caused by hot high-speed machinery.

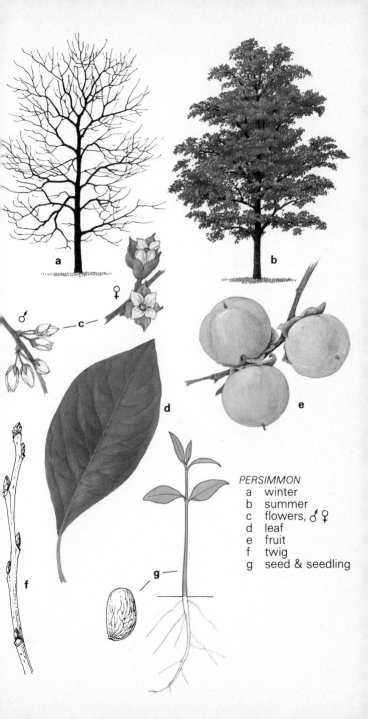

PERSIMMON
a winter
b summer
c flowers, ♂ ♀
d leaf
e fruit
f twig
g seed & seedling

ASH

FRAXINUS genus   OLEACEAE

Ash trees can be told, even in winter, by **hard black buds set in opposite pairs** with three at twig tips, and by smooth greenish-grey twigs **flattened** at the nodes or budding points. Any damage to a large terminal bud causes the stem to develop two branches, and hence ash trunks are usually **forked**, often repeatedly. The general branch system shows bold angular divisions, each limb keeping clear of its neighbours.

Ash leaves, which open late, are compound, with around nine oval leaflets, with toothed edges and pointed tips, springing from one centre stalk. They fall late also, often in one piece, being then **drab grey** with no bright autumn colour.

The flowers of ash open just before the leaves, in catkin clusters that may hold all male or all female flowers, or flowers that mix both sexes. All these versions look like green tassels, for each long-stalked flower lacks petals, and pollination is effected by wind. Male flowers, or elements of mixed ones, are simple stalked stamens, two per flower. Female ones are solitary flask-shaped pistils that enlarge, by autumn, to winged seeds called 'keys', from their resemblance to keys used in medieval locks. The **single twisted wing, holding one oval seed at its base** ripens from green to dull brown, then falls and is carried away on winter winds.

When an ash seed sprouts, eighteen months after ripening, it sends up two pale green oval seed leaves, followed by two simple **undivided pointed oval leaves**; the next pair of leaves have three leaflets apiece; normal compound leaves follow.

Ash bark gradually develops a beautiful **even network of shallow fissures**, firm though rough to the touch. The tough, strong, timber within is a uniform pale brown colour. Very large vessels at the start of each annual ring appear as **large pores on cross-cut surfaces** and **long streaks like scratches** on surfaces cut lengthwise. Used for heavy-duty tool handles—hammers, spades, axes, cart shafts, oars, and hockey sticks, it withstands rough treatment.

Common ash, *Fraxinus excelsior*, is native throughout Europe, and often planted in America. White ash, *F. americana*, the typical North American kind, has larger leaves, grows more vigorously. Manna ash, *F. ornus*, from southern Europe, bears **white petals**, and is occasionally planted for ornament; its name arises from an edible gum or 'manna' obtained by making cuts in its bark.

ASH
a winter
b summer
c Manna Ash
d flowers
e leaves
f fruit
g twig
h seedling

OLIVE

OLEA EUROPAEA   Oleaceae

Olive trees are known by **slender grey-green, evergreen leaves set in pairs** on slender twigs. Each leaf is a long pointed ellipse, virtually stalkless. Dark green above, greyish or brownish white and hairy below, with inrolled unbroken margin, well adapted to resist drought. Leaf is willow-like, but willow leaves are set singly. Wild olives are thorny, cultivated ones thornless.

Trees are remarkable for irregular branching and gnarled appearance of old stems, often centuries old. Bark is thin, grey, and broken into many irregular oblong islands by shallow fissures. Boles are often pitted with deep hollows, or holes you can see through; this tough character can survive damage fatal to any other tree, and live for 500 years.

Olive's hard, smooth timber has bright yellow sapwood, orange brown heartwood, both shot through with **black streaks**. Very decorative, an excellent material for carving and turnery; valued by craftsmen making attractive woodware, particularly tourist souvenirs.

Olive's small flowers arise in little sprays from leaf axils in spring. At first they appear pale yellow, but when they expand their four petals, the insides of these become white, and only the flower centre remains yellow. There are four sepals, two stamens, and a central two-celled pistil.

Fruits, which ripen slowly through summer, have a tough outer skin surrounding first a mass of soft pulp, then a very hard brown stone, the seed. Green olives are gathered early in autumn, for eating in various ways. They are at first very bitter. To render them palatable, they are first steeped for a few days in an alkaline lye, either quicklime, or caustic potash or caustic soda. This is washed away, and the olives are next pickled in a solution of common salt. Black olives, gathered early in winter when fully ripe, are eaten in very similar ways.

Olive oil is extracted from fully ripe, black olives, formerly by simple stone presses, but nowadays by powerful hydraulic plant that extracts the maximum oil possible. Oil is used for cooking or dressing many kinds of food.

Olives sprout readily when cut back; growers harvest valuable wood, leaving four shoots to renew their orchard. Propagation is usually by cuttings. The hard seed takes about four months to sprout. It then sends up a sturdy shoot bearing a pair of seed-leaves, next a pair of small true leaves, then typical alternate true leaves.

Commercial cultivation is limited to countries around the Mediterranean, plus Portugal and California. Olives are too sensitive to exceptional frosts to be grown in the north; some are said to survive in Cornwall. Though wild olives grow in France, the cultivated strain or *elaifa* arose in Greece.

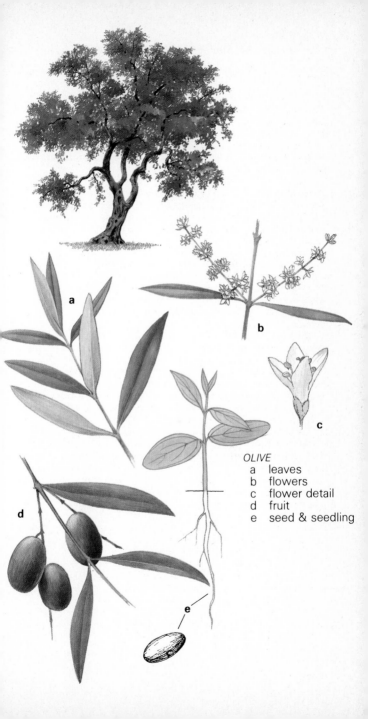

OLIVE
a leaves
b flowers
c flower detail
d fruit
e seed & seedling

CATALPA OR INDIAN BEAN

CATALPA genus   BIGNONIACEAE

This magnificent tree, native to mid-western and southern States of America, has been widely planted further north, over much of Europe, and in the southern half of England. Its unique feature is the grouping of **large buds and leaves in threes.** The stout winter twigs, spotted with pale breathing pores, show **prominent raised leaf scars**, likewise in threes.

Catalpa leaves, last to open of any tree, are long-stalked, long-pointed and exceptionally large, often 10 cm (4 in.) across. **Pale green** in colour, their shape normally resembles a **conventional playing-card heart**, but may be an oval or a conventional diamond. They fall early, without autumn colour.

Catalpa's showy blossoms, quite unmistakable, open in late summer in large clusters carried clear of the foliage. Each individual white flower is **shaped like an open bell**, markedly uneven between top and bottom, and divided at its edges into four crinkly petals, two above, two below. Within, a pattern of **reddish-purple, brown or yellow spots or lines** serves as a 'honey-guide' to direct visiting insects past five stamens to the central pistil, and nectaries.

The equally distinctive fruit ripens as a green pod in autumn and persists as a brown one through winter. Its **long, slender outline**, hanging downwards, has earned catalpa its nickname of (Red) Indian bean, but you cannot eat it. When ripe, the pod splits, to release scores of small seeds, each **surrounded by a membranous wing, bearing a tuft of hairs at each end**. When it sprouts this seed raises two peculiar **two-lobed seed-leaves**, followed by normal foliage.

Catalpa trunks are clad in fawn-grey rough bark with a definite **pinkish tinge**. The timber within is pale brown with **bluish-brown heartwood**. Light, yet strong and naturally durable, it is used for fence posts in America. Elsewhere catalpa is grown only for its flowers and effective spreading crown of leaves. The commonly grown species is *Catalpa bignonioides*, from the south-eastern states. Catawpa is the original Red Indian name.

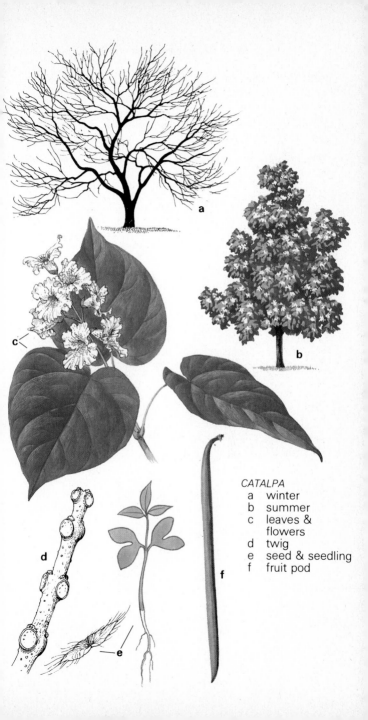

CATALPA
a   winter
b   summer
c   leaves &
    flowers
d   twig
e   seed & seedling
f   fruit pod

ELDERS

SAMBUCUS genus   CAPRIFOLIACEAE

Though elder is usually a low bush, occasional specimens grow up to tree height, even reaching 22 m (65 ft) tall. Large stems form remarkably **hard smooth white wood**, used by watchmakers, in finely divided 'toothpicks' for cleaning delicate mechanisms. At the heart of an elder stem there is a **conspicuous round hole**—the relic of its original pith.

Exceptionally thick, light, white pith forms in small elder twigs, which **snap easily**. You can hollow twigs out to make whistles or pop-guns. The pith itself is used by botanists to hold fine specimens, especially leaves, when using a razor to cut thin slices for their microscopes. Twigs bear obvious breathing pores on corky bark. Older stems develop networks of deeply fissured **soft** yellow-brown bark; badgers scratch it to clean their claws.

Elder buds, which **lack external scales**, appear as **purplish-brown leaf and shoot elements** in midwinter; they start growth and turn green very early in spring. Leaves are set, like the buds, in opposite pairs with boat-shaped bases. Each leaf is compounded of about five-short-stalked oval leaflets with **toothed edges** and pointed tips. Colours: dark green, mid green, yellow.

Flowers open in midsummer in pretty umbels, or umbrella-shaped clusters. Many **minute** individual blossoms, creamy white in colour, are carried on a **much-branched** system of stalks. They have a **strong musky odour** and can be used to brew elder-flower tea. Each flower holds five sepals, five petals, five cream-coloured stamens and a central pistil. The berries that follow in autumn hang down in **loose clusters** until stripped by hungry birds, which eat them whole. The hard black ridged seed at the heart of the soft pulp passes through the bird's digestive tract and sprouts next spring. Seedlings raise two seed-leaves, followed in turn by simple leaves with toothed edges, tri-foliate ones, then compound ones.

Common elder, *Sambucus nigra*, bears purplish-black berries, edible but with a sickly taste when raw. They are however baked in elderberry pies or used to make elderberry jelly or wine. Red-berried elder, *S. racemosa*, native to Scandinavia and upland Europe, is naturalized locally in Britain. The commonest American species is blue elder, *S. canadensis*, with bright blue berries.

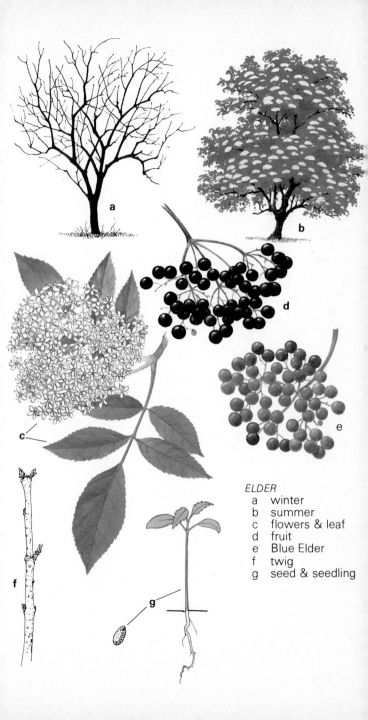

ELDER

- a winter
- b summer
- c flowers & leaf
- d fruit
- e Blue Elder
- f twig
- g seed & seedling

CABBAGE TREE

CORDYLINE AUSTRALIS   LILIACEAE

Native to New Zealand, cabbage tree, also called cabbage palm, is planted around the coasts of the British Isles, the Channel Islands, and regions of mild climate elsewhere, to give a suggestion of tropical luxuriance. Resembles true palms in bearing a **tuft of leaves at the tip only** of an otherwise leafless stem, that does not taper and seldom branches. Leaves differ from true palms in being long, often 75 cm (30 in.) long, and **narrow**, around 5 cm (2 in.) wide. Evergreen, dark green, hard and pointed, these leaves are extremely strong, holding fibres akin to sisal. Young leaves grow almost upright, radiating from tree's tip. After a few years they bend outwards, fading to greyish brown, finally drooping round stem. Bark is fawn grey, finely fissured into deep corky ridges.

Cabbage trees flower when well established, sending out long curved main flower stalks from their foliage tuft. Each sturdy main stalk is deep green, ribbed and flattened, up to 1 m (3 ft) long. It carried many long side branches which in turn carry many small stalkless creamy-white fragrant blossoms. Each star-shaped flower has six pale yellow petals, six broad stamens and a central ovary. Fruits, ripe in autumn, are bluish-white berries, holding several hard black seeds.

A sprouting seed sends forth a single green seed-leaf, like a blade of grass. True leaves, also grass-like, follow and a woody stem slowly develops. Suckers sometimes spring up from underground roots, but cabbage tree is, in practice, propagated from stem cuttings. Old trees that have flowered often develop side branches, and build up a domed crown.

In its native New Zealand, cabbage tree grows along forest margins and stream-sides, or in clearings. Its Maori name is *ti kouka*. Botanically, these 'palms' are really lilies, and our familiar species is actually the tallest lily in the world.

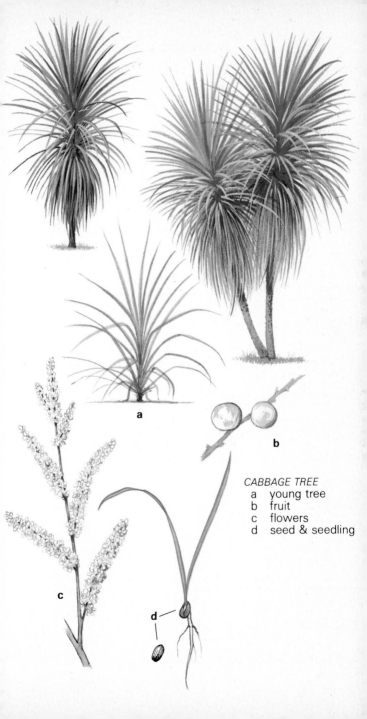

CABBAGE TREE
a   young tree
b   fruit
c   flowers
d   seed & seedling

PALMS

WASHINGTONIA, TRACHYCARPUS and
CHAMAEROPS genera   PALMACEAE

Palms differ from other trees in bearing all their leaves, always evergreen, **at the tip** of an otherwise leafless, unbranched trunk, almost the same thickness from foot to top. Most are tropical; three fan-leaved species described here grow in mild northern climates.

California washingtonia, *Washingtonia filifera*, is a tall erect tree, up to 25 m (75 ft) tall and 3 m (9 ft) in circumference. **Enormous fan-shaped leaves**, with blades up to 2 m (6 ft) across, spring from its top on stout spiny stems averaging 1·5 m (4·5 ft) long. These leaves are light green, with numerous folds, split into narrow rays, about half way down; edges carry threadlike fibres. When each in turn fades it bends down and persists for years; several years' dead leaves form a **brown skirt** around trunk.

Washingtonia flowers in mid-summer. Branching clusters of small fragrant yellow blossoms, often 3 m (9 ft) long overall, spring from the centre. They ripen an equally huge cluster of fleshy, black shiny fruits, each about 1 cm (0·4 in.) long, and holding a central seed or stone. Introduced to southern France, called *Prilchardia* there.

Chusan palm, *Trachycarpus fortunei*, hardiest known kind, is often grown in northern gardens to give a hint of the tropics. Native to mountains of southern China, introduced in 1836, may grow 10 m (30 ft) tall, 1 m (3 ft) round. Unbranched stem completely clad in hard brown fibres and triangular upward-pointing bases of fallen leaves; no visible bark. Fibrous roots emerge at its foot.

Dark green live leaves radiate from top, on spiny stalks about 50 cm (18 in.) long. Each blade is fan-shaped, around 75 cm (27 in.) broad, with about fifty folded segments, split into rays half way down. New leaves unfold through summer, last about two years, turn yellow, finally brown, then bend over. Faded grey-brown leaves form round 'skirt' below living green leaf-tuft.

Yellow flowers expand in summer in large inflorescences, about 50 cm (20 in.) long. A long leafy spathe splits to reveal four or five long pale yellow stalks, which bear many short-stalked flowers. Male and female flowers usually in separate inflorescences. Orange at first, clear yellow later. Males have six stamens. Female flowers ripen round purplish grape-like fleshy fruits, about 1·5 cm (0·75 in.) long, each holding one hard seed.

The shoot that emerges from a sprouting seed grows very slowly, forming a broad base before upward growth begins. All palms form stems, leaves and flowers from a single growing point at their tip; they die if this is damaged. Early leaves are narrow. Timber consists of bundles of fibres, with no annual rings.

Europe's only native kind, Mediterranean fan palm, *Chamaerops humilis*, resembles Chusan palm but has stiffer leaf fans. It bears brown fruits on female trees; males are separate.

CHUSAN PALM
a   leaf
b   flowers emerging
c   seed & seedling
d   fruit

YEWS

TAXUS genus TAXACEAE

Yews are easily known by **dark green, almost black** foliage, made up of two-ranked narrow needles. **Pale green undersides** of yew needles lack white resin or wax found on conifer needle undersides; whole tree is **non-resinous**. Tiny buds at twig tips are yellowish green, with leaf-like scales. Needles **snap off** when pulled but when shed naturally fall singly, leaving rough scars. Young twigs are green, older twigs brown.

Yew's swarthy aspect arises from capacity to absorb more light, casting denser shade, than other trees. Forms **solid crown**, since inner leaves are not readily killed through overshading. Can be clipped to form a dense hedge, or fanciful figures such as peacocks, by skilled topiary. No green plants whatsoever grow on the floor of a yew wood, but yew itself thrives in the shade of other trees.

Yew forms an **irregular, much-fluted bole**, with many ribs. Bark is **rusty-brown, thin and flaky**. Strong durable heartwood is **purplish rusty red**, surrounded by a **narrow zone of dead-white sapwood**. Used for decorative furniture, or carvings, that display its irregular shape, rich colour and fascinating grain. Rough stuff goes for durable fence posts or firewood. Selected yew provides long-bows for archers, for it has outstanding strength and elasticity.

Each yew tree is wholly male or wholly female. Male trees bear, in spring, dainty clusters of yellow flowers that shed golden, wind-borne pollen. On female trees small green bud-like female flowers develop, after fertilization, into conspicuous **rose-red berries**, ripe in autumn. Each berry has a green cup-shaped base, a circular aril of pink, soft, sticky, sickly-flavoured sweet pulp, and an exposed **single central** seed, hard and greenish black. Birds swallow pulp and seed, voiding the latter unharmed. Seeds sprout, eighteen months after ripening, as seedlings bearing only two strap-shaped seed-leaves.

Bark, foliage, and seeds are poisonous to man; pink pulp is harmless. Cattle, sheep and horses nibble green foliage without ill effects, but are poisoned by withered foliage.

Exceptional yews expand slowly to great girths, forming short trunks, hollow within. Record: Tandridge Church, Surrey, 14 m (45 ft) in diameter, estimated age 2,500 years. Churchyard tradition began with Christian missionaries preaching in shelter of venerated yews, evergreen symbols of eternal life.

Common yew, *Taxus baccata*, thrives in Europe and Asia. Irish yew is a sport, cultivar 'Fastigiata', with all branches upright. Both widely planted as ornamentals in North America. Pacific yew, *T. brevifolia*, is native to forests on America's western seaboard. Canadian yew, *T. canadensis*, grows as a low shrub from Newfoundland south to Virginia.

YEW
a Irish yew ♂♀
b flowers, ♂♀
c fruit & leaves
d seed & seedling

MONKEY PUZZLE OR CHILE PINE

ARAUCARIA ARAUCANA   ARAUCARIACEAE

Monkey puzzle trees are easily known by their **regular, symmetrical pattern of branching**, which suggests that an engineer designed them! Their distinctive leaves are **evergreen, thick, leathery and triangular in outline, with sharp points**. They persist on the tree for twelve years or more, **giving the long stems continuous cover**. There are no obvious buds; each terminal bud is hidden by a protecting **rosette of immature pale green needles**.

Monkey puzzle bark is smooth and dark purplish-brown in colour. Even on largest trees it bears **traces of the leaves** that once grew out around the stem—now stout and sturdy—that then formed the tree's leading shoot. The base of a large tree often becomes buttressed. It may also develop an all-round leathery texture, and come to resemble an elephant's foot.

Usually, each monkey puzzle tree bears only male flowers, or only female ones. Exceptionally, flowers of both sexes may appear on the same tree at the same time as illustrated here from a specimen growing in Sussex. They open at midsummer and remain visible for several months. Male catkins, about 10 cm (4 in.) long are outstanding **cylindrical clusters of long, narrow leaf-like stamens, at first green, then yellow, finally brown**, which arise below the branch tips. They bear yellow anthers on their inner surfaces, and these shed abundant pollen. Each stamen has a narrow bent-back tip.

Female catkins are **large upright golden-green globes**, about 7·5 cm (3 in.) across set very close to branch tips. Each is made up of leafy green scales tipped by golden hair-like appendages. They ripen over the course of two to three years to **brown globular cones**, around 15 cm (6 in.) across, as big as pineapples. These huge structures can be clearly seen from the ground. The spirally-ranged scales, now woody and resinous, fall away when ripe. They release **huge bright brown seeds**, 2·5 cm (1 in.) long by 1·25 cm (0·5 in.) thick which are quite good to eat. Each seed is attached to a thick, broad, long-oval, brown bract, fused to a thinner portion which has a long pointed tip.

When the seeds sprout, their two seed-leaves remain below ground, the first upright shoot, which emerges from a bulbous enlargement at the top of the young root, bears normal foliage.

'Monkey Puzzle' is a nickname, arising from a chance remark at a tree-planting ceremony: 'it would puzzle a monkey to climb that tree'.

MONKEY PUZZLE
a flowers, ♂♀
b leaf
c ripe cone
d seed & seedling

PINES I: SCOTS PINE

PINUS SYLVESTRIS   PINACEAE

The name 'pine' is loosely applied to various conifers and their timbers. All 'true pines' belong to the distinct genus called *Pinus*. All are evergreens with tough green needles **grouped in twos, threes or fives**. Needle number is constant for most species, helps sort different pines out. All alike, in their first year, bear **solitary needles on their first upright shoot**.

Scots or Scotch pine, *Pinus sylvestris*, a typical example, is so-called because its native range includes Scotland. Also found elsewhere in British Isles, all Europe, Siberia and Turkey. Extensively grown in the United States, where it has become, remarkably, the 'traditional' Christmas tree. Naturalized in New England.

Scots pine begins life as a winged seed which raises its husk on a slender pink stalk. Husk splits, to release a rosette of about six seed-leaves. Primary shoot grows up from this, bearing single needles. On later shoots needles appear **in pairs**, about 2·5 cm (1 in.) long, pointed, **bluish green**. Each needle lives about four years, then turns brown; each pair falls as one unit. Winter buds **cylindrical, rusty-brown, bluntly-pointed**.

Shoots, pinkish green at first, gradually develop the beautiful **rose-red or pinkish-orange bark** that is Scots pine's handiest distinguishing feature. On larger trunks plates, divided by shallow fissures, develop; colour again becomes pinkish grey. Branch patterns are symmetrical at first. Older trees develop **irregular rounded crowns**, unlike those of other conifers, but similar to broadleaved trees.

Scots pine timber has pale creamish brown sapwood and well-marked red-brown heartwood. Annual rings distinct, with clear bands of red-brown summerwood. Not naturally durable but strong, easily worked. Uses: building, box-making, everyday furniture, telegraph poles, mine supports, fencing, chipboard, paper pulp. Trade name 'redwood'.

Scots pine bears male flowers, in late spring, in oval **yellow clusters** around shoots formed in previous year. Each flower holds many stamens that shed clouds of golden wind-borne pollen. Female flowers open as **crimson globes at very tips of newly-expanded shoots**, above still unopened needles. In their first summer they ripen partially to become **round, brown, pea-sized immature cones**, which persist thus through winter. Next summer they mature to become **soft, green unripe cones**, conical in shape, with rounded bases and blunt tips. These finally turn greyish brown as they ripen in autumn. Each scale bears a **blunt** projection, or umbo. Next spring, **two years** after flower first appeared, cone scales open and two winged seeds are released from each.

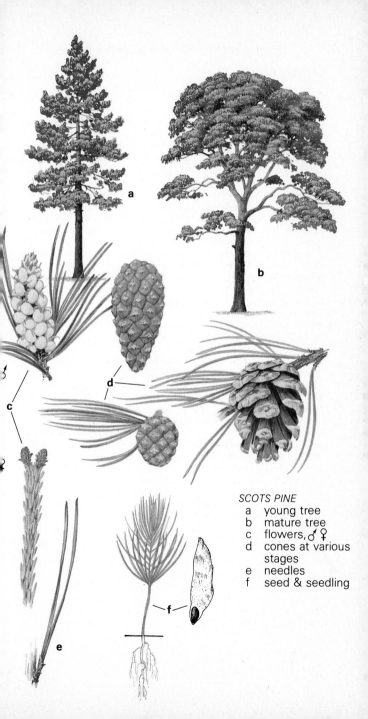

SCOTS PINE
a young tree
b mature tree
c flowers, ♂ ♀
d cones at various
  stages
e needles
f seed & seedling

PINES II: SHORT NEEDLES IN PAIRS

PINUS genus   PINACEAE

Pines described here bear needles shorter than 10 cm (4 in.).

Mountain pine, *Pinus mugo*, grows on higher mountain ranges of Europe, above general level of timber forests. A **straggling much-branched bush**, valued by conservationists as the highest woody cover. Identified by dense foliage **arranged in whorls** and **cone-scales bearing bent-back hooks**. Bark greyish-pink, becoming black, **cracked into small squares**. *P. uncinata*, Pyrenean mountain pine, is similar, but achieves tree form.

Jack pine, *P. banksiana*, most northerly species, is found across Canada, except far west, also in Michigan; occasionally planted elsewhere. Usually a **ragged, straggling tree** as name suggests, yet yields some lumber and pulpwood. **Scaly**, dark grey to red-brown bark. **Very short, dark green needles in whorls. Weird cones, smooth yet lumpy, tapering and twisted forward towards stem**, borne in whorls, **persist unopened** on twigs for many years.

Lodgepole pine, *P. contorta*, a variable tree, occurs naturally from Alaska to California, inland to Alberta. Selected strains are planted locally in Scotland, Ireland, as best timber tree for poor soils under harsh climates. **Bark thin, scaly, black**. Leaves **mid-green**. Cones **remain closed** for years, but a forest fire opens scales, releases seeds; enables seedlings to re-colonize burnt land. **Stiff prickle** on every cone scale aids identification. 'Lodgepole' recalls use of straight young poles to support Red Indian lodges or wigwams.

Virginia pine, *P. virginiana*, also called Jersey pine and aptly, **scrub pine**, grows plentifully on poor soils in the eastern United States, but yields little timber. Red-brown scaly bark. **Straggly shoots** change colour with age from pinkish brown to **purple**; each main shoot bears **two or three curved side shoots. Tapering cylindrical cones** have a prickle on each scale.

Aleppo pine, *P. halepensis*, native to countries around the Mediterranean, invades abandoned pastures and vineyards. Known by **bright green needles** on shoots that change from **green to orange and grey, buds with bent-back, grey-fringed scales. Tapering cones bent back** towards shoot, **orange-brown** with raised **grey patch** on each scale. They **persist** on the tree in whorls. Bark **purple-brown, scaly, with orange fissures**.

Aleppo pine resists drought and proves useful for shelterbelts to check soil erosion. Low-grade timber has red-brown heartwood, yellow sapwood.

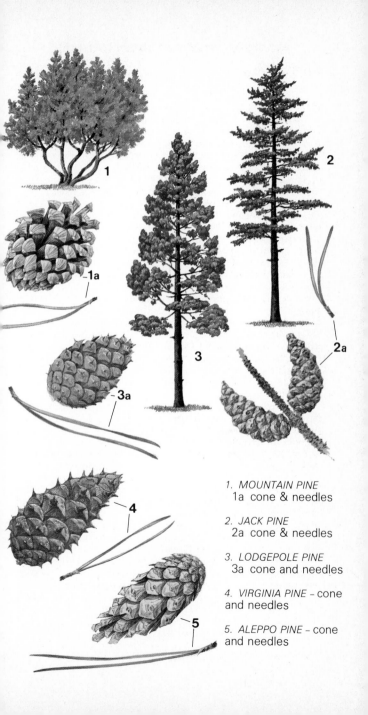

1. *MOUNTAIN PINE*
   1a cone & needles

2. *JACK PINE*
   2a cone & needles

3. *LODGEPOLE PINE*
   3a cone and needles

4. *VIRGINIA PINE* – cone and needles

5. *ALEPPO PINE* – cone and needles

PINES III: LONG NEEDLES IN PAIRS

PINUS genus   PINACEAE

Pines described here bear needles over 10 cm (4 in.) long.

Stone pine, *Pinus pinea*, draws name from large edible seeds. Also called umbrella pine because of **broad spreading crown**. Native to Mediterranean, planted for ornament in northern Europe, North America, South Africa. Resists salty sea winds. Stout bole clad in **orange-grey** platy bark, with grey fissures. Stout branches radiate low down, **like umbrella ribs**, supporting dark dome of foliage. Oval buds have reflexed scales, fringed grey. Needles straight, sometimes twisted, dark grey-green. **Large round brown cones**, 10 cm (4 in.) diameter, with flat bases, take three years to ripen. **Scales rounded. Seeds large**, pea-size with stone-hard, mottled brown and black husk which explains name; **bear minute wings**; harvested commercially for eating as confectionery; called 'pine kernels', *pignons, pinocchi*. Timber, reasonably strong, holds little resin. Juvenile, solitary-needled, blue-grey foliage persists on seedlings for several years.

Corsican pine, *P. nigra* variety *maritima*, is widely planted in Europe, for rapid timber production in **straight-boled, lightly branched** trunk. Bark thick, **grey**, platy, deep fissures. Needles long, **grey-green, twisted in wavy fashion. Round terminal bud narrows suddenly to sharp point**. Cones large, shiny pale brown, markedly **oblique or lop-sided**; seeds large, winged. Timber has cream coloured sapwood, pale brown heartwood; used for building, box-making, fencing, mine supports, chipboard, paper pulp.

Austrian pine, *P. nigra*, var. *nigra*, bears **straight-needles**, and has **rugged, close-ranked branches**, causing knotty, inferior timber. Widely planted for shelterbelts in Europe and North America. American red pine, *P. resinosa*, native from Quebec south to Pennsylvania, resembles Corsican pine, but shoots are **orange**, needles in **whorls**, male flowers **red**, cones disintegrate before falling; **sheath persists** at base of thin needles, which snap easily.

Maritime pine, *P. pinaster*, native to Mediterranean, is planted extensively in south-west France, Portugal, South Africa, locally in south-west England. Vigorous **sinuous** trunk, clad in **rusty-grey to purple bark, broken into squares**. Open crown. Stout shoots, often crimson, end in **big, cylindrical red-brown buds with reflexed scales**. Needles change from bright to dark green, exceptionally **long, tough, leathery inrolled. Huge cones**, cylindrical to oblong, shiny red-brown, persist on branches, thick scales bear minute prickles. Big winged seeds. Timber deep red-brown with yellow sapwood, very resinous, used for building, joinery, paper pulp. Trees tapped commercially in France, using chisel-shaped tools. Resin which exudes is scraped away, distilled to yield turpentine and yellow, waxy rosin.

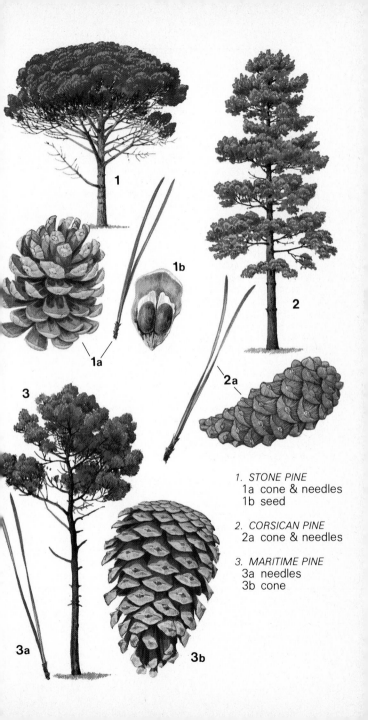

1. *STONE PINE*
   1a cone & needles
   1b seed

2. *CORSICAN PINE*
   2a cone & needles

3. *MARITIME PINE*
   3a needles
   3b cone

PINES IV: NEEDLES IN THREES

PINUS genus   PINACEAE

Pitch pine, *Pinus rigida*, the only three-needled species native to the north-east United States, was once tapped for resin. Vigorously invades abandoned farm lands, as a **straggling tree** with red-brown platy bark. Bears twisted yellowish-green needles around 12·5 cm (5 in.) long. Egg-shaped, mid-brown, persistent cones have scales with **sharp reflexed prickles**. Timber is hard, dense, resinous, serves well for building, especially flooring, and ship-building. Heartwood dark red-brown, sapwood yellowish.

Short-leaf pine, *P. echinata*, found farther south, forms a larger timber tree. Its shorter needles, around 8 cm (3·25 in.) long, are **sometimes in pairs, sometimes in threes**, even on same tree. Long-leaf pine, *P. palustris*, found still farther south, reaching Florida, has **exceptionally long** needles, up to 50 cm (20 in.) always grouped in threes. Buds long, green, torpedo-shaped. Main source of commercial resin, for naval stores, obtained by tapping living trees. Huge cones, up to 25 cm (10 in.) long. Grass-like juvenile, single-needled, foliage. (These pines are shown on p. 216.)

Lobolly pine, *P. taeda*, another southern resin-producer, has moderately long needles, around 25 cm (10 in.). Big cylindrical cones, 12·5 cm (5 in.) long, bear reflexed prickles on their scales. Other key features: bluish-green shoots, non-resinous buds, reflexed bud-scales. Rapidly invades abandoned farmland, hence local name 'oldfield pine'.

Ponderosa pine, *P. ponderosa*, grows on lower slopes of the Rocky Mountains as a splendid shapely tree, reaching 60 m (180 ft) tall, a major timber producer. Bark, dark brown at first, matures to **bright reddish orange** with scaly plates that fit together like pieces of a jigsaw puzzle. Needles, in twos or threes on same tree, are dark yellow-green and **form tufts near ends of branches. Crown appears sparse and open.** Oval cones, around 12·5 cm (5 in.) long, bear prickle-tipped scales.

Monterey pine, *P. radiata*, found wild only on Monterey peninsula, southern California, has become a major timber producer in Spain, South America, South Africa, Australia, and New Zealand. Grown as specimen tree or seaside shelterbelt in France, western Britain. **Bark becomes exceptionally thick, very deeply fissured, dark grey to purplish-black. Needles densely massed in grass-like tufts; bright-emerald green at first, darkening to blue-green. Large ovoid oblique cones, lop-sided, apparently deformed, pale brown, blunt,** persist on branches for many years, gradually opening to release big winged seeds. Timber has yellow sapwood, bright red-brown heartwood, striking summerwood zones; used for building, packaging, furniture, chipboard, paper pulp.

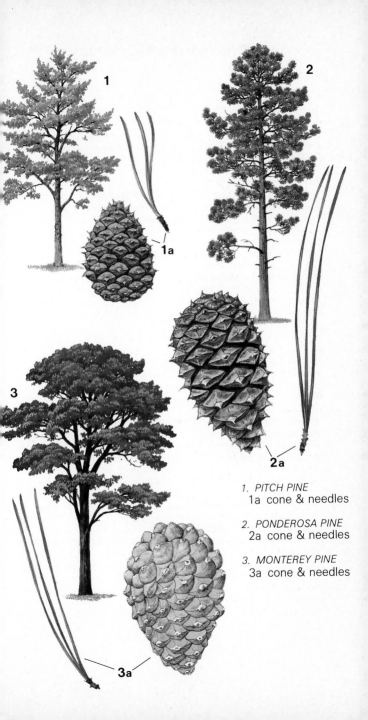

1. *PITCH PINE*
   1a cone & needles

2. *PONDEROSA PINE*
   2a cone & needles

3. *MONTEREY PINE*
   3a cone & needles

PINES V: NEEDLES IN FIVES

PINUS genus   PINACEAE

Sugar pine, *Pinus lambertiana*, world's tallest pine, bears longest cone. Grows in Rocky Mountain States to 80 m (250 ft.). Bole beautifully straight, cylindrical. Bark with irregular grey ridges. Branches, of irregular lengths, stand out horizontally, building up narrow pyramidal crown. Shoots, olive-green, have downy covering of red-brown hairs. Needles, massed, deep green outside, brilliant blue-white within, slightly twisted. Cones cylindrical, 45 cm (18 in.) long, 10 cm (4 in.) wide; have broad, soft, brown scales. Valued timber tree. Owes name to sweet, sugary white substance which oozes from cut heartwood.

Bristle-cone pine, *P. aristata*, grows in high alpine deserts in California, Utah, Nevada, 3,500 m (11,000 ft) above sea level. Called 'fox-tail pine' because **needles are closely massed and curved inwards**, forming a 'brush'. Orange shoots. Needles shining green on outer surface, white with resin within; may endure for 15 years. Oval brown cones have a **distinct bristle** 6 mm (0·25 in.) long on each scale. Though a stunted tree, rarely exceeding 13 m (40 ft) tall or 2 m (6 ft) in girth, bristle-cone pine outlives all others. Archaeologists, dating Indian artefacts, have recorded patterns of annual ring growth approaching 5,000 years!

Arolla pine, *P. cembra*, thrives at high elevations—2,000 m (6,000 ft) on Alps, Carpathians, growing to moderate size, but enduring to 1,000 years. Crown dense, columnar; branches with upturned ends. Bark dark grey to orange brown, with red-brown fissures between thin scales. Greenish-brown shoots end in **sharp-pointed conical buds**, bearing long, sharp, appressed scales. Needles dark green without, **shining blue-white within**. Cones, **squat ovoid cylinders**, with **broad, pointed scales**; ripen from dark red female flowers, through purple conelets, and blue stage, to red-brown. **Large edible seeds, bearing minute wings** often remain in cone till it falls; spread by mice or marmots. Timber valued for carving, especially ornaments (Swiss stone pine).

White pine, *Pinus strobus*, is largest conifer in eastern North America. Called 'Weymouth pine' in England, due to planting by Lord Weymouth, circa 1710; blister rust fungus and aphids now make cultivation unprofitable in Britain. Magnificent, straight bole bears outstretched, horizontal branches with upturned ends. Bark dark grey, thin, fissured. Shoots hairy. **Buds conical, sharp-pointed, resinous.** Needles slender, bluish green. Cones, **hanging downwards, banana-shaped, are long curved cylinders with broad scales** that open readily and bear **white blobs of sticky resin.** Timber, has pinkish-brown heartwood, yellow sapwood; adaptable to joinery, carpentry box-making, everyday furniture. Bhutan pine, *P. wallichiana*, from Himalayas, is similar, but has **long (20 cm or 8 in.) needles, very slender, bent half way along.** Pesists pests and diseases.

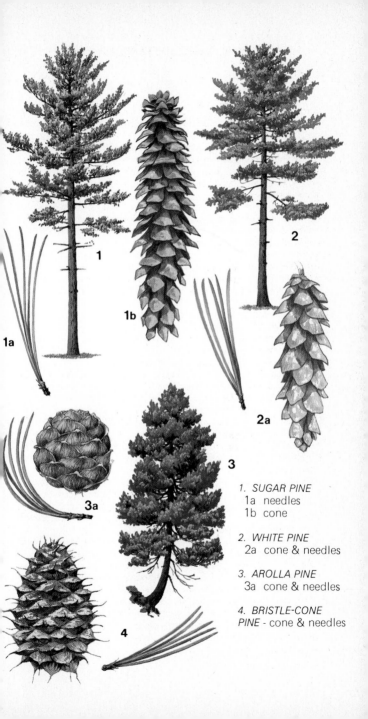

1. *SUGAR PINE*
   1a needles
   1b cone

2. *WHITE PINE*
   2a cone & needles

3. *AROLLA PINE*
   3a cone & needles

4. *BRISTLE-CONE PINE* - cone & needles

TRUE CEDARS

CEDRUS genus   PINACEAE

The name 'cedar' has been applied to many trees that have fragrant foliage or wood, but true cedars all belong to a distinct genus of conifers native only to Asia and North Africa. All are evergreens that bear **hard, dark green needles in tufts** on short shoots. These shoots elongate slowly, **leaving rough scales**, which mark each year's growth. At the ends of branches needles are borne singly, but many have **knobs** at the base, which will become short shoots next year.

Cedars flower, remarkably, **in autumn**. You can then find conspicuous **cone-shaped** groups of male flowers, laden with yellow pollen, standing upright from foliage; they are often mistaken for cones. Bud-like green female flowers, at twig tips, receive wind-borne pollen and then develop slowly over two years, into **large upright barrel-shaped cones** with **hollow tips**. Individual cone scales look **very flat**. They fall away slowly, release seeds, and leave a **hard woody erect central axis**. Seeds are large, with **triangular** wings. On germination, they expand a whorl of numerous seed leaves, then a shoot bearing solitary needles. Tufted foliage first appears in second year.

Cedars develop grey bark broken into many **small oblongs**. Trunks have a thin outer zone of pale brown sapwood surrounding dark brown heartwood that is pleasantly **fragrant**. This is due to cedarwood oil that makes heartwood, already strong, exceptionally durable. Annual rings have a characteristic **wavy outline**. Cedar timber has been used since prehistoric times for building, shipbuilding, and furniture. The best-known example is recorded in the Bible, First Book of Kings. This tells how Hiram, King of Tyre, shifted huge quantities of cedar wood from Mount Lebanon—where cedars still flourish—to Israel, to be used by King Solomon in building his great temple.

Four species of cedar, outwardly much alike, grow on four isolated mountain ranges in sub-tropics, thriving in snow climates surrounded by hot deserts. All have been introduced to most temperate and sub-tropical lands, where they are widely planted for ornament. Three can be named at a distance from their growth habits—note the initial letters.

Cedar of Lebanon, *C. libani*, which grows wild on Mount Lebanon, spreads **level branches** and forms a flat or shallow dome-shaped crown. **D**eodar or Indian cedar, *Cedrus deodara*, from Himalayan foothills, also bears level branches, but with distinctive **drooping tips**. **A**tlas cedar, *Cedrus atlantica*, from the Atlas Mountains of Morocco, has **a**scending branches, set at an acute angle to the trunk. It is most popular in its beautiful blue-foliage variety, *C. atlantica glauca*. Cyprus cedar, *C. brevifolia*, of Troodos Mountains, has *short* needles.

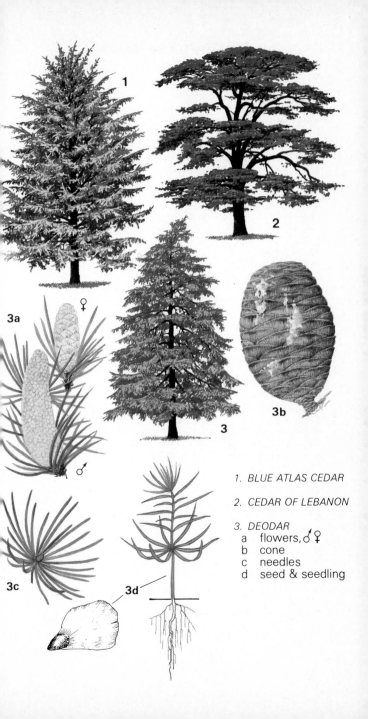

1. *BLUE ATLAS CEDAR*

2. *CEDAR OF LEBANON*

3. *DEODAR*
   a flowers, ♂ ♀
   b cone
   c needles
   d seed & seedling

LARCHES OR TAMARACKS

LARIX genus   PINACEAE

Larches are the only common cone-bearing trees that lose their leaves in winter. They are easily known at that time by their **knobbly twigs**. Along the **ridged** main shoots you find round 'short shoots' or 'knobs', minute near the tips, larger further back. In spring, a **circular cluster of needles** springs out around each knob, but needles near twig tips are always set singly. Larch needles are softer in texture than those of other conifers. **Vivid emerald green** in spring, they darken later, fade in autumn to **brilliant orange shades**, then fall.

Male larch flowers, opening just before leaves, are golden clusters of stamens. Female flowers, usually **rose-red** but sometimes white, are exceptionally pretty **rosettes of scales**, aptly called 'larch roses'. Each brown cone is **barrel-shaped with hollow top** and scales tightly adpressed at their bases. Small brown seeds within bear broad, triangular wings. Seedlings have a whorl of about six seed-leaves, then a slender long shoot, with evergreen solitary needles. The first knobs appear in second season of growth.

Larch timber shows a marked difference between pale brown outer sapwood, and **dark red-brown to terracotta-coloured** heartwood. There are distinct bands of darker summerwood throughout. Naturally durable and remarkably strong, larch is used for fencing, gates, buildings, and as planking for hulls of fishing boats. Larch bark is thick and **markedly fibrous**, with a meshwork pattern of ridges and hollows. The erect tapering trunk carries gracefully **downswept side branches**, with **ascending ends**.

European larch, *Larix decidua*, grows typically near tree-lines of Alps and other central European ranges. It is nowadays widely planted for ornament and timber in both Britain and America. It has **straw-coloured twigs, true green needles** and **straight** cone scales. Japanese larch, *L. kaempferi*, native to Mount Fuji and neighbouring peaks, is widely planted for faster growth. It bears **rust-red twigs, blue-green needles, reflexed** cone scales. Hybrid between them, × *eurolepis*, is intermediate, grows faster still. American larch, *L. laricina*, also called tamarack, or hacmatack (Red Indian names) is distinguished by smaller, more open cones. Western larch, *L. occidentalis*, has larger cones with ragged, wavy scales.

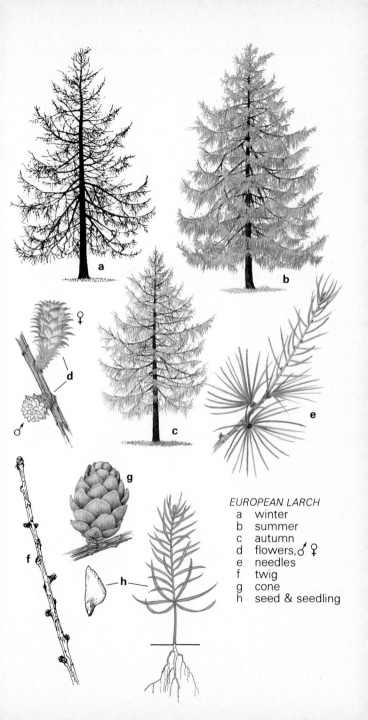

EUROPEAN LARCH
a winter
b summer
c autumn
d flowers, ♂ ♀
e needles
f twig
g cone
h seed & seedling

SPRUCES I: NORWAY AND WEEPING SPRUCES

PICEA genus   PINACEAE

The large genus *Picea*, spruces, includes fifty species. Norway spruce, *P. abies*, grows wild throughout Europe. Extensively planted in Britain for timber, it is traditional Christmas tree. An established ornamental tree in North America.

Spruces carry an unmistakable character: **woody peg at base of every needle**. Pull a needle and peg **tears away with it**. Let it die naturally, and it will break off, **leaving peg behind like hat peg**; hence old spruce twigs are **always rough**. Spruces form **symmetrical trees with solid conical crowns. Side branches, in regular whorls, sweep down in arcs**, resisting snow breakage. On German mountains spruces live 1,000 years, reach 60 m (200 ft). Trunk, often buttressed, bears **thin, unfissured, rough-surfaced, red-brown bark**, harsh to touch.

Short needles, around 1·5 cm (0·5 in.) form two-ranked pattern on level twigs; stiff, four-sided, pointed. On upright shoots needles stand all round. Terminal buds red-brown, oval, pointed. In spring, **bright green** needles emerge, bunched together; they last about four years, turn brown, then drop.

Male flowers, groups along side shoots, are crimson oval clusters of stamens that turn yellow in early summer, then shed yellow wind-borne pollen. Female flowers, near side-shoot tips, are dark red, upright, oval mini-cones. After fertilization they turn green, enlarge rapidly, bend over, ripening by autumn to **long cylindrical red-brown cones with regular diamond-shaped, round-ended scales, pointing downwards**. In spring they release seeds, two per scale, each lightly attached to its oval papery wing, resting in cup at wing's base.

The sprouting seedling raises a whorl of five to ten seed-leaves, sickle-shaped, upcurved. Primary leaves follow, all round first shoot. Two-ranked foliage appears later, on side shoots.

Timber is uniform pale cream, without obvious distinctions of heartwood; summerwood bands thin, pale; no natural durability. Moderately strong, easily worked; employed, world-wide, for building, packaging, furniture, chipboard, paper pulp. Branches, ranked in whorls, leave dark brown knots through wood; **smaller knots**, formed by branchlets between whorls, aid identification.

Two lovely ornamental weeping spruces originate on high mountains where pendent foliage lessens snow damage. Himalayan weeping spruce, *P. smithiana*, bears long dark needles **quadrangular in cross section, incurved**, spread evenly round drooping twigs. Brewer's weeping spruce, *P. brewerana*, from Siskiyou Mountains, California, has similarly-arranged **flat** silvery blue-green needles, **with white resin bands on inner surfaces**; tips bend **outwards**. After rain foliage forms silver curtains shimmering in sunshine.

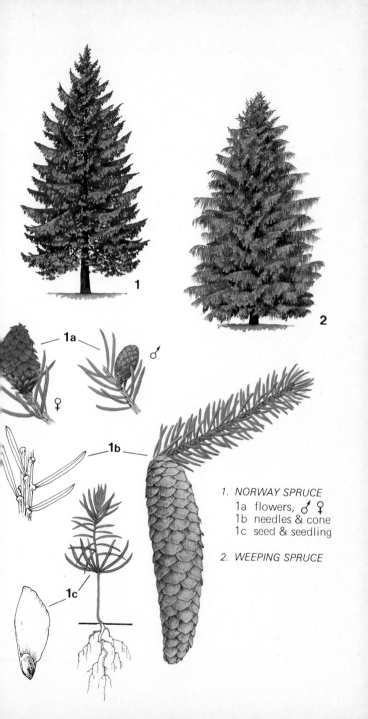

1. NORWAY SPRUCE
   1a flowers, ♂ ♀
   1b needles & cone
   1c seed & seedling

2. WEEPING SPRUCE

SPRUCES II: OTHER KINDS

PICEA genus   PINACEAE

Four of the spruces chosen for a closer look are major sources of timber and paper pulp; the other two, Serbian and blue spruce, admirable garden trees.

White spruce, *Picea glauca*, one of the world's most northerly growing trees, is found right across North America, from Alaska through Canada and Maine to Newfoundland. Foliage is rather sparse, with bluish or silvery green needles pointing outward. Relatively long, 2·5 cm (1 in.), they have a **pungent odour when crushed, resembling blackcurrant jam**. White spruce bears cylindrical cones with rounded scales. It has been planted on many exposed hillsides in Britain and Europe, as a possible hardy pioneer tree, but has rarely grown well.

Black spruce, *P. mariana*, which has a similar natural range, has shorter, mid-green needles on hairy shoots. It bears **small, squat cones**.

Red spruce, *P. rubens*, found only in Maine and adjoining territories, and along the Appalachian mountains, has still shorter needles, set in crowded ranks, pointing forwards. Its short cones are distinctly **red**.

Blue spruce, which is the variety *glauca* of the species *Picea pungens*, the Colorado spruce, comes from high-elevation regions in the Rocky Mountains that have hard cold winters and hot dry sunny summers. It is easily known by its stiff, sharp-pointed needles, which have beautiful blue-white shining surfaces. This is due to a waxy resin, which lessens water loss under bright sunshine, and helps this spruce to survive droughts. Twigs are bright yellow-brown or orange-brown. Blue spruce grows slowly, remaining a bush-size tree, handy for the front lawn, for many years.

Serbian spruce, *P. omorika*, native only to a small mountainous region around Sarajevo in Yugoslavia, forms an extremely narrow crown of deep green foliage. Usually planted for scenic effect—as the 'Lombardy poplar of the conifers'. It can also achieve a high timber yield.

Sitka spruce, *Picea sitchensis*, takes its name from Sitka, the capital of Alaska in its Russian colonial days. Its natural range extends south through Canada to Oregon, but is narrow, along the western seaboard only. The wet, misty, but mild climate there is matched by that of the western British Isles, and Sitka spruce has become the leading conifer for afforestation in Ireland, Wales, Scotland, and upland England. Easily picked out by vigorous upward growth, often 1 m (3 ft) taller each year, **and silvery grey-green needles with sharp points**. The pretty cones are **oval, pale brown** and have **crinkly scales with wavy edges**. Grows erect in the face of the wildest westerly gales, and resists sea salt.

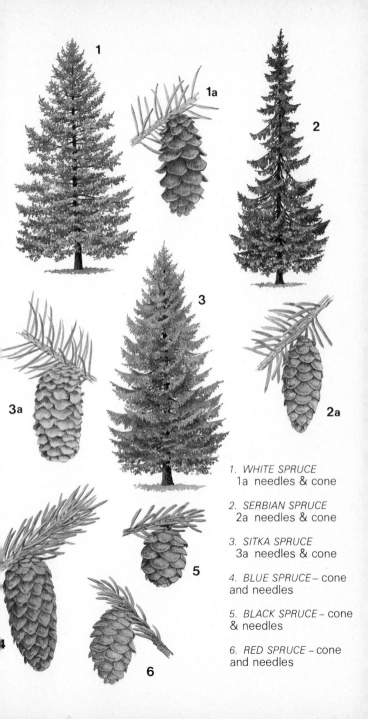

1. *WHITE SPRUCE*
   1a needles & cone

2. *SERBIAN SPRUCE*
   2a needles & cone

3. *SITKA SPRUCE*
   3a needles & cone

4. *BLUE SPRUCE* – cone
and needles

5. *BLACK SPRUCE* – cone
& needles

6. *RED SPRUCE* – cone
and needles

HEMLOCKS

TSUGA genus   PINACEAE

Foliage sprays made up of **short flat needles all apparently of irregular lengths** immediately distinguish hemlocks from other evergreen conifers; actually only three lengths are present, all intermixed. These needles are dark green above, but look white below because of bands of wax that shield the breathing pores, or stomata, and check water loss. This decorative foliage is of low value for indoor ornament because the needles quickly wither and fall—another identification point.

Hemlocks form graceful, pyramidal trees often planted as specimens. The slender **leading shoot of each tree droops gracefully downwards**, though quick upward growth continues none the less. Crimson male flowers, grouped in clusters amidst needles, open in spring and scatter yellow pollen. Plum-purple bud-like female flowers are borne at branch tips. They ripen in autumn through green and lilac-purple stages to small pale brown egg-shaped cones, which droop downwards from the twigs. They soon expand their scales, and release **tiny, oval, wrinkled seeds**, each carrying an oblong papery wing, much larger than itself. Hemlock seedlings are unique in bearing **three seed-leaves**; these are followed by lax juvenile needles, ranked in threes, and even in length; uneven length, adult needles follow.

Hemlock's reddish brown bark remains smooth for years, then develops shallow plates and fissures. It is harvested in America as tanbark for tanning leather. The uniform pale brown timber has good strength properties, and is used on a large scale for building, joinery and paper pulp.

Eastern hemlock, *Tsuga canadensis*, native to eastern North America, bears needles with tapering sides, and cones on short stalks. Western hemlock, *T. heterophylla*, native to America's Pacific seaboard from Alaska south to Oregon, has parallel-sided needles and unstalked cones. The western race is now widely planted in Europe, including the British Isles, because of vigorous growth and rapid timber production.

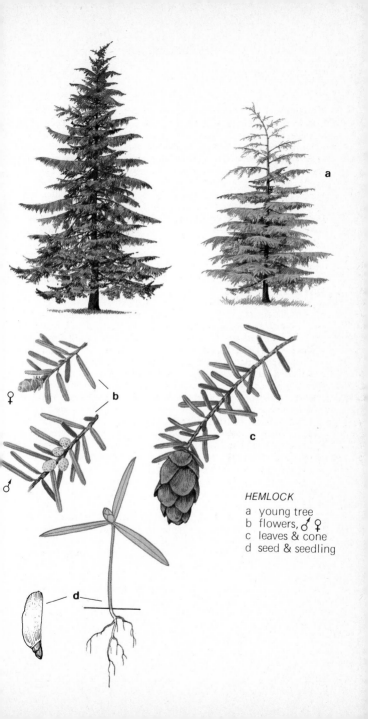

HEMLOCK
a young tree
b flowers, ♂ ♀
c leaves & cone
d seed & seedling

DOUGLAS FIR

PSEUDOTSUGA genus   PINACEAE

Though their name suggests a Scottish origin, all Douglas firs are native to western North America or eastern Asia. Their title commemorates David Douglas, a Scottish botanist and explorer, who first sent seed to Britain from Oregon in 1827. They are now extensively planted throughout Europe, in Australia and also New Zealand, as valuable commercial timber trees. Douglas firs can reach great size; one unfortunately felled on Vancouver Island, British Columbia, in 1895 had reached 133 m (417 ft), taller than any tree standing today. Outstanding American specimens still reach 80 m (250 ft), with diameters around 4 m (12 ft) at the base. British records are 55 m (175 ft) for height and 2·2 m (7 ft) for diameter. Timber, usually marketed as 'Oregon pine' or 'Columbian pine' from its general resemblance to true pine (*Pinus*) timber, has red-brown heartwood and pale brown sapwood. **Annual rings are very distinct** because Douglas fir, whether it grows fast or slow, always lays down **thick dark bands of summerwood**.

Douglas fir foliage resembles that of silver firs or *Abies* species; the solitary flat needles, dark green above, and paler below, have **short stalks** and leave round **raised scars** when pulled from the twigs; silver firs leave **depressed** scars and **lack** stalks. A **pinched-in base** is another key point for Douglas fir needles. **Reddish brown, slender, tapering pointed buds**, like those of beech, provide a ready means of identification. Male flowers are pretty yellow oval structures, placed near twig tips, which open and shed wind-borne pollen in spring. Female flowers, borne right at twig tips, are tufts or 'brushes' of scales and bracts; colour is variable— green, crimson, purplish or white. They ripen in autumn to **drooping brown egg-shaped cones**, easily recognized by the **straight three-pointed bract** that protrudes behind every cone-scale. The pale-brown seeds are oval; each is fixed to a papery-brown wing, also oval. Seedlings, when they sprout next spring, raise a whorl of about six slender seed-leaves, followed by normal foliage.

Douglas fir bark is at first grey-brown and smooth, with prominent **resin blisters that release delicious fragrance if you break them**. As the trunk expands it develops great character, splitting to open deep fissures showing **tawny orange-brown shades** with irregular smooth **purple-brown panels** between them.

The kind usually planted is green or coastal Douglas fir, *Pseudotsuga menziesii*. Its variety *glauca*, the blue or inland Douglas fir, known by bluer needles and reflexed cone scales, grows more slowly to lesser sizes.

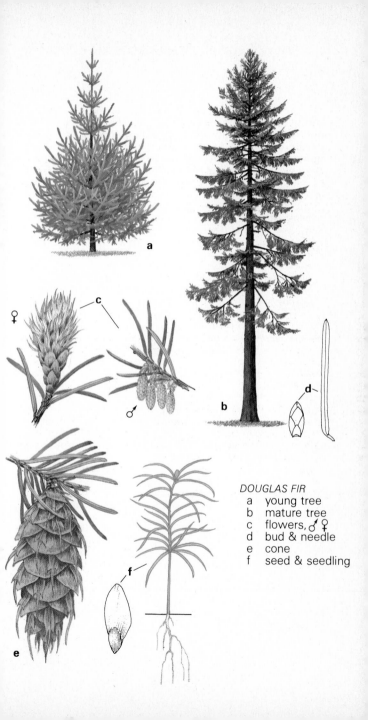

DOUGLAS FIR
- a young tree
- b mature tree
- c flowers, ♂ ♀
- d bud & needle
- e cone
- f seed & seedling

SILVER FIRS I: TWO EUROPEAN KINDS

ABIES genus   PINACEAE

Silver firs, also called 'true firs', form the distinct *Abies* genus, and are distinguished by a simple key-sign. **The base of each stalkless needle fits into a circular depression on the stalk; pull any needle away and it leaves a neat round scar**. For comparison, spruces, genus *Picea*, have needles set on pegs; Douglas firs, genus *Pseudotsuga*, have stalked needles, leave raised scars. Needles arise all round twigs, but in some kinds their stalks bend so that they appear **two-ranked, with dark upper surfaces, pale under-sides**. Others have bushy foliage, like a carpet pile, or needles standing straight out. Upright shoots bear all-round-the-twig foliage, never flatter types. Leaves fragrant, resinous; white resin-bands along their undersides give silver firs their name. **Blunt buds** are resinous in some kinds, not all. **Resin blisters** are frequent on young, otherwise smooth, bark.

Timber is pale brown throughout, lacks natural durability, is only moderately strong. Good enough for general building and packaging jobs; yields excellent paper pulp.

Male flowers open in oval clusters of golden blossoms near twig-tips in late spring. Female flowers appear as odd **upright torpedo-shaped green structures, with protruding green bracts**, also near twig tips; mature into **brown oval cones that always stand upright**; they never droop like spruce or Douglas fir. Early in autumn the **cones shatter**; scales and bracts fall away from a **central stalk, or candle**, which can be seen through winter. Obviously, no whole cones can be found later. **Two large triangular seeds with roughly triangular wings** are released from each scale. When a seed sprouts, it raises a whorl of about four long seed-leaves, alternating with an adjacent whorl of four short primary leaves. Thereafter normal solitary needles appear on first upright shoot.

European silver fir, *Abies alba*, bears foliage in two flat ranks. Native to Europe's main mountain ranges, it forms magnificent forests, self-sustaining despite regular timber harvests. Throve in British Isles until 1910 but since devastated by the minute aphid, *Adelges nordmannianae*—a few giants survive. Cone cylindrical; flat scales; **small reflexed pointed bracts**. Smooth bark, eventually cracking into rough squares. Winter buds, small, oval, **non-resinous**.

Spanish fir, *Abies pinsapo*, found wild only around Sierra Nevada, is known by **stiff thick leathery needles standing out in all directions around every twig**. Hence its other names: 'hedgehog fir' and 'bottle-brush fir'. Male flowers tinged red; cones are tapering cylinders. Rough black platy bark. Park trees elegant, mountain ones rugged, picturesque.

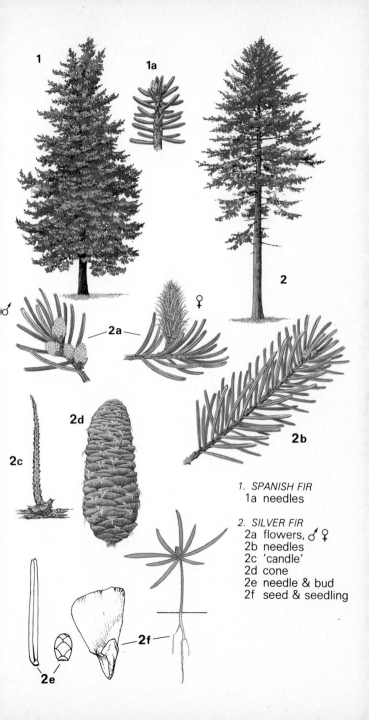

1. SPANISH FIR
1a needles

2. SILVER FIR
2a flowers, ♂ ♀
2b needles
2c 'candle'
2d cone
2e needle & bud
2f seed & seedling

SILVER FIRS II: THREE AMERICAN KINDS

ABIES genus   PINACEAE

Balsam fir, *Abies balsamea*, is very common over the north-eastern United States, and Canada east of the Rockies. A major source of general building, packaging and joinery timber, also pulp for paper-making. Name arises from thick resin blisters on smooth young bark, source of transparent, pale yellow fluid known as 'Canada balsam'. This is widely used by biologists for mounting specimens on glass slides for microscopic examination; soft, it soon dries, through evaporation of turpentine, becoming a solid yet transparent fixative. Old bark cracks into brown scales.

Balsam fir is known by its beautiful, symmetrical, spire-shaped crown, Needles are closely crowded along twigs, **short**, around 2·5 cm (1 in.), **blunt or notched at the tip**, shiny dark green above, silvery because of two white waxy bands below. They form two ranks, but **rise forwards** along the twig, never lying flat. **Buds are red**, resinous, shiny. Male flowers at twig tips are yellow, small, numerous. Female flower, a slender cylinder, shows bracts at first, but **only tips of bracts can be seen on ripe cone. Cone is short, squat**, cylindrical to egg-shaped. Seedlings have only four seed-leaves.

Very hardy, balsam fir grows right to the fringes of tundra of northern Canada, being eventually reduced to a stunted bush. Further south, thrives high up on mountains. Introduced to Scotland in 1697, but remains rare in Europe, even in botanical collections.

Grand fir, *Abies grandis*, is native to British Columbia and western United States. Popular plantation tree in Britain and western Europe, where climate makes a good match with its homeland. Fast growing, forms a magnificent symmetrical crown, reaches 55 m (175 ft)—(hundred-year-old specimen at Ardkinglass, Argyll, Scotland). Easily known by **long needles**, reaching 5 cm (2 in.), **very flat**, and arranged in **very flat ranks** too. When crushed, a **strong smell of oranges**. Dark green above, mid-green with white wax bands below. **Small brown winter buds**, at twig tips, conical, resinous. Large cylindrical cones have bracts hidden below scales. Bark becomes purplish-brown, cracks into small squares.

Noble fir, *A. procera*, native from Washington south to California, is widely planted elsewhere in North America and also western Europe for ornament and sometimes for timber. Known by **silvery blue-green needles curving forward and upward. Winter buds at twig tips oval, stout, purple-brown, exude white resin. Huge cylindrical cone displays spiral pattern of scales. A reflexed, pointed, pale brown bract appears below every scale**; hence called 'feathercone fir'. **Stout bole has smooth grey bark, tapers markedly near base.**

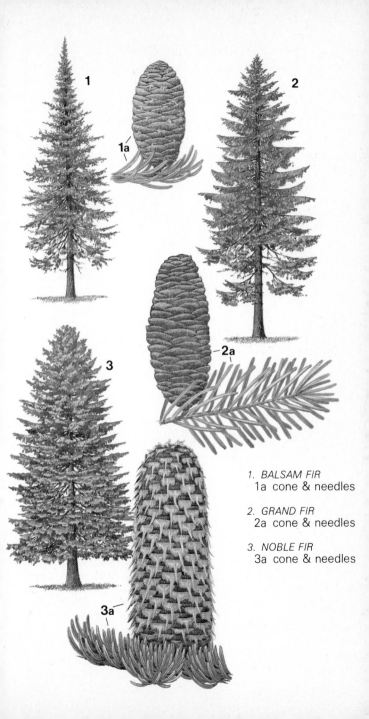

1. *BALSAM FIR*
   1a cone & needles

2. *GRAND FIR*
   2a cone & needles

3. *NOBLE FIR*
   3a cone & needles

GIANT SEQUOIA

SEQUOIADENDRON GIGANTEUM   TAXODIACEAE

Aptly called 'giant' because it is the world's largest tree, sequoia is named after Sequoyah, a Cherokee Indian leader in the east, who never actually saw it! In Britain, it is often called 'wellingtonia' in honour of the great Duke of Wellington, victor of the Napoleonic wars, who never saw it either! Native only to Sierra Nevada or the Snowy Mountains of central California; grows in valleys at heights of 4,000–8,000 ft. First reported to incredulous Western world by John Bidwell, explorer, in 1842. Too scarce to be exploited for timber, most trees are preserved in National Parks, including famous Calaveras Grove. 'General Grant', one of the largest 'national monument' trees, is 81·5 m (267 ft) tall, and 24·3 m (80 ft) round. Trunk has an estimated weight of 3,000 tonnes (tons) for a volume of some 3,000 m³. Only coast redwood grows taller.

Introduced to the eastern United States and Europe in 1853, giant sequoia became fashionable for garden, park and estate planting. Today it can often be picked out as the **largest conical evergreen** in many broad landscapes. It has already achieved 50 m (153 ft) in England, after 122 years growth. An age of 3,400 years, by ring counts, is recorded for one Californian specimen; 4,000 years is estimated for larger trees.

Giant sequoia bears **very thick, very soft, rust-red bark** which later matures to a **pinkish grey**, up to 60 cm (2 ft) thick on old trees. Deeply fissured, with holes where branches have fallen. Trunk **swells markedly at base**, often buttressed. Always dead straight, it carries a **symmetrical crown of downswept branches**. Foliage consists of **uniform, pointed, grey-green, tapering needles, directed forwards, which completely hide young shoots and minute buds**. Main shoots bear cord-like branchlets.

Timber, not available commercially, has red-brown durable heartwood, white sapwood.

Male flowers of giant sequoia form short, oval, yellow catkins at tips of branchlets and shed pollen in spring. Female flowers arise singly at tips of other branchlets; like green oval buds, with bristles below scales. After fertilization, they expand in one summer to become oval green knobbly cones. Seed within takes a further year to mature. Grey-brown, fully ripe cones are made up of **flat scales with hollow creases across their outer faces**. Tight at first, they shrink and separate later, making an 'open' cone. Each scale sheds about five tiny seeds, each a long-oval brown grain with a broad half-oval paler wing on either side. Seedling bears a whorl of four seed-leaves. These are followed by normal spirally-ranged needles, somewhat lax at first, later firm as on adult, upright shoots.

GIANT SEQUOIA
a   young tree
b   mature tree
c   flowers, ♂ ♀
d   leaves
e   cone
f   seed & seedling

COAST REDWOOD

SEQUOIA SEMPERVIRENS TAXODIACEAE

California's coastal region, with much rain and frequent sea fogs, is the home of this magnificent evergreen, the world's tallest tree. A giant in a valley near Dyerville Flats has reached 120 m (394 ft). Girths reach 20 m (61 ft). Redwood's **dead-upright tapering columnar trunk** marks it out, in forests, parks and gardens; extensively planted throughout America and Europe.

Rufous red bark, very thick, very spongy, with deep fissures and holes left by fallen branches is a key feature that can only be confused with pinker bark of giant sequoia. Hit it hard and it softly absorbs the blow from your fist! Bole spreads out near base, often bearing sprouts carrying dark green needles. Yew-like foliage has **two distinct leaf types**. Main shoots carry **single, flat, dark green needles** pointing forwards and arranged spirally. Branchlets, bear two ranks of needles; when needles wither after three or four years, each branchlet falls in one piece. Every branchlet has a cluster of green bracts at its base; next come large needles, then needles becoming progressively smaller. General outline is boat-shaped. Branchlets sometimes bear mini-branchlets at their tips. Each individual needle is **hard, sharp-pointed, dark green above, with two white bands beside midrib on paler green underside**; yew has no such bands. If pulled, redwood needles **tear from stem**; yew needles snap off. Buds are minute, surrounded by scales that turn brown and persist around shoot bases.

Male flowers form in winter in very small whitish-yellow catkins, terminal to smallest side-shoots. They become yellow with pollen in spring. Female flowers, at tips of other branchlets, are bud-like structures of green scales with bristle-tipped bracts. They are borne on short individual stalks clad in small, pointed, scale-shaped needles. They ripen in one season to **knobbly oval cones** made up of scales that present **diamond-faced surfaces, each with a central hollow**, to the outer world. Green at first, these scales ripen to brown, shrink, and separate along their edges. About six minute seeds escape from beneath each scale. Each is a triangular brown grain edged on each side with a narrow rudimentary wing.

A sprouting redwood seedling expands from two narrow seed-leaves at tip of its first slender stem. First shoot beyond this carries needles of typical main-shoot type, placed spirally around it, the first ones lax and spreading. Yew-type branchlets develop later, commonly in second year.

Redwood, as name suggests, has strong red-brown, durable heartwood, surrounded by paler, pinkish-brown sapwood. Adaptable to building construction, joinery and fencing, it is the basis of a substantial lumber trade. Ring-counts prove oldest trees have attained 2,600 years.

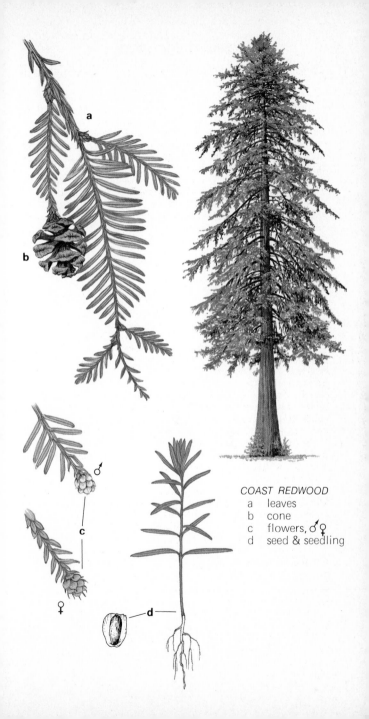

COAST REDWOOD
a   leaves
b   cone
c   flowers, ♂♀
d   seed & seedling

JAPANESE CEDAR

CRYPTOMERIA JAPONICA   TAXODIACEAE

Slender, claw-shaped, yellowish-green needles, arched to point towards shoot tips, are the key-note of the magnificent Japanese cedar, or *sugi* tree. The only similar foliage is that of giant sequoia, which has shorter, grey-green needles. Bark at once distinguishes them; Japanese cedar has thin tight, hard, stringy red-brown bark; giant sequoia bark is thick, loose fibrous.

When fully mature, the brown cones of Japanese cedar show unique feathery scales. These round, short-stalked structures look oddly like frilly globe-flowered chrysanthemums. Green at first, they develop from odd tufts of scales—the female flowers —at twig tips. Ripe cones release from two to five seeds from beneath each scale. Each tiny brown oval seed-grain has a very narrow pale brown wing on either side. Red-brown male flowers open in spring near twig tips, in club-shaped catkins—holding many blossoms that scatter yellow wind-borne pollen.

Japanese cedar seedlings carry a whorl of three seed-leaves on a short stalk. The first shoot to rise amid this whorl bears straight juvenile needles in groups of two or four, standing straight out around it. Incurved adult needles follow, usually in the second year, first in three ranks, later in five ranks.

Japanese cedar timber has red-brown, strong, naturally durable heartwood, surrounded by a narrow band of pale-brown sapwood. A major commercial timber in Japan, it is used for all kinds of building and heavy construction work, including shrines and temples, bridges, docks and harbours; also for furniture, panelling, joinery and boxes. Natural forests, mainly on the central island of Honshu, form a valuable, well-tended lumber resource.

Japanese cedar has been planted as an ornamental tree in all parts of Europe and North America that do not suffer hard winters; in Britain it thrives best in coastal lowlands. Forms a shapely, conical tree, up to 50 m (150 ft) high in Japan, and may stand for 500 years.

The variety *elegans*, a natural sort found centuries ago in some unrecorded Japanese forest, is often planted in parks, streets and gardens. It looks quite unlike its respectable parent, or indeed, anything else! A floppy, bushy tree, it satisfies the landscape architects' occasional need for something shapeless. Long, lax, bent juvenile needles, blue-green in summer, turn warm bronze in winter, as though the tree were dying, but resume green shades next spring

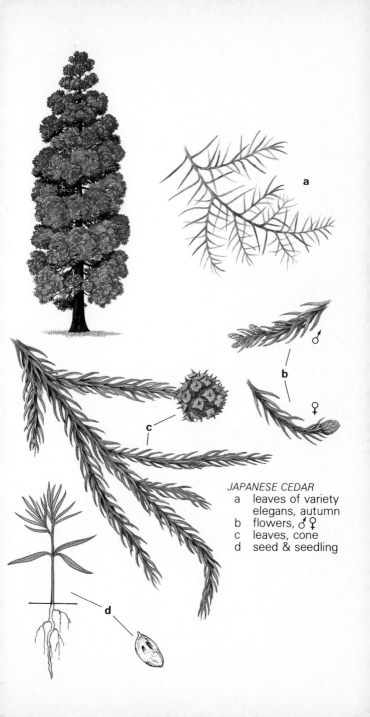

JAPANESE CEDAR
a   leaves of variety
     elegans, autumn
b   flowers, ♂ ♀
c   leaves, cone
d   seed & seedling

SWAMP CYPRESS

TAXODIUM DISTICHUM   TAXODIACEAE

Feathery foliage, that turns brilliant orange in autumn, then falls to leave twigs leafless through winter, marks out this lovely waterside tree. It grows naturally in freshwater swamps in Florida, and neighbouring southern states, north up the Mississippi valley. Planted extensively elsewhere in America and Europe, nearly always along watersides, or in bogs few other trees tolerate. To gain oxygen for its roots, when growing in waterlogged soil, swamp cypress roots send up conspicuous **knee roots**, or **pneumato-phores**, easily seen as **brown knobbly projections** from the soil; they have soft spongy tissue within, adapted to transport air. Also called 'bald cypress' because it is leafless in winter.

Most of the foliage consists of **short deciduous branchlets**, rather than separate leaves. Single needles, spirally set, occur only near twig tips. Farther back, **branchlets spring alternately** from permanent brown shoots. Each branchlet has a green central midrib and about twenty slender pointed needles **set alternately** on either side; outline is boat-shaped, with longest needles near centre, shorter ones near base and tip. Leaves appear **very late**, as a pale blue haze in June, turn red-brown in late autumn, then fall; branchlets drop as whole units. Dawn redwood has similar foliage, but opposite buds and opposite needles.

Swamp cypress bark is hard, tight, red-brown, stringy. Boles become fissured near base and often **develop buttresses** that help support trunk on soft wet muddy soil. Strong, though soft timber has yellowish-white outer sapwood, and red-brown, naturally durable, heartwood. Boats are used to harvest it from tree's native swamps. Valued for greenhouse construction, window sills, barrels, joinery, furniture and other work needing fine finish with minimum shrinkage and good resistance to damp.

Slender, bright brown winter twigs carry many scars left by fallen branchlets, also small side buds from which next year's branchlets will arise. Rounded buds at twig tips prolong shoot growth.

Male flowers open at twig tips in early spring, in **long-stalked purplish catkins**. Many tiny blossoms, strung along main stalk, shed golden pollen. Female flowers, set farther back, singly or in small groups, are green bud-like structures holding seed-bearing scales. Cone ripens in autumn as a **brown globe** made up of broad close-set scales that open later. Seeds, two per scale, are small, hard, dark brown, **triangular** objects, with thick, horny, warted coats. No wings—they spread by floating.

Swamp cypress seedlings sprout in summer on wet mud. The rootstalk raises the horny coat, and five slender seed-leaves emerge from it before it falls. First upright shoot bears solitary needles; branchlets appear in second season, often later.

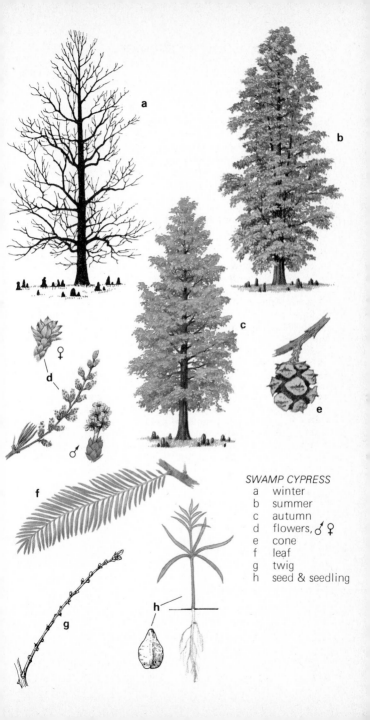

SWAMP CYPRESS
 a   winter
 b   summer
 c   autumn
 d   flowers, ♂ ♀
 e   cone
 f   leaf
 g   twig
 h   seed & seedling

DAWN REDWOOD

METASEQUOIA   TAXODIACEAE
GLYPTOSTROBOIDES

Unknown to the western world until 1941, this Chinese tree is now commonly planted, usually along watersides in European and American gardens. Resembles swamp cypress but dawn redwood bears **needles and branchlets in opposite pairs**, not alternately. Key feature, unique among all the world's trees, is placement of **scars on twigs beside or above buds**; all other trees have scars below buds.

Discovered by Chinese forester Tsang Wang during wartime timber hunt, dawn redwood, called in Chinese *shui-sa* or water-fir, grows wild only in the land-locked Shui-sa-pa, or Water-fir Valley, of Szechuan. Its soft red-brown timber, though scarce, is favoured for coffins. Because its extinct ancestors were previously known in fossil form, it has been aptly called 'a living fossil'. A lively tree today, growing readily from cuttings.

Dawn redwood boles, clad in thin, tight, red-brown bark, have a **bizarre appearance caused by deep, irregular hollows**. Long slender shoots bear small oval pale-brown, **opposite** buds. Slender, flat, pale-green paired needles open along these shoots late in spring. At the same time paired green branchlets also expand their own ranks of paired, pale-green needles. Vivid orange autumn colour. Branchlets drop all as one piece.

Male flowers, in oval yellow catkins, open early in spring along outer portions of certain main shoots and associated branchlets. Whole structure resembles a flowering panicle. Female flowers arise farther back, singly, with long 5 cm (2 in.) stalks. Oval in shape, at first soft and green, later form dark brown, hard, woody cones, with pointed tips, which hang down on long red stalks like Chinese lanterns. Cone scales have swollen ends. Below each scale are five to nine compressed, oval, brown seeds, each surrounded by a yellow wing. A sprouting seedling bears two seed-leaves, then simple paired needles, before the adult branchlet-type foliage appears.

DAWN REDWOOD
a   winter
b   summer
c   autumn
d   flowers, ♂ ♀
e   cone
f   leaves
g   seed & seedling
h   twig & bud

INCENSE CEDAR

CALOCEDRUS DECURRENS   CUPRESSACEAE

As seen in Europe and eastern North America, this beautiful evergreen first attracts attention by its **columnar growth habit**. Its tall dark cylindrical crown is built up of countless, much-divided, rich green, flat branchlets. Crush these and you are rewarded 'with an unmistakable **aromatic scent** recalling that of church incense. Needles are set in obvious **whorls of four**. The base of each needle clasps the stem, running along it—*decurrens* means 'running along'. Tips of four needles swell to make a bump.

Incense cedar's fragrant timber has pale pinkish-brown heartwood, surrounded by pinkish white sapwood. Fairly soft and very smooth, it works evenly and can be used for lead pencils and fine carving. More general uses include carpentry, joinery, fencing and furniture.

Native to California, incense cedar has been planted as an ornamental tree in most temperate lands. Many handsome specimens grow in English parks, contrasting strangely with broader-crowned hardwood and tapering conifers. Curiously, on their home ground many incense cedars form, in youth, dense conical crowns. Many mature trees develop spreading rounded ones: the striking columnar habit is rarely seen in the wilds.

Male flowers, born in groups near twig tips, are small greenish structures that shed yellow wind-borne pollen. Female flowers arise at very ends of branchlets, as green **vase-shaped structures**, each composed of six **oval scales with reflexed points**. They become brown when they ripen in autumn, and open widely like pointed stars. Small oval seeds, each with a large oval wing, and a smaller rudimentary wing, then escape and drift away on the wind. These seeds bear resin glands.

Incense cedar seedlings raise only two seed-leaves. Peculiar straight juvenile needles succeed them, followed in turn by flattened fern-frond foliage.

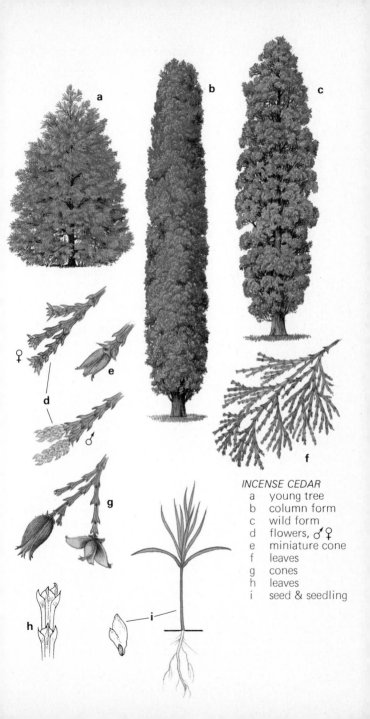

INCENSE CEDAR
a   young tree
b   column form
c   wild form
d   flowers, ♂ ♀
e   miniature cone
f   leaves
g   cones
h   leaves
i   seed & seedling

WESTERN RED CEDAR, NORTHERN WHITE CEDAR

THUJA genus   CUPRESSACEAE

Two evergreens of similar appearance, belonging to same genus, *Thuja*, originate far apart in North America. Western red cedar, *Thuja plicata*, is native to southern Alaska, British Columbia, Washington and Oregon. Northern white cedar *T. occidentalis*, grows in eastern Canada, the Lake States and on the Appalachian mountains. Both have been widely planted as ornamental trees elsewhere in America and Europe; Western red cedar is planted for timber in Britain and France.

Thujas have foliage like that of Lawson cypress and Atlantic white cedar, both of *Chamaecyparis* genus, that is, **flat much-branched fern-fronds**. Look towards the base of each branchlet for **red-brown faded needles and shoots** that indicate *Thuja*. Feel outer ends of branchlets for **thickness of hidden buds** below enveloping green needles; Lawson cypress has buds too thin to feel. *Thuja* cones are quite distinct, being **slender brown ovals with scales that separate from base to tip**, not round globes. Leading shoot of Lawson cypress usually droops; *Thuja* **shoot is upright**. Gardeners and nurserymen call a *Thuja* tree an 'arbor-vitae'. This Latin phrase, meaning 'tree of life', stems from the fact that the evergreen foliage is sustained without any obvious buds.

Names of these two, almost identical, cedars help sort them out. Western red cedar has redder bark; no white bands on underside of foliage, and a **tiny prickle outside the tip of every cone scale; strongly aromatic foliage smells of pineapple**. Northern white cedar has greyer bark; **white wax bands on underside of foliage; smooth rounded tips to cone scales**; its foliage smells of apples cooked with cloves.

Both *Thuja* cedars bear small oval reddish male flower groups, later yellow with pollen, near shoot bases in spring. Minute female flowers, cone-like, green or purple, arise on very short stalks on outer branchlets. Cones ripen brown, leaf-like scales in autumn, then open from tight ovals to spreading clusters. Tiny brown oval seeds, each with a narrow pale brown wing on either side, escape and are spread by wind. Seedlings raise two oval seed-leaves, then a shoot with simple narrow needles projecting all round. Adult fern-frond foliage first appears on side shoots, usually in second year.

Both these cedars have exceptionally strong, yet very light, timber. Sapwood white. Heartwood red-brown, naturally very durable, weathers to beautiful silver grey. Wood cleaves readily so is used for cleft roofing tiles called shingles, and cleft boards, called clapboard, for sides of houses, also fence posts and rails. Western red cedar, used traditionally for Indian dwellings, dug-out canoes and totem poles, is exported world-wide for cedar buildings, especially greenhouses. Ideal for ladder poles.

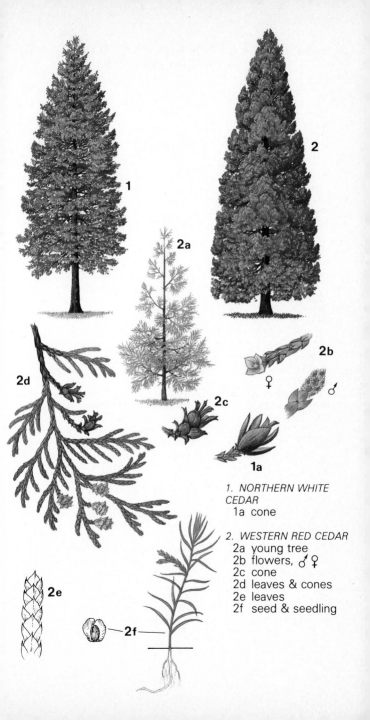

1. *NORTHERN WHITE CEDAR*
   1a cone

2. *WESTERN RED CEDAR*
   2a young tree
   2b flowers, ♂ ♀
   2c cone
   2d leaves & cones
   2e leaves
   2f seed & seedling

FERN-FROND CYPRESSES I: LAWSON AND LEYLAND CYPRESSES

CHAMAECYPARIS and   CUPRESSACEAE
CUPRESSOCYPARIS genera

The term 'fern-frond' aptly describes the foliage of trees in the genera *Chamaecyparis* and *Cupressocyparis*, which include trees variously known as 'cypress' from botanical relationships, and 'cedars' from fragrant foliage. This consists of short needles, grouped in fours, which hug hidden twigs, hide buds and form flat planes. **Cones are always round, scales have central stalks.** *Thuja* and *Calocedrus* have similar foliage, different cones.

Lawson cypress, *Chamaecyparis lawsoniana*, is so-named after Peter Lawson, Edinburgh nurseryman who promoted botanical exploration on America's Pacific coast, and introduced it to Scotland in 1854. Also called Port Orford cedar. Native only to small area in Oregon. Now cultivated in gardens everywhere, very common, highly variable in colour, foliage type, and form.

Typical Lawson cypress is known by dense pyramidal shape with **leading shoot at top bent over, drooping down.** (Western hemlock, with needle foliage, does this too.) Foliage is **very flat**, all buds and twigs hidden. Dark green, tinged blue. Fragrant when crushed. Twigs dark **bluish-grey** (no hint of red). Bark bluish grey, becoming ribbed as trunk expands. Trunk develops buttresses at foot. **Main stem usually forks.** Pale yellow-brown timber, with darker heartwood, is strong and serviceable, but forking habit restricts forest planting.

Flowers, at twig tips, minute, open in spring. **Males resemble little crimson paint-brush heads**, become yellow with pollen. **Females**, on other twigs, **look like tiny** open buds, coloured blue. Cones ripen through green to brown-and-cream stage, finally brown. **Pea-sized, round**, with swellings on broad scales. Seeds oval, dark brown, with **pale brown wings on either side**.

Seedling raises **two strap-shaped seed leaves**. First upright shoot bears **needle-shaped primary leaves in whorls of four**. Fern-frond foliage first appears on side shoots, often delayed till second year.

Leyland cypress, *Cupressocyparis × leylandii*, was bred accidentally in 1888 by a Mr Leyland, owner of Leighton Hall, Welshpool, mid-Wales. Male parent, Californian Monterey cypress, *Cupressus macrocarpa*; female parent, Alaskan white cedar, *Chamaecyparis nootkatensis*. Known by **shoot pattern with major shoot repeatedly dividing into minor off-shoots. Consistently mid-green to bright green. Foliage in flattish planes, not truly flat.** Shoots visible below green needles, first **greenish yellow, then copper-coloured, then purplish brown**; dark red-brown fissured bark on trunk. Open-grown trees become **bottle-shaped**, with solid crowns. **Top bends but does not droop.** Vigorous, hardy, fast-growing. Cones, pea-sized, brown, with straight knobs on scales.

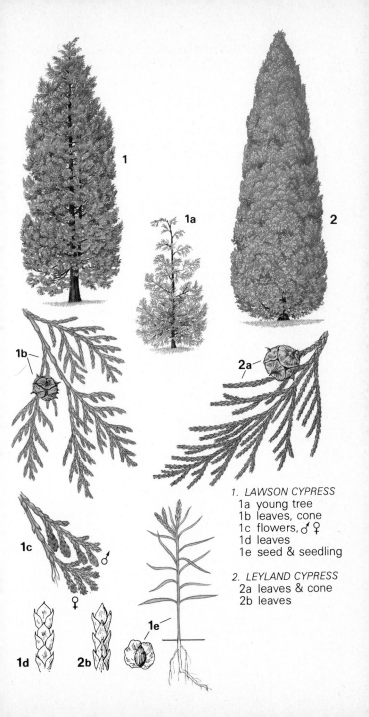

1. *LAWSON CYPRESS*
   1a young tree
   1b leaves, cone
   1c flowers, ♂♀
   1d leaves
   1e seed & seedling

2. *LEYLAND CYPRESS*
   2a leaves & cone
   2b leaves

FERN-FROND CYPRESSES II: ALASKA CEDAR, ATLANTIC WHITE CEDAR, JAPANESE CYPRESSES

CHAMAECYPARIS genus   CUPRESSACEAE

These trees bear **round cones** like those of Lawson cypress; **Western red cedar** and **northern white cedar** have, by contrast, **long slender** cones and belong to the genus *Thuja*, described earlier. On typical wild or plantation trees the foliage is fern-frond. Gardeners often prefer abnormal foliage strains, especially those of Japanese cypresses.

Alaska cedar, *Chamaecyparis nootkatensis*, is native to the Pacific coast region, from Alaska south to Oregon. Planted for ornament elsewhere, including European parks and gardens. In Britain it is called 'Nootka cypress'. Very like Lawson cypress, but foliage has **strong, rank odour when crushed**, hence forester's name: 'stinking cedar'. Small cones carry a **curved prickle on every scale**. Foliage always droops, giving tree a **wilted look**, as though it needs watering. **Shaggy grey bark** forms thin elongated strips, loose at ends. **Yellow timber**—hence called 'yellow cedar', valued for fine joinery. Weeping form, cultivar 'Pendula', is remarkably decorative.

Atlantic white cedar, *C. thyoides*, grows in coastal fresh-water swamps from Maine south to Florida, thence west to Mississippi. Slender, narrow-crowned tree bearing thin ash-grey to reddish brown bark. Small **blue-green needles on slightly flattened branchlets**. Small, rather fleshy **cones become wrinkled, resembling dried raisins**; they ripen from green through blue to purple, finally reddish-brown. Reddish-brown, durable wood valued for roofing shingles, fence posts, telegraph poles, mine supports.

Most **shapeless** evergreens with **feathery foliage** encountered in parks prove to be *plumose* varieties of Japanese Sawara cypress, *C. pisifera*. Wild form, rarely seen, resembles Lawson cypress, but has spreading needle tips. Cones, infrequent on decorative varieties, are small, brown, pea-shaped, knobbly when open. Cultivar 'Plumosa', introduced from Japan in 1961, has **short distinct needles**, forming dense **soft masses of floppy, yellowish grey-green foliage**; golden form 'Plumosa aurea' common too. Cultivar 'Squarrosa' bears **longer, more distinct, blue-grey needles**, building up sprays that are **fluffy and open**, rather than **floppy and close**.

Japanese Hinoki cypress, *C. obtusa*, differs from others in having **stubby blunt-pointed needles**. These build up elegant bright-green sprays, bearing a pattern of white lines on under surfaces. Foliage smells pleasantly, like eucalyptus, when crushed. Bark red-brown. Straw-coloured timber is valued in Japan for joinery, furniture, lacquer-ware and temple building.

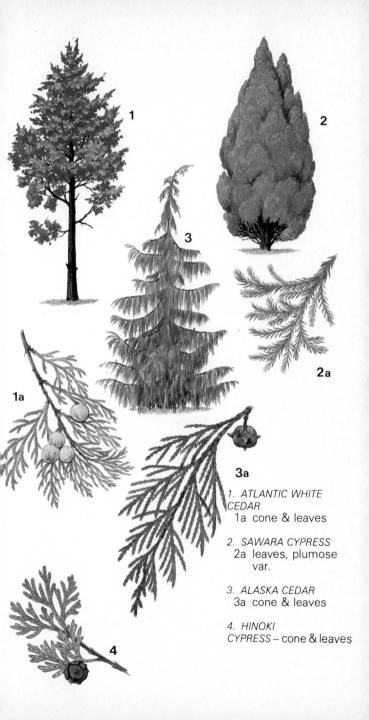

1. *ATLANTIC WHITE CEDAR*
   1a cone & leaves

2. *SAWARA CYPRESS*
   2a leaves, plumose var.

3. *ALASKA CEDAR*
   3a cone & leaves

4. *HINOKI CYPRESS* – cone & leaves

TRUE CYPRESSES

CUPRESSUS genus   CUPRESSACEAE

Many trees are called 'cypress'. The true one of classical times is
Italian cypress, *Cupressus sempervirens*. In this genus the short
**evergreen needles clasp their hidden twigs evenly on four
sides**. Buds are hidden, each **twig resembles a green rod**.
Branching repeatedly, these twigs build up **dense dark crowns**.
Needles, mid-green at first, become dull green, sombre; fading to
brown, they fall after some five years life. Italian cypress has two
growth forms. Best-known has **fastigiate narrow spire shape**,
like Lombardy poplar, and is familiar in Mediterranean landscapes.
Broad-crowned form, commoner in forests, spreads wider, yields
better timber. Both survive to great ages, 500 years or more.

Trunk, usually **buttressed at base**, bears **thin red-brown bark
shredding away in ribbons**. White sapwood surrounds red-
brown heartwood, strong, very durable, used by Romans for
house-building, ship-building, furniture.

Minute flowers open in spring at twig tips. Male groups are
club-shaped, 3 mm long, shed yellow wind-borne pollen. Solitary
female flower is bud-like, green without, flecked purple within,
about 5 mm across. Takes eighteen months to ripen, through green
stage to grey-brown, hard, woody cone, about 2·5 cm (1 in.) across,
roughly barrel-shaped to round, and knobbly. It is built up of **flat
scales with central stalks below and curved woody outgrowths above. Closed cones resemble a tortoise shell**. Scales
open slowly and release tiny seeds, four per scale. Seeds are dark
brown, oval, and carry a narrow, tough pale brown wing on either
side.

Seedlings bear three or four short, pointed seed-leaves on
reddish stem. Narrow, pointed, juvenile needles, standing well-
clear of shoot, follow. Adult needles, clasping shoot, appear in
second year.

Californian Monterey cypress, *C. macrocarpa*, native only to
Monterey Bay, is almost identical with Italian cypress. Recognize it
by **bright green foliage smelling of lemon when crushed**.
(Italian cypress is scentless). Needles are swollen at tips. Shoots of
Monterey cypress, below the needle-clad extremities, are reddish
to pinkish-brown; Italian cypress has coppery-brown to purple-
brown shoots. Seeds of Monterey cypress bear tiny resin blisters;
none appear on Italian cypress seeds.

Widely planted as ornamental tree, hedge bushes, or as a timber
producer throughout sub-tropics. Valued for rapid growth, up to
3 m (9 ft) taller each year.

Varieties include columnar forms, cultivar 'Fastigiata', and
yellow-foliaged one, 'Lutea'. Often used as seaside shelter, because
it tolerates salt-laden gales. Cannot survive long-sustained frosts.

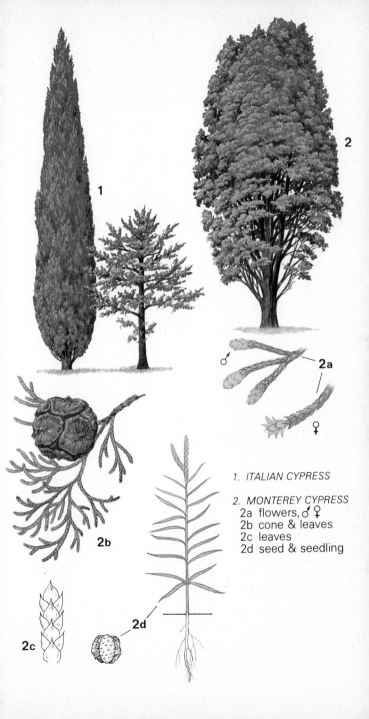

1. ITALIAN CYPRESS

2. MONTEREY CYPRESS
   2a flowers, ♂ ♀
   2b cone & leaves
   2c leaves
   2d seed & seedling

JUNIPERS I: COMMON JUNIPER

JUNIPERUS COMMUNIS   CUPRESSACEAE

Common juniper is the only tree that grows unchanged right round the Northern Hemisphere, across the cold tundras of Alaska, Canada, Scandinavia and Siberia. Further south it is common on high mountain ranges, like the Alps and the Alleghanies. In Britain it has two main centres, the Scottish Highlands and, surprisingly, the chalk downs of the south, including the Chiltern Hills and Wiltshire Downs near Salisbury.

Juniper is usually a low spiky shrub, but occasionally attains tree form, with heights up to 5 m (15 ft). Though it resembles a gorse bush, it can be known at once by **blue-green aromatic foliage**. Each sharp-pointed needle bears white wax bands. Examine foliage closely and you will find that needles are **grouped in threes**. Crush them, and a **sharp odour recalling gin** becomes apparent—for gin is flavoured with juniper berries. Cultivated forms include the fastigiate form 'Suecica' or Swedish juniper; prostrate forms grow in the far northern tundra.

A juniper bush bears both male and female flowers. As the fruits take two or even three years to ripen you can find flowers, unripe green berries, and ripe blue ones all at the same time. Male flowers open in spring, as bunches of yellow blossom near twig tips. Female flowers, which receive wind-borne pollen from males, are very small and bud-like, no more than a cluster of open scales. After fertilization they develop slowly into **hard round green berries**, with a blunt point on each of their scales, which number four to eight. Later they turn **dark blue**, with **white waxy bloom**, and become softer. At this stage they attract the birds who scatter their small seeds. They also attract berry-pickers who seek them for flavouring grain spirits to make gin.

Juniper seeds are small, hard, triangular and **unwinged**. When they sprout, eighteen months after ripening, they raise two slender seed-leaves, normal spiky needles follow.

The bark of juniper is very **thin, flaky, and bluish grey**. It often breaks away from the thin stem, which is often irregular and much-divided. The wood has a bluish-brown heartwood, with paler sapwood; both have a **pungent, pleasant, aromatic** smell. Being small, juniper wood is used only for decorative work or tool handles. The dry, resinous foliage, which burns freely, is used as kindling for fires, or else to smoke choice hams or cheeses.

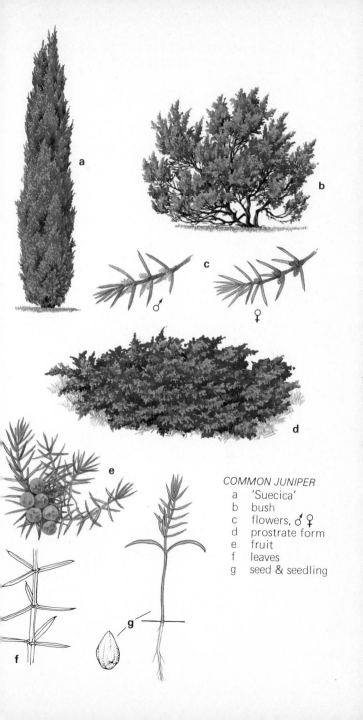

COMMON JUNIPER
a   'Suecica'
b   bush
c   flowers, ♂ ♀
d   prostrate form
e   fruit
f   leaves
g   seed & seedling

JUNIPERS II: SPECIES WITH ADPRESSED OR VARIABLE NEEDLES

JUNIPERUS genus   CUPRESSACEAE

The large genus *Juniperus*, distinguished from other conifers by its **fleshy, fragrant berries**, includes several kinds that develop cypress-like foliage, with needles closely **adpressed to the twigs**. This is regarded by botanists as the adult form, because it never appears until the tree has first produced juvenile foliage like that of the common juniper, *J. communis*. Several species appear undecided whether to remain adult or not; they bear a bewildering mixture of both kinds of foliage on fully mature twigs that also carry flowers and berries. Occasionally a whole twig carries one kind or the other.

Chinese juniper, *J. chinensis*, is often encountered in large gardens or churchyards, either as its typical race or in some colour or form variety. It bears male and female flowers **on separate trees**. The berry has an **irregular, lumpy outline**; it ripens from bluish green to dark purple, with a pale grey waxy bloom.

Sabine juniper, or savin, *J. sabina*, grows as a pale green bush high on European mountains. A low, spreading, very green form called 'Tamariscifolia' is often used by landscape planners to cover vacant ground.

Alligator juniper, *J. deppeana* variety *pachyphloea*, also known as oakbark juniper, thick-barked cedar, or mountain cedar, forms a sturdy broad-crowned tree on the dry hills of Texas and adjacent states. As a protection against drought and scorching sun, it grows reddish-brown bark up to 20 cm (4 in.) thick, divided by deep fissures into scaly squares 2·5–5 cm (1–2 in.) long, like an alligator's hide.

Eastern red cedar, also called pencil cedar, or Virginian juniper, *J. virginiana*, is a very common tree along America's eastern seaboard, from Florida to southern Canada, extending westwards beyond the Mississippi. It forms a beautiful columnar tree, up to 16 m (50 ft) high and 60 cm (2 ft) in diameter. It thrives on poor soils. Its berries are carried everywhere by birds, and this helps it to invade abandoned pastures, forming juniper thickets. Adult foliage consists of adpressed dark green scales, each about 10 millimetres (0·05 in.) long. The round berries ripen from green to dark blue, covered with white waxy bloom. The pinkish-brown, fragrant timber can be cut evenly to fine dimensions. It is the world's best wood for making lead pencils, and never splinters when they are sharpened. Knotty wood makes durable fence posts.

1. *EASTERN RED CEDAR*
   1a leaves

2. *CHINESE JUNIPER* – golden bush form
   2a variable leaves

3. *SABINE JUNIPER*
   3a leaves

4. *ALLIGATOR JUNIPER*
   4a leaves

GINKGO OR MAIDENHAIR TREE

GINKGO BILOBA   GINKGOACEAE

This weird and way-out tree is the sole survivor of a group that flourished in the far prehistoric past, 200 million years ago. Remains of almost identical trees are often found in coal seams laid down then. Ginkgo persisted as a very rare tree in south China, but was extensively grown in Chinese and Japanese temple gardens. Introduced to the West in 1758, it is now widely planted in Europe and America as a decorative street or garden tree.

In summer ginkgo is easily known by its **fan-shaped two-lobed pale green leaves with undivided parallel veins**, like the ribs of a fan. Most of these leaves spring from the **rough knobbly shoots** that are another key feature, especially in winter, when the tree stands leafless. Other leaves spring singly from longer shoots at the tips of branches. Autumn leaf colour is bright gold. The tree, always tall and slender, has a bizarre outline, especially in winter, due to fine angular branching. The bark is brown to dull grey and deeply fissured. The trunk, which tapers very evenly, often bears smooth bosses. Leafy twigs persist low down.

Ginkgo rarely flowers; when it does so, each tree proves wholly male or wholly female. Yellow male catkins open when the leaves do, in clusters on the short shoots or spurs. Female catkins are groups of two or three long-stalked, very small, green acorn-shaped structures. After pollination by wind, they ripen to yellow fruits that resemble plums. Later, in autumn, they become dull brown in colour; at that stage they decay and give out a foul smell. A single large seed, resembling a plum stone, lies within. It sprouts readily if sown in spring. The seedling bears typical foliage, with fan-shaped leaves set singly on its first shoot.

Ginkgo is seldom felled for timber; its yellow-brown wood, light and brittle, is used only for small carvings. The common name of 'maidenhair tree' springs from a fanciful resemblance of ginkgo's foliage to the fronds of a maidenhair fern. One Chinese name, *pa kuo*, means duck's foot, from the shape of the leaf.

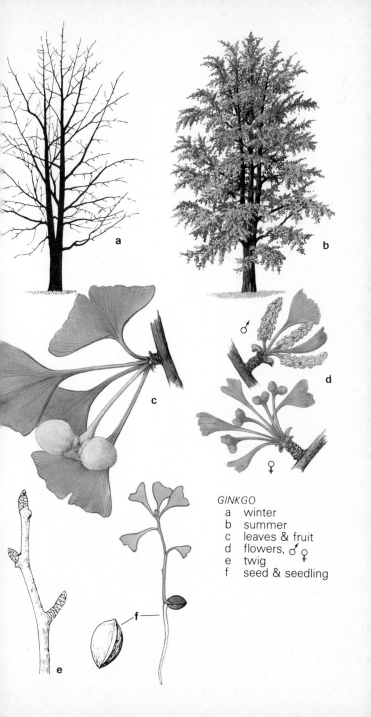

GINKGO
  a winter
  b summer
  c leaves & fruit
  d flowers, ♂ ♀
  e twig
  f seed & seedling

Bole Photographs

Unless otherwise stated, all illustrations are by
MAURICE NIMMO

1 white willow (*Salix alba*), 2 weeping willow (*Salix babylonica*), 3 crack willow (*Salix fragilis*), 4 white poplar (*Populus alba*), 5 aspen (*Populus tremula*), 6 black Italian poplar (*Populus* 'Serotina'), 7 Lombardy poplar (*Populus nigra* 'Italica'), 8 walnut (*Juglans regia*), 9 shagbark hickory (*Carya ovata*), 10 silver birch (*Betula pendula*), 11 paper birch (*Betula papyrifera*), 12 alder (*Alnus glutinosa*).

13 hornbeam (*Carpinus betulus*), 14 hazel (*Corylus avellana*), 15 beech (*Fagus sylvatica*), 16 sweet chestnut (*Castanea sativa*), 17 pedunculate oak (*Quercus robur*), 18 sessile oak (*Quercus petraea*), 19 turkey oak (*Quercus cerris*), 20 red oak (*Quercus borealis*), 21 live oak (*Quercus virginiana*), 22 cork oak (*Quercus suber*), 23 wych elm (*Ulmus glabra*), 24 English elm (*Ulmus procera*).

25 black mulberry (*Morus nigra*), 26 fig (*Ficus carica*), 27 magnolia (*Magnolia grandiflora*), 28 tulip tree (*Liriodendron tulipifera*), 29 sweet bay (*Laurus nobilis*), 30 sweet gum (*Liquidambar styraciflua*), 31 London plane (*Platanus × hispanica*), 32 hawthorn (*Crataegus monogyna*), 33 European mountain ash (*Sorbus aucuparia*), 34 whitebeam (*Sorbus aria*), 35 wild service tree (*Sorbus torminalis*), 36 apple (*Malus*).

37 wild crab apple (*Malus sylvestris*), 38 plum (*Prunus domestica*), 39 peach (*Prunus persica*), 40 almond (*Prunus amygdalus*), 41 wild cherry (*Prunus avium*), 42 cherry laurel (*Prunus laurocerasus*), 43 Judas tree (*Cercius siliquastrum*), 44 honey locust (*Gleditsia triacanthos*), 45 laburnum (*Laburnum anagyroides*), 46 robinia (*Robinia pseudocacia*), 47 tree of heaven (*Ailanthus altissima*), 48 box (*Buxus sempervirens*).

49 staghorn sumac (*Rhus typhina*), 50 holly (*Ilex aquifolium*), 51 spindle tree (*Euonymus europaeus*), 52 spindle tree twigs showing bright green bark, 53 European sycamore (*Acer pseudoplatanus*), 54 field maple (*Acer campestre*), 55 sugar maple (*Acer saccharinum*), 56 moosebark maple (*Acer pensylvanicum*), 57 horse chestnut (*Aesculus hippocastanum*), 58 buckthorn (*Rhamnus purshiana*), 59 lime (*Tilia × vulgaris*), 60 tamarisk (*Tamarix anglica*).

61 tupelo (*Nyssa sylvatica*), 62 eucalyptus (*Eucalyptus gunnii*), 63 strawberry tree (*Arbutus unedo*), 64 persimmon (*Diospyrus virginiana*) (from A–Z BOTANICAL COLLECTION), 65 ash (*Fraxinus excelsior*), 66 olive (*Olea europaea*) (by HEATHER ANGEL), 67 catalpa (*Catalpa bignonioides*), 68 elder (*Sambucus nigra*), 69 cabbage tree (*Cordyline australis*) (by JOHN CLEGG), 70 Chusan palm (*Trachycarpus fortunei*), 71 yew (*Taxus baccata*), 72 monkey puzzle tree (*Araucaria araucana*).

73 Scots pine (*Pinus sylvestris*), 74 lodgepole pine (*Pinus contorta*), 75 stone pine (*Pinus pinea*), 76 ponderosa pine (*Pinus ponderosa*), 77 Weymouth pine (*Pinus strobus*) (by HERBERT EDLIN), 78 Atlantic cedar (*Cedrus atlantica*), 79 larch (*Larix decidua*), 80 Norway spruce (*Picea abies*), 81 Sitka spruce (*Picea sitchensis*), 82 eastern hemlock (*Tsuga canadensis*), 83 Douglas fir (*Pseudotsuga* genus), 84 silver fir (*Abies alba*).

270

85 grand fir (*Abies grandis*), 86 giant sequoia (*Sequoiadendron giganteum*), 87 coast redwood (*Sequoia sempervirens*), 88 Japanese cedar (*Cryptomeria japonica*), 89 swamp cypress (*Taxodium distichum*), 90 dawn redwood (*Metasequoia glyptostroboides*), 91 incense cedar (*Calocedrus decurrens*), 92 western red cedar (*Thuja plicata*), 93 Monterey cypress (*Cupressus macrocarpa*), 94 common juniper (*Juniperus communis*), 95 Virginian cypress (*Juniperus virginia*), 96 maidenhair (*Ginkgo biloba*).

Index to Trees

Italic numerals indicate colour plates

277

279